Solicitors' Negligence

Hope you do not
need to consult
this too often!

Solicitors' Negligence

Robert Rennie LLB, PhD
Solicitor, Professor of Conveyancing,
University of Glasgow

Butterworths/Law Society of Scotland
Edinburgh
1997

United Kingdom	Butterworths, a Division of Reed Elsevier (UK) Ltd, 4 Hill Street, EDINBURGH EH2 3JZ and Halsbury House, 35 Chancery Lane, LONDON WC2A 1EL
Australia	Butterworths, SYDNEY, MELBOURNE, BRISBANE, ADELAIDE, PERTH, CANBERRA and HOBART
Canada	Butterworths Canada Ltd, TORONTO and VANCOUVER
Ireland	Butterworth (Ireland) Ltd, DUBLIN
Malaysia	Malayan Law Journal Sdn Bhd, KUALA LUMPUR
New Zealand	Butterworths of New Zealand Ltd, WELLINGTON and AUCKLAND
Singapore	Reed Elsevier (Singapore) Pte Ltd, SINGAPORE
South Africa	Butterworth Publishers (Pty) Ltd, DURBAN
USA	Michie, CHARLOTTESVILLE, VIRGINIA

Law Society of Scotland
26 Drumsheugh Gardens, EDINBURGH EH3 7YR

 A CIP Catalogue record for this book is available from the British Library.

ISBN 0 406 99610 5

Typeset by Phoenix Photosetting, Chatham, Kent
Printed and bound in Great Britain by
Clays PLC, St. Ives Ltd

Foreword

In the late 1960s and early 1970s, professional negligence on the part of solicitors was not an issue which impinged on the daily thinking of a practitioner, far less on the budget of a solicitors' firm – if indeed it had one. My firm maintained a professional indemnity policy not because of the fear of claims but rather because my predecessors thought it prudent to do so. By 1973, however, there had been a dramatic change. Consumerism and claims emanating therefrom exploded in the USA and like most developments there, they worked their way – wanted or not – to the UK. The immediate problem for Scottish solicitors was both to obtain professional indemnity insurance and to pay for it. By 1976, the problem of professional indemnity insurance was so critical that the Law Society of Scotland sought and obtained powers in terms of the Solicitors (Scotland) Act 1976 to make professional practice rules regulating indemnity insurance for solicitors. So was born the Master Policy for Professional Indemnity Insurance.

That policy and its premiums, because of a rapidly increasing frequency of claims and an inexorable rise in their cost, have become a real issue which significantly affects firms' budgets – which by now most, if not all firms, have! It was inevitable that the Law Society would introduce a risk management strategy. The purpose is to heighten awareness of the proper management of risk and claims and to secure their avoidance.

Professor Rennie has been involved with the Law Society's risk management strategy from the very start. He is, of course, a recognised teacher of outstanding knowledge and abililty. His seminars are sell-outs. More and more his formal Opinion in regard both to professional practice and to professional negligence has been sought. His Opinions are highly regarded and hugely persuasive. Professor Rennie does not, however, simply confine himself to an academic view of the law involved. As a practising solicitor of great experience, he recognises that the client needs help and guidance which he gives in an eminently practical way. It is not a matter of surprise that he is, as an Opinion giver, in great demand.

I am particularly delighted that Robert Rennie has written this work. Nobody is better qualified from both the academic and practical aspects of professional life to do so. It will be a work to which all practitioners both newly qualified and greatly experienced will seek recourse: to do so will be greatly to the advantage of their peace of mind and of their bank balance.

Kenneth W Pritchard
The Secretary
The Law Society of Scotland
December 1996

Preface

It used to be said that it was the most difficult thing in the world to take on a lawyer and win. When I first qualified, negligence claims against solicitors were something of a rarity. Indeed, some solicitors would never have taken on a case against a fellow practitioner. These days have now gone and there are very few (if any) firms in Scotland who have not faced a claim of one sort or another. Formerly, professional negligence tended to feature only as a chapter in a general textbook relating to delictual liability. Jackson and Powell produced the first edition of their standard work on Professional Negligence in 1982 and this work is now in its third edition with supplements. When I was appointed to the Chair of Conveyancing in 1993, I anticipated that there would be a large volume of opinion work. What I did not appreciate was that a large percentage of opinions sought would relate to matters of negligence. It soon became clear to me that professional negligence was a fast developing branch of the law and that the duty of care owed by a solicitor to his or her clients was a moving concept. There is no question in my mind that the recent English cases relating to disclosure of information have radically altered the notion that a solicitor's liability extends only to the actual legal work undertaken.

I formed the view that such were the developments in the law of professional negligence so far as solicitors were concerned, that there was merit in trying to put together a textbook on the topic.

I have greatly benefited from the advice of Neil Cochran and Colin MacLeod, both panel solicitors appointed by the insurers under the master policy. They have made many valuable suggestions and prevented me from making, I hope, too many errors. The manuscript was typed by Mary Love and Jean Steele in Motherwell, who have both typed more words for me over the years than any of the three of us care to remember.

Finally, I think it is appropriate to thank Kenneth Pritchard, the Secretary of the Law Society of Scotland, for his unfailing encouragement and support in this project.

The law is stated as at 31 December 1996.

Robert Rennie
31 December 1996

Contents

Table of statutes

Table of orders, rules and regulations

Table of cases

Abbreviations

Cases and journals

AC	Law Reports, Appeal Cases (House of Lords and Privy Council) 1890–
Ad & El	Adolphus and Ellis's Reports (Queen's Bench), New Series 1841–1852
All ER	All England Law Reports 1936–
App Cas	Law Reports, Appeal Cases (House of Lords and Privy Council) 1875–1890
B & Ald	Barnewall and Alderson's Reports (King's Bench) 1817–1822
B & C	Barnewall and Cresswell's Reports (King's Bench) 1822–1830
BCLR (2d)	British Columbia Law Reports, Second Series
Beav	Beavan's Reports (Rolls Court) 1838–1866
Bell Oct Cas	P Bell's Octavo Cases (Court of Session) 1790–1792
Bing	Bingham's Reports (Common Pleas) 1822–1834
C & P	Carrington and Payne's Reports (Nisi Prius) 1823–1841
CB	Common Bench Reports 1845–1856
CBNS	Common Bench Reports, New Series 1856–1865
CP	Upper Canada Common Pleas, 1850–1881
Camp	Campbell's Reports (Nisi Prius) 1807–1816
Ch	Law Reports, Chancery Division 1890–
Ch D	Law Reports, Chancery Division 1875–1890
Cl & Fin	Clark and Finnelly's Reports (House of Lords) 1831–1846
Cr & J	Crompton and Jervis's Reports (Exchequer) 1830–1832
D	Dunlop's Session Cases 1838–1862
D (HL)	House of Lords cases in Dunlop's Session Cases 1838–1862
DLR (2d)	Dominion Law Reports (Canada), Second Series 1956–1968
DLR (3d)	Dominion Law Reports (Canada), Third Series 1969–1984
E & E	Ellis and Ellis's Reports (Queen's Bench) 1858–1861
EG	Estates Gazette 1858–
EGCS	Estates Gazette Case Summaries 1988–
Exch	Exchequer Reports 1847–1856
F	Fraser's Session Cases 1898–1906
F & F	Foster and Finlason's Reports (Nisi Prius) 1856–1867
FC	Faculty Collection (Court of Session) 1752–1825
Fam	Law Reports, Family Division 1972–
GWD	Green's Weekly Digest 1986–
HL	House of Lords
Hume	Hume's Decisions (Court of Session) 1781–1822
JLSS	Journal of the Law Society of Scotland 1956–
KB	Law Reports, King's Bench Division 1901–1952
LJ	Law Journal newspaper 1866–1965
LJ Ch	Law Journal, Chancery 1831–1946
LR (vol no) Eq	Law Reports, Equity 1865–1875
LT	Law Times Reports 1859–1947
Lloyd's Rep	Lloyd's Law Reports 1968–

M	Macpherson's Session Cases 1862–1873
Macl & R	Maclean and Robinson's House of Lords Appeals Cases 1839
Macq	Macqueen's House of Lords Reports 1851–1865
Mor	Morision's Dictionary of Decisions (Court of Session) 1540–1808
NLJ	New Law Journal 1965–
NZLR	New Zealand Law Reports 1883–
Pat	Paton's House of Lords Appeals Cases 1726–1822
PN	Professional Negligence
PNLR	Professional Negligence and Liability Reports 1996–
QB	Law Reports, Queen's Bench Division 1891–1901, 1952–
R	Rettie's Session Cases 1873–1898
Robin	Robinson's House of Lords Appeals Cases 1840–1841
S	P Shaw's Session Cases 1821–1838
SC	Session Cases 1907–
SC (HL)	House of Lords cases in Session Cases 1907–
SCLR	Scottish Civil Law Reports 1987–
SJ	Solicitors' Journal 1856–
SLPQ	Scottish Law and Practice Quarterly 1995–
SLT	Scots Law Times 1893–
SLT (Notes)	Notes of Recent Decisions in Scots Law Times 1946–1981
SLT (Sh Ct)	Sheriff Court Reports in Scots Law Times 1893–
Taunt	Taunton's Reports (Common Pleas) 1807–1819
WLR	Weekly Law Reports 1953–

For abbreviations used for **textbooks**, see **Bibliography**.

Bibliography

(Some authors' names appear originally in italics: this indicates the abbreviations used for frequently cited textbooks.)

Begg	J H Begg *The Law of Scotland relating to Law Agents* (2nd edn, 1883)
Bell	G J Bell *Principles of the Law of Scotland* (10th edn, 1899, ed W Guthrie)
Cusine and Rennie	D J Cusine and Robert Rennie *Missives* (1993, Butterworths/Law Society of Scotland)
Erskine	John Erskine *An Institute of the Law of Scotland* (8th edn, 1871, ed J B Nicolson)
Glegg	A T Glegg *The Law of Reparation in Scotland* (2nd edn, 1905, W Green)
Gloag	W M Gloag *The Law of Contract* (2nd edn, 1929, W Green)
Gretton and Reid	G L Gretton and K G C Reid *Conveyancing* (1993, W Green/Sweet & Maxwell)
Halliday	J M Halliday *Conveyancing Law and Practice in Scotland*, vol I (1985) and vol II (1986) (W Green)
Halliday	*The Conveyancing Opinions of J M Halliday* (ed D J Cusine, 1992, W Green/Sweet & Maxwell)
Jackson and Powell	R Jackson and John L Powell *Professional Negligence* (3rd edn, 1993, Sweet & Maxwell)
McBryde	W W McBryde *The Law of Contract in Scotland* (1987, W Green)
Ryder	Jane Ryder *Professional Conduct for Scottish Solicitors* (1995, Butterworths/Law Society of Scotland)
Sinclair	John H Sinclair *Handbook of Conveyancing Practice in Scotland* (3rd edn, 1995, Butterworths/Law Society of Scotland)
Smith	T B Smith *A Short Commentary on the Law of Scotland* (1962, W Green)
Stewart	W J Stewart *Delict* (2nd edn, 1993, W Green/Sweet & Maxwell)
Thomson	J M Thomson *Delictual Liability* (1994, Butterworths)
Walker	D M Walker *The Law of Contracts and Related Obligations in Scotland* (3rd edn, 1995, T & T Clark)
Walker	D M Walker *The Law of Prescription and Limitation of Actions in Scotland* (4th edn, 1990, W Green)

CHAPTER 1

Introduction

The public attitude to professions

1.01 When the author qualified in 1967, the status of any professional, be they solicitor, doctor, teacher, architect or anyone else, was still something which had a special quality. The term 'professional' stems from the fact that professionals used to profess an oath. Indeed many professionals still do take an oath at some stage in their training. Members of the general public who consulted professional people tended to treat them with a fair amount of respect and in some cases that respect bordered on awe if not fear. Professions had their own professional bodies who dealt with matters of conduct but not matters relating to the adequacy or otherwise of professional services. Complaints to professional bodies tended to be made only in cases where the professional had been guilty of serious misconduct.

In so far as solicitors were concerned, the Law Society of Scotland was the appropriate body and although it owed dual duties to the profession and to the public, the level of complaints lodged could not be said to be out of the ordinary. Many complaints were dealt with without any particular sanction being imposed on the solicitor concerned. There is no doubt that the attitude of the general public to professionals in general and solicitors in particular has changed dramatically since 1967. This has occurred for a variety of reasons and in some ways it can be said that the change has been evolutionary rather than revolutionary. There is no doubt, however, that deliberate government policy in relation to professionals in general and the legal profession in particular has had an effect not only on the status of the professions but also on the attitude of those who employ professionals. What is clear is that negligence claims against professionals in general and solicitors in particular are now very common. Complaints to the Law Society of Scotland, whether relating to conduct or inadequate professional service, are also on the increase.

The author recently had occasion to look at the late Professor J M Halliday's index of opinions. The author was mildly surprised that in going through the various headings there appeared to be no mention of negligence. It is a salutary fact that of the 600 opinions given by the author since taking the Chair of Conveyancing in the University of Glasgow, well over a third relate to negligence claims. In these cases the author is not asked to interpret a deed or give an opinion on the adequacy of a description. The question posed is whether the solicitor who framed the deed or description has failed to meet the required standard of care. It is appropriate to look at the various factors which may be said to have brought about this increase in the number of claims.

Professionalism and competition

1.02 In 1967, there was a very clearly held view that solicitors should not compete with each other for business, especially if this involved price competition. Indeed, many fees such as conveyancing fees were on a fixed scale approved by the Law Society of Scotland. In Scotland it was, however, always possible to agree to provide legal services for an established client for a lesser fee than the approved scale fee, but any reduction was generally a percentage reduction of the scale fee so that there could always be said to be some benchmark. Other fees were worked out on a time and line basis by bookkeepers employed by firms and it was common practice to have such accounts taxed by independent auditors. While it is fair to say that clients never like paying solicitors' fees, there was some degree of certainty for the client that payment of a professionally regulated fee would mean a professional standard of service. Law Society regulations prohibited solicitors from advertising their services at all and even where solicitors acted as estate agents, regulations regulated the size of any heading and tail in any advert which publicised the solicitor's name and address.

It is doubtful whether anyone now would seriously regard the strict regulations which were in place in 1967 as wholly necessary for the maintenance of professional standards. Nevertheless, in 1967 few practising solicitors could have envisaged the dramatic changes which were to take place in the decades which followed. Government policy favoured competition in all areas of commerce. Scale fees were abolished and solicitors were allowed to compete for work on the basis of price. The difficulty was and is that the professional standards by which solicitors were judged remained and remain the same as they were in 1967. If anything the professional standards imposed are higher than they were in 1967. There never has been any principle of law to the effect that a client who pays a low fee must accept a lower standard of professional service[1]. In so far as matters of negligence are concerned, however, it is not just the question of lower fees which has brought about the increase in the number of claims. It is rather the sense among the public that solicitors are just purveyors of services. Clients do not just expect value for money; they also expect that when they entrust work to a solicitor, it will be done properly. If things go wrong, clients now expect to know the reason and then to know whether there is fault in some quarter. There is no doubt in the author's mind that in 1967 a client would have been reluctant to sue a solicitor for negligence except in the most obvious of cases. Indeed many solicitors would have been reluctant to sue another member of the profession. In 1996 there are no such taboos. The whirlwind of competition has not just brought lower fees; it has also brought a keener awareness in the public of their right to sue solicitors when they fail to come up to the required standard of care.

1 *Currie v Colquhoun* (1823) 2 S 407.

The role of the Law Society

1.03 Since its inception the Law Society of Scotland has regulated the solicitors' branch of the legal profession. Initially, its primary function was not only to promote the interests of the profession but also to deal with matters of conduct. Solicitors could be found guilty of professional misconduct or unprofessional conduct. In so far as the level of service provided was concerned, originally it was a firm rule that the Society did not deal with matters of negligence. It would, however, have been accepted, even in 1967, that the line between conduct and negligence or inadequate service was never very distinct. Delay on the part of a solicitor may result in loss and there is no doubt that unconscionable delay would be negligence. Delay, however, might also be unprofessional conduct or professional misconduct. Things changed dramatically with the passing of the Solicitors (Scotland) Act 1988.

This Act contained new provisions which provided that the Council of the Law Society of Scotland should not only deal with matters of conduct but also with matters relating to the level of professional service provided. The Law Society of Scotland is now empowered, where it thinks there has been an inadequate professional service, to reduce the amount of fees and outlays charged, to direct the solicitor to do certain work, to refund fees and to pay compensation. There can be no doubt that these new statutory powers have led to an increase in the level of complaints to the Law Society of Scotland but they have also raised public awareness of the duty of any solicitor to carry out work to a certain standard.

It is the stated policy of the Law Society of Scotland when dealing with a complaint which relates to the level of service to point out, where necessary, that the complainer may have a remedy under the law of negligence. It is also the practice of the Law Society of Scotland to advise complainers that, if they intend to pursue a claim for negligence, the complaint relating to the adequacy of service cannot be entertained until the negligence claim has been determined. The reason for this is to guard against the possibility that the solicitor may give information in the course of answering the complaint which could prejudice any defence to the negligence action. The dividing line between an inadequate professional service and negligence is difficult to determine but in the author's view, while it may be possible to have inadequate service which does not amount to negligence, it is unlikely that there can be negligence which does not amount to inadequate professional service (see further Chapter 11 below).

The availability of professional indemnity insurance

1.04 Many prospective litigants have in the past been deterred from taking action against a solicitor by the cost of civil litigation. It is often said that civil litigation is something for the very poor or the very rich. There are two reasons why this statement is true. In the first place civil litigation is costly and can be funded only by someone who is entitled to legal aid or has unlimited resources. In the second place actual recovery of the sum sued for is by no means certain. It is one thing to obtain a decree against a person for £10,000; it is quite another thing to recover that amount. Prior to the requirement for motorists to have compulsory third party insurance cover, many claimants did not sue a driver simply because the driver might not be able to pay the sum awarded. Since compulsory insurance has been in place claims of this nature are commonplace, and there are many instances of members of a family suing each other as a result of a motor vehicle accident simply because an insurance company will settle whatever is awarded at the end of the day.

Most firms of solicitors have always carried some form of professional indemnity insurance but it has not always been compulsory. Because of the relatively low level of claims insurance companies in the past regarded the legal profession as a reasonably safe risk. An insurance company, of course, accepts a risk on the basis of the insured's track record. As negligence claims increased it was felt that the public would be better protected if all solicitors in Scotland were insured under a master policy. Since May 1978, solicitors' firms have been insured under a master policy organised by the Law Society of Scotland[1]. Since its inception the master policy has undergone many changes but one thing has remained, and that is that every practising solicitor is covered for negligence claims by an insurance policy no matter how bad his or her track record. This fact is well known to the general public and has undoubtedly had an effect on the number and frequency of claims made.

1 The current rules are the Solicitors (Scotland) Professional Indemnity Insurance Rules 1995.

The effects of recession

1.05 Although many claims against solicitors are made by aggrieved individuals, the largest claims are made by institutions, often lending institutions. It is fair to say that in 1967 there was a cosy relationship between solicitors and lending institutions. Even before the days of the Financial Services Act 1986 and the plethora of regulations thereunder, firms of solicitors had informal ties with their favourite banks, building societies, insurance companies, surveyors and accountants. In those days there was a reluctance on the part of institutions to make claims which might upset a long-standing relationship, especially claims which were not perhaps the result of an obvious mistake but more the result of some error of judgment or lack of disclosure. In the boom times of the late 1980s there was a considerable amount of economic and commercial activity involving the sale and acquisition of commercial properties, with financial institutions lending freely. In good times, institutions lend freely and take profit; in bad times, financial institutions are less and less inclined to take losses as they fall. Some financial institutions now have special departments devoted entirely to the investigation of losses, the function of these departments being to attempt to attach liability to third parties such as surveyors, solicitors and accountants. The fact that solicitors must carry professional indemnity insurance is something well known to financial institutions. There is no doubt that the recession has brought in its wake a number of claims against solicitors which would not have been made in better times.

The claim conscious society

1.06 After a discussion with members of the solicitors' profession in relation to negligence claims, one might be forgiven for coming away with the impression that only solicitors were being subjected to an increased number of claims. This is, of course, not the case. Hardly a day goes by without reading of some enormous claim being made against an international firm of accountants or a health trust, doctor, architect, engineer or some other professional. In the United States of America there are apparently more lawyers per head of population than in any other country and many of these lawyers deal with nothing else but negligence claims of one sort or another. Perhaps this is because the individual citizen in the United States has always had rights which are enshrined in a written constitution and a Supreme Court to enforce these rights. There is no doubt that British citizens are following in their transatlantic cousins' footsteps. Whatever the reason for the increase in claims may be, there is no doubt that the public is no longer afraid to make claims in all sorts of situations and the very concept of negligence is continually being pushed well beyond the limits originally envisaged when Lord Atkin pronounced his famous dictum on the general duty of care[1]. Solicitors have had to accept their fair share of the increased number of negligence claims which have arisen in society in general.

1 *Donoghue v Stevenson* 1932 SC (HL) 31 at 44, 1932 SLT 317 at 323.

The expanding duty of care

1.07 Claims against solicitors are brought either under contract or under delict and usually under both heads. In either case the general standard of care required of the solicitor is much the same. The standard required is the normal standard expected in the profession. Lord Atkin's view of the law of delictual liability is based on a neighbourhood principle[1]. Because of the difficulties surrounding matters of economic loss in delictual claims and because there will always be a contract between solicitor and client, most claims are actually brought under the contractual head, on the basis that the solicitor owes the client a similar standard of care under contract. In the past, most claims have related to mistakes or omissions in the actual carrying through of a particular legal task. Obvious examples would be a failure to raise a court action for personal injury within the appropriate time limit, or a failure to obtain a valid marketable title to a property.

More recently, however, the ambit of the duty of care has been increased to include duties of disclosure in relation to matters which might be regarded as peripheral to the legal transaction. The most common example of this type of claim is a claim by a lender to recover a loss resulting from the fact that the value of a security is less than the lender had supposed. This type of claim is now routinely made in circumstances where the solicitor who acted for the lender has failed to disclose to the lender that the titles indicated that the security subjects had recently been bought for a price significantly lower than the price being paid by the borrower[2].

1 Thomson *Delictual Liability* (1994) p 54 et seq.
2 See *Mortgage Express v Bowerman & Partners* (1995) Times, 1 August; *Target Holdings Ltd v Redferns* [1995] 3 All ER 785, [1995] 3 WLR 352; *Bank of East Asia Ltd v Shepherd & Wedderburn, WS* 1995 SCLR 598, 1995 SLT 1074; Rennie 'Negligence, Instructions and the Lender's Need to Know' (1994) 39 JLSS 135; Rennie 'Negligence, Securities and the Expanding Duty of Care' (1995) 40 JLSS 58.

The importance of contractual instructions

1.08 Since most actions against solicitors tend to be based on breach of contract, professional negligence nowadays can be said to be very much a matter of contract. This is especially true where the client is an institutional lender. A solicitor may come up to the required standard of care in a general sense but still be liable in damages if he or she has broken one of the express terms of the contract with the client. It may be possible to show that any solicitor exercising the appropriate standard of care would accept a letter of comfort from a local authority in respect of an alteration which was carried out 15 years prior to the purchase of a property. That will not help a solicitor if the written instructions from the lending institution state in terms that the solicitor *must* obtain a building warrant and completion certificate for any alterations of whatever age. Quite apart from specific provisions relating to specific matters in transactions, many lenders' instructions now contain general obligations imposed on the solicitor to act at all times in the best interests of the lender and to disclose to the lender any matter which might affect the lender's decision to lend. Many claims by lenders are brought for breach of a specific instruction as well as for breach of the general duty of care. The fact that lenders can often do this has led to an increase in the number of claims.

Third party claims

1.09 It may be said that the law of Scotland has resisted the principle that a solicitor can be liable to anyone other than the client with whom that solicitor has a direct relationship. Although solicitors may be in no different position from any other professional where they make a negligent misrepresentation which is relied on by a third party[1], there is no doubt that Scottish courts have hitherto been wary of saddling solicitor with wider duties to third parties especially where there may be no reliance[2]. English courts, on the other hand, have held that a solicitor is liable to a disappointed beneficiary where that prospective beneficiary suffers loss because the solicitor has failed to have the will completed and signed within a reasonable time, the testator having died in the meantime[3]. In the old Scottish case of *Robertson v Fleming*[4] it was, however, decided that in similar circumstances the solicitor owed no duty of care to the third party. While this peculiarly Scottish standpoint has been criticised it does not appear likely that it can be altered except by a decision in the House of Lords[5].

Solicitors can, however, expressly undertake a contractual liability to a third party. For many years solicitors had been giving reports on title to institutional lenders. More recently solicitors acting for one client have given such a report or a certificate of title to a client of another firm. This can occur where, for example, there is a company takeover and the solicitors acting for the acquiring company do not wish to examine the title deeds of all the properties owned by the company being acquired. In these circumstances it is normal practice for the solicitor who acts for the company being acquired to grant a certificate of title to the acquiring company. This produces a direct contractual relationship outwith the normal solicitor/client relationship. More recently the practice has grown up of a borrower's solicitor giving a certificate of title to a lender even in circumstances where the lender is separately represented. The purpose of this certificate is to avoid the unnecessary expense and delay which can arise when two firms of solicitors have to examine the same set of titles. In practice, of course, the adjustment of the certificate of title can sometimes take as long as an independent title examination. Certificates of title represent another way in which solicitors may be liable, quite apart from the normal rules of negligence[6].

1 *Hedley Byrne & Co Ltd v Heller & Partners Ltd* [1964] AC 465, [1963] 2 All ER 575; *Caparo Industries plc v Dickman* [1990] 2 AC 605, [1990] 1 All ER 568.
2 *Midland Bank plc v Cameron, Thom, Peterkins & Duncans* 1988 SCLR 209, 1988 SLT 611; *Weir v J M Hodge & Son* 1990 SLT 266.
3 *Ross v Caunters* [1980] Ch 297, [1979] 3 All ER 580; *White v Jones* [1995] 2 AC 207, [1995] 1 All ER 691.
4 (186l) 23 D (HL) 8, (1861) 4 Macq 167.
5 See Thomson *Delictual Liability* p 136.
6 See Rennie 'Certificate of Title, Legal Context' (1995) 40 JLSS 377.

Expert evidence

1.10 The standard of care owed by a solicitor is measured by a negative evidential test. What must be shown is that no solicitor exercising due care and skill would have acted in the manner complained of. The conduct is judged against the standard in the profession at the time of the alleged negligence and not at the time of the claim. Where a client has suffered loss because something has gone wrong it is often difficult for the solicitor to find another solicitor who is an expert in the particular field and who despite his or her expertise is prepared to state that he or she might have taken the same action with the same disastrous consequences for the client. It is sometimes easier for the client to obtain expert evidence that the solicitor has not attained the required standard of care than for the solicitor to obtain expert evidence to the contrary.

The increase in standards

1.11 It may be stating the obvious to say that claims against solicitors whether based on delict, contract or some third party right are likely to increase rather than decrease in number, amount and scope. The standard of care in a general sense will change from time to time as the general practice of solicitors changes. In many ways solicitors set their own standard of care and what was standard practice in 1967 may be negligence in 1997. For example, in 1967 it was not standard practice to insert clauses in missives dealing with the following:

(1) The exhibition of a planning inquiry report except in cases of flatted property in obvious redevelopment areas.
(2) The exhibition of building warrants, planning permissions and completion certificates in respect of alterations.
(3) The granting of a warranty concerning the state of repair of the central heating system and any other moveable items of a working or running nature.
(4) The payment of penal interest for failure to settle with a right to rescind for non-payment after a certain time.
(5) The exhibition of a title which, where the minerals were reserved, would provide for adequate compensation and no rights to enter the surface.
(6) The exhibition of a title containing no unusual or onerous burdens and conditions[1].
(7) The passing of risk of accidental destruction.

Who can doubt that a failure to insert any of these provisions in 1997 would be professional negligence? The law, however, has not changed from 1967 to 1997. What has changed is the practice of solicitors in relation to these matters. It is a salutary fact that the more protection solicitors seek for their clients, the higher the standard will be by which the same solicitors are judged by these same clients.

1 The common law would probably have implied this.

CHAPTER 2

The Standard of Care

The choice between contract and delict

2.01 The term 'negligence' immediately conjures up the notion of a delictual liability. The law of delict is based on *culpa* or fault and for a person to recover it must be shown that another person actually intended harm or caused harm negligently in circumstances where a duty of care existed. Most claims against solicitors are based on contract. This is because the party who has suffered the harm or loss is generally in a contractual relationship with the solicitor as a client. Claims can sometimes lie against solicitors at the instance of third parties but these can be brought only under delict. The difficulty with a delictual claim against a professional person such as a solicitor is that pure economic loss cannot always be recovered unless the loss derives from injury to the party or his or her property[1]. Pure economic loss can be recovered if it can be shown that harm was actually intended as where, for example, someone deliberately induces breach of contract[2]. Claims for pure economic loss are also entertained in certain cases of negligent misrepresentation[3]. In claims against solicitors pure economic loss is frequently a part of the claim and accordingly most claims are brought under contract. The odd thing is that except in cases where there is a breach of a specific instruction, claims under contract are generally founded on an implied term of the contract that the solicitor will bring to the performance of his or her obligations the standard of care normally to be expected in the profession. The general duty of care is really the same whether the claim is brought under contract or delict and, as presently formulated, the standard of care required is measured by what is an essentially negative evidential test. It has been held by the House of Lords to be competent to bring an action in contract and delict under the same action[4]. It is important to trace the nature of the duty of care and the way in which the courts have interpreted it up to the present time.

1 *Murphy v Brentwood District Council* [1991] 1 AC 398, [1990] 2 All ER 908. For a general discussion of liability for pure economic loss see Thomson *Delictual Liability* pp 67, 68.

2 For a discussion on deliberate economic delicts, see Thomson *Delictual Liability* Ch 2; Stewart *Delict* (2nd edn, 1993) Ch 3.
3 *Hedley Byrne & Co Ltd v Heller & Partners Ltd* [1964] AC 465, [1963] 2 All ER 575; *Caparo Industries plc v Dickman* [1990] 2 AC 605, [1990] 1 All ER 568.
4 *Henderson v Merrett Syndicates Ltd* [1995] 2 AC 145, [1994] 3 All ER 506.

The early decisions

2.02 Originally there seems to have been a tendency to separate the basis for liability into two categories namely, circumstances where there had been a positive breach of duty, involving gross negligence and circumstances where there had been something less than that such as a want of skill or care. It has to be remembered, of course, that earlier decisions, which were mainly based on contract, occurred before the general definition of negligence was set out in *Donoghue v Stevenson*[1]. The notion of a positive breach of duty tended to relate in the main to failure to follow instructions or a professional code. The dividing line, however, between gross negligence or *culpa lata* and lack of skill and care appears always to have been blurred[2]. It is fair to say that some of the professional breaches are now dealt with as conduct matters by the Law Society of Scotland, whereas in the past they might only have founded damages claims.

1 1932 SC (HL) 31, 1932 SLT 317.
2 Begg *The Law of Scotland relating to Law Agents* (2nd edn, 1883) p 233 et seq.

Positive breach of duty

2.03 In earlier cases clients brought actions against solicitors, or law agents as they were commonly known, alleging loss where there had been some professional wrong such as a breach of confidentiality. In *Bogle v Cameron*[1] a law agent acted for purchaser and seller. On examining the seller's title he found that it was in fact the seller's son who owned the property. He informed the purchaser of this and the purchaser then concluded a contract with the son, thus cutting out the father. The father sued the law agent for damages founding on breach of confidentiality. The court held that the loss had not been sustained because of the breach of any confidentiality but because of the lack of title and did not uphold the claim. A similar case of breach of confidentiality involving a doctor, however, was held relevant to support a claim[2]. Other instances of alleged breach of a positive duty included acting contrary to instructions or without authority[3].

1 (1844) 6 D 682.
2 *AB v CD* (1851) 14 D 177.
3 See *Thomson v Incorporation of Candlemakers of Edinburgh* (1855) 17 D 765 where the court pointed out that if a party's name had been used in an action without authority, expenses would still be due from that party although the party might have a remedy against the agent who used the name.

Gross negligence

2.04 The concept of gross negligence in relation to the conduct of professional people appears to derive from the well-known maxim that a professional person promises to perform in accordance with the generally accepted standards of his or her profession. The maxim is *spondet peritiam artis*. In dealing with the hiring of skilled labour Bell puts it in these terms[1]:

'The engagement here is to bestow attention, art and skill on the act to be performed; skill being presumed in all professional persons according to the rule *spondet peritiam artis et imperitia culpae enumeratur.*'

Even when Bell was pronouncing on the standard of care to be expected, he recognised that it was only ordinary skill which was promised. He stated that the employer might specify for a higher level of skill in the contract but if not the employer was entitled to expect only the ordinary level of skill of the profession.

1 *Principles* s 153.

Lack of skill

2.05 The modern law of professional negligence would not recognise any particular distinction between gross negligence, ordinary negligence and lack of skill. Older authorities tend to treat negligence as being in some way culpable and lack of skill as simply involving carelessness. A professional person was not expected to guarantee success for the client[1]. In *Hamilton v Emslie*[2] the court appeared to take the view that a law agent who acted to the best of his own ability could be liable only if the advice was so inaccurate as to be inexcusable in any man who professed himself capable of practising in the particular profession. Older decisions certainly seemed to favour law agents. It is fair to say that the later decisions in *Donoghue v Stevenson*[3] in relation to negligence in general and *Hunter v Hanley*[4] in relation to professional negligence in particular have drawn the threads of these concepts firmly together.

1 *Cooke v Falconer's Reps* (1850) 13 D 157.
2 (1868) 7 M 173.
3 1932 SC (HL) 31, 1932 SLT 317.
4 1955 SC 200, 1955 SLT 213.

The quality of skill

2.06 Bell sets out rules of responsibility in relation to the hiring of skilled labour[1]. He introduced the notion that where a skill was exercised by a professional person it was to be done according to a standard in that profession, or, in his own words, in accordance with a professional rule of responsibility. He states that:

'By a professional man, a specific act is to be done according to rule if a rule be fixed. When the rule is obscure, professional usage may excuse error.'

Bell also suggests that where express instructions are actually given to a professional person, that person may deviate from these instructions within the fair limits of professional discretion. Bell also points out that if there is a known method of carrying through the particular task, the professional who follows that method takes less risk than one who deviates from that method, although in general Bell affirms that the criteria are still reasonable care and skill. As with many of the succinct statements in Bell's *Principles*, there is encapsulated here one of the modern problems which surround the standard of care, namely, whether or not there may be said to be some sort of absolute duty on solicitors to perform strictly in accordance with written instructions, or whether the duty is only a duty to use ordinary professional practice in the attempt to fulfil instructions[2]. The ingredient of skill and care in the professional contract involving a law agent was described by Lord Justice Clerk Inglis in the following terms[3]:

'The agent, on the one hand, engages that he possesses the requisite skill, and will employ it with all due diligence in the client's service; and the client, on the other hand, becomes bound to supply funds for disbursements, and to pay the agent at the proper time reasonable remuneration for his services. These correlative obligations are all implied, unless any of them be expressly dispensed with; and in a contract of this ordinary kind I think nothing but an express agreement can alter or release either of the parties from the obligations which are *inter essentialia* of the contract.'

The more modern distinction is not so much between gross negligence and lack of skill as between negligence or lack of skill and an error of judgment which might be made by another solicitor.

Glegg states[4] that a law agent like any other professional person is presumed to be possessed of a fair and average knowledge of the practice of his calling, but does not require to be a specialist and is not liable simply for an error of judgment or a misinterpretation of the law. Glegg quotes Lord Chancellor Cottenham in the case of *Hart v Frame & Co*[5]:

'Professional men possessed of a reasonable portion of information and skill, according to the duties they undertake to perform, and exercising what they so possess with reasonable care and diligence in the affairs of their employers, certainly ought not to be held liable for errors in judgment, whether in matters of law or of discretion. Every case, therefore, must depend upon its own peculiar circumstances, and where an injury has been sustained, which could not have arisen except from the want of such reasonable information and skill or the absence of such reasonable skill and diligence, the law holds the attorney liable.'

Glegg points out that there is a difference between a failure to carry out instructions and an error in judgment or discretion[6]. The older authorities leave us with the notion that the following were important points in relation to claims for negligence against law agents or solicitors and indeed other professionals:

(1) The professional person had to profess a skill, although only in the general manner of his or her own particular profession.
(2) The professional person contracted to provide an ordinary level of skill, but not necessarily a specialist level of skill.
(3) If the particular profession had a set method or rule for the carrying out of a particular task that would be relevant and a professional person would be more likely to be negligent if he or she deviated from that particular method or rule.
(4) There was a clear difference between a failure to exercise the appropriate degree of skill and the making of an error of judgment in a particular matter, only the former giving rise to a claim.
(5) Liability tended to arise in cases of gross negligence only.
(6) The particular terms of the contract or instructions could impose particular duties quite apart from any general duty to perform with the required skill, but some professional discretion could still be exercised in relation to particular instructions.

1 *Principles* s 154.
2 See Chapter 3 below.
3 *Bell v Ogilvie* (1863) 2 M 336 at 341.
4 A T Glegg *The Law of Reparation in Scotland* (2nd edn, 1905) p 591.
5 (1839) Macl & R 595 at 614.
6 *Reparation* p 593.

The modern standard: *Hunter v Hanley*

2.07 In modern cases involving professional negligence the test which is universally applied is the test set out in *Hunter v Hanley*[1]. That case may be said to have buried for ever the notion that a professional person will be liable only for gross negligence. Lord President Clyde laid down a general test for the establishment of liability on the part of a professional person. The case itself was a case involving a doctor, but the test is applicable to solicitors and to any other professionals. In the Outer House the Lord Ordinary had charged the jury to the effect that the test was whether there had been such a departure from normal and usual practice as could reasonably be described as gross negligence. In the Outer House Lord Patrick charged the jury in the following manner[2]:

'There must be such a departure from the normal and usual practice of general practitioners as can reasonably be described as gross negligence . . . there must be a serious departure from a normal practice, if that normal practice has been proved, and the serious departure must involve a substantial and serious fault.'

The jury found for the doctor and the patient enrolled a motion for a new trial on the ground of misdirection on the standard of care. The Inner House held that the Lord Ordinary had misdirected the jury in relation to the test for negligence. The case was heard before a bench of five judges. Lord Russell stated[3]:

'. . . It appears to me that in civil claims based on negligence and including claims against professional men, there is, as recognised in recent precedents and practice only one standard, viz, the absence of reasonable care in the circumstances or ordinary *culpa*.'

Lord Sorn, when comparing the modern authorities with older authorities, stated[4]:

'I think that these and other cases have resulted in a development which makes it doubtful whether in a question of civil liability such as we have here, there remains any room for the conception of "gross negligence" as distinct from "negligence". Liability follows negligence and negligence consists in the failure to perform a duty of care. Of course it must be seen to that the proper test for negligence is applied. Whether it is lack of skill that is alleged, or lack of diligence, or both, the defender must not be judged by too high a standard and I endorse what your Lordship has said on this matter.'

Lord Sorn was endorsing the judgment of the Lord President and it is that judgment which now contains the classic definition of the standard of care in professional negligence cases. Before defining the standard of care Lord President Clyde highlighted three matters concerning professional negligence:

(1) That in the case of a professional person the concept of negligence was not as clear as it was in the general law.
(2) That there would be scope for a genuine difference of opinion in relation to medical or other professional matters.
(3) That there would, in any profession, be differing levels of skill.

The Lord President was of the view that the true test was whether or not the professional person had been proved to be guilty of such a failure as no other member of that profession of ordinary skill would be guilty of if acting with ordinary care[5]. The Lord President appeared to accept the words of the Lord Chancellor in *Hart v Frame & Co*[6], but redefined the phrase 'gross negligence' as indicating so marked a departure from the normal standard as to infer a lack of ordinary skill and care. The Lord President did not believe that there was really any difference in levels of negligence, nor did he accept that it was necessary to show that a professional person had been grossly negligent for a claim to succeed. The basic standard by which a professional should be judged was whether that professional had been guilty of such failure as no other professional of ordinary skill would be guilty of if acting with ordinary care. The Lord President also considered claims which are based on a deviation from normal practice. Drawing together all the arguments the Lord President set out the test for negligence arising from a deviation from normal practice in the following terms[7]:

'It follows from what I have said that in regard to allegations of deviation from ordinary professional practice – and this is the matter with which the present note is concerned – such a deviation is not necessarily evidence of negligence. Indeed it would be disastrous if this were so, for all inducement to progress in medical science would then be destroyed. Even a substantial deviation from normal practice may be warranted by the particular circumstances. To establish liability by a doctor where deviation from normal practice is alleged, three facts require to be established. First of all it must be proved that there is a usual and normal practice; secondly it must be proved that the defender has not adopted that practice; and thirdly (and this is of crucial importance) it must be established that the course the doctor adopted is one which no professional man of ordinary skill would have taken if he had been acting with ordinary care. There is clearly a heavy onus on a pursuer to establish these three facts, and without all three his case will fail. If this is the test, then it matters nothing how far or how little he deviates from the ordinary practice. For the extent of deviation is not the test. The deviation must be of a kind which satisfies the third of the requirements just stated.'

This quotation is fuller than is normally given. The author takes the view that it is necessary to look at everything said by the Lord President. Many claimants think that if something goes wrong there must be a claim. Many practitioners acting for claimants think that if a solicitor does something unusual and this results in a loss, there must be a claim. Neither of these two propositions is actually accurate. A claim for negligence will succeed only if a solicitor has failed to exhibit the level of skill which would normally be exhibited by another solicitor exercising ordinary care. Many claims are also based on deviation from normal practice, such deviation being treated as evidence that the usual and normal level of skill has not been exhibited. The Lord President remarked that where the claim was based on deviation from normal practice, *three* things required to be proved and the onus of proof would always be heavy. The standard of care is essentially a negative evidential test. What must be shown where deviation is alleged is not just that some members of the particular profession would have acted in a different way. It may not even help to show that the vast majority of professional persons would have acted in a different way. It must be shown that *no* other professional acting with *ordinary* skill would have acted in the manner complained of. In general terms ordinary skill is not necessarily the best skill, and there is clearly a difference in relation to claims against solicitors between ordinary practice and best practice. Apart from what is contracted for in special contracts with solicitors, the implied standard is one of ordinary skill. This is a notion which is often overlooked. Where the claim is based on deviation from normal practice, there are three elements to the test for negligence and it is appropriate to look at each one of them separately while bearing in mind that a court can still hold that there has been negligence where ordinary skill and care has not been exhibited irrespective of the practice employed by the solicitor.

1 1955 SC 200, 1955 SLT 213.
2 Quoted at 1955 SC 202.
3 1955 SC 200 at 207.
4 Ibid at 208.
5 Ibid at 205.
6 (1839) Macl & R 595.
7 *Hunter v Hanley* 1955 SC 200 at 206, 1955 SLT 213 at 217.

Ordinary skill and the usual and normal practice

2.08 Bell indicated[1] that a practice or a rule of a particular profession would be relevant in assessing the degree of skill and care required from a professional person. *Hunter v Hanley*[2] formalises this part of the test where the claim is based on deviation from a normal practice. Apart from a breach of a specific instruction or a breach of the general standard of skill and care where there is an alleged deviation, for negligence to be proved it will have to be shown that whatever task the solicitor was performing was normally performed by solicitors in a particular way. This first part of the test is often ignored. There is a tendency simply to examine the conduct of the solicitor and then to cast around for evidence that other solicitors would not have acted as he or she acted. That rather pre-supposes that there must always be some sort of general practice in the profession in relation to every task undertaken. It is, however, perfectly possible to obtain the evidence of another solicitor as to differing practice without actually establishing a general practice in the first instance.

It may be, for example, that a number of solicitors would give evidence to the effect that they would not accept a letter of comfort from a local authority in relation to major alterations recently carried out to a property in place of a building warrant and completion certificate. That, however, may not be the same as saying that there actually exists in the profession a usual and normal practice in relation to letters of comfort at the present time. It seems to the author that there are various practices adopted by the profession in relation to letters of comfort depending on the age and extent of the alterations and the precise amount of comfort offered in the letter. A usual and normal practice sometimes takes years, if not decades, to establish. When the author entered his apprenticeship in 1967, an offer for heritable property generally ran to half a dozen clauses. Only occasionally did an offer provide that the seller must produce a clear planning report from a local authority. No one would now seriously suggest that there was not a usual and normal practice among solicitors to insert such a clause. Equally, however, it is doubtful whether anyone could say with certainty when that particular practice was adopted by the profession.

In a very real sense, the profession sets its own standards of care by setting its own usual and normal practice. A usual and normal practice is not so much a matter of law as a matter of evidence. The existence and extent of the practice is usually established by expert evidence taken from other solicitors who are recognised as experts in the particular field and who generally have a considerable number of years' experience. Where an action goes to proof it is not uncommon for each side to lead evidence from an expert. The opinion given is, of course, based on a particular version of the facts, but there can be genuine differences of opinion among experts as to the usual and normal practice. Theoretically, if a solicitor can show that he or she adopted one of the usual and normal practices there should be no question of negligence[3]. There have, however, been cases where the court has preferred the evidence of one expert to another[4]. In *Peach v Iain G Chalmers & Co*, a case involving surveyors, Lord Caplan said[5]:

'However I do not regard any of the cases that I have cited as precluding the rejection of one strand of expert opinion if grounds exist for so doing.'

Although the existence of a usual practice is generally a matter for evidence, it must always be borne in mind that deviation from a usual practice is only one matter which can be used to prove negligence. The court does still have a residual authority to hold that there has been a failure to exhibit ordinary skill and care and that there has therefore been negligence as a matter of law[6].

1 *Principles* s 154.
2 1955 SC 200, 1955 SLT 213.
3 *Bolam v Friern Hospital Management Committee* [1957] 2 All ER 118 at 121, [1957] 1 WLR 582 at 587; *Maynard v West Midlands Regional Health Authority* [1985] 1 All ER 635, [1984] 1 WLR 634; *Gordon v Wilson* 1992 SLT 849.
4 *G & K Ladenbau (UK) Ltd v Crawley and de Reya* [1978] 1 All ER 682, [1978] 1 WLR 266.
5 1992 SCLR 423 at 427.
6 See the comments of Oliver J in *Midland Bank Trust Co Ltd v Hett, Stubbs & Kemp* [1979] Ch 384 at 402, [1978] 3 All ER 571 at 582; *Brown v Gould & Swayne* [1996] PNLR 130.

Failure to adopt the practice

2.09 In cases involving alleged deviation from normal practice, even if it is proved that there is a normal practice, it must then be proved that the solicitor concerned failed to adopt that practice. In many ways, this should be the easiest branch of the test to satisfy. It ought to be obvious from the evidence whether or not the solicitor has conformed to the usual and normal practice. Nevertheless, it is in this area that there may be evidential difficulties, especially if the failure relates to a lack of communication, failure to follow an instruction or the taking of an alleged instruction to deviate from normal practice.

It may be obvious from a solicitor's file that there has been a failure to obtain a title which contains a properly constituted servitude right of access over a private road. On the other hand, the file may not disclose the content of oral communings between the solicitor and the client over this point. In a number of cases, the solicitor will allege that the client was fully advised of the lack of a formally constituted servitude right of access but nevertheless instructed the solicitor to proceed. It is in this part of the test that the solicitor's file and file notes may be of crucial importance. A solicitor who has given full and adequate advice will not normally be negligent if the client refuses to follow that advice and gives an instruction which if followed must carry a risk for the client[1]. The same will not be true if the instruction is the result of wrong or inadequate advice[2].

1 *Waine v Kempster* (1859) 1 F & F 695.
2 *Lee v Dixon* (1863) 3 F & F 744.

Ordinary skill and ordinary care

2.10 The third branch of Lord President Clyde's test for negligence is that 'it must be established that the course . . . adopted is one which no professional man of ordinary skill would have taken if he had been acting with ordinary care'[1]. It is significant that the word 'ordinary' is used twice in this part of the definition. It is this part of the definition which often causes the most difficulty because, in a way, it faces both ways. On the one hand, it accepts that there may be a usual and normal practice in the profession and that that practice may not have been followed. On the other hand, it lays down quite clearly that that may not matter if an ordinary professional exercising ordinary care might also have deviated from the usual course. Here the Lord President ties in the question of deviation from normal practice with the general duty to exhibit ordinary skill and care.

It is at this point that one wonders whether or not the test comes very close to saying that a professional person is only liable for gross negligence or *culpa lata*. In the first place, who is the mythical 'professional man of ordinary skill' in the legal profession today? At one time, it was thought that a solicitor or law agent was the client's general man of business capable of seeing a client through every stage in life: the purchase of a property, the making of a will, the acquisition of a business, the framing of a partnership agreement, the formation of a private company, the ultimate floatation of the business as a public company, the handling of a divorce and, finally, the winding up of an estate. It has to be accepted that modern practice, even in a small or middle sized firm, is not like this. Even in a two-partner firm, one generally finds that one partner handles the conveyancing and chamber practice and another the court practice. In larger firms, there are various departments and sub-divisions within these departments. It would be difficult nowadays to find a solicitor who claimed to be a general man of business with expertise in all areas of law.

Accordingly, it must now be accepted that this part of the definition will require to be taken against the background of specialisation. It cannot be seriously argued that just because a general practitioner in an outlying country practice has never been involved in a share purchase agreement, he or she would not require to exercise that degree of skill appropriate to ordinary practitioners in that particular area of law. Those who practise in that area of law know that it is normal practice for the seller of the shares to grant a number of warranties in relation to the company. A solicitor who simply carried through a transaction of this type for a purchaser on the basis of executed share transfers would undoubtedly be negligent, unless specifically instructed to proceed in this manner. It would not be a defence to show that many solicitors engaged in general practice with no real experience of company transactions might have proceeded in the same manner. It seems, therefore, that the words 'in the particular area concerned' must now be added after the words 'professional man of ordinary skill' in the original test, whether the negligence claim is based on a breach of the ordinary standard of skill and care or an alleged deviation from normal practice. Conversely, where a client chooses a solicitor who is known to be a specialist, that solicitor must exhibit the skill normally exhibited by other solicitors specialising in the same field[2].

1 See *Hunter v Hanley* 1955 SC 200 at 206, 1955 SLT 213 at 217, and para 2.07 above.
2 See the remarks of Megarry J in *Duchess of Argyll v Beuselinck* [1972] 2 Lloyd's Rep 172 at 183, as discussed in R Jackson and John L Powell *Professional Negligence* (3rd edn, 1993) para 4–52.

2.11 Even if it can be shown that the course adopted in deviating from normal practice is one which no professional man of ordinary skill would have taken, it still has to be shown that he was not acting with ordinary care. It is at this point that the difference between negligence and an error of judgment arises. It has long been regarded as essential that those who profess a skill do so on an almost personal level. In other words, they have or ought to have some individual spark which makes them worth consulting. It has also long been accepted that the carrying through of a task by a professional may involve some degree of risk, however small, to the client or customer. No surgeon can guarantee that each and every operation will be a success, nor even that a routine operation is free from risk. Similarly, no solicitor can guarantee that a particular title may not be subject to a servitude which has been constituted by prescription, as opposed to one which is constituted in a recorded or registered deed. Few solicitors would ever dare to predict the outcome of a court action.

Accordingly, failure to achieve the client's particular purpose does not of itself signify that there has been negligence. The doctrine of *res ipsa loquitur* has no application in professional negligence claims. The difficulty for anyone attempting to prove negligence is, of course, that there may be differences of opinion within a profession as to the appropriate level of skill and care or the usual and normal practice. This is very often the difficulty with medical negligence cases, where there can be responsible bodies of medical opinion on either side of the argument. Thus in *Gordon v Wilson*[1] it was held that a doctor was not negligent in delaying to refer a patient to a specialist, despite the fact that there was clear evidence from medical experts that a reasonable doctor would have referred the patient at an earlier date. There was also a body of medical opinion to the effect that a reasonable doctor would have delayed referral. Where there is a divergence of views among experts it is not normally a question of lining up the experts on either side of the argument and accepting that the majority view represents the standard of care by which the professional is to be judged. If there is a substantial minority view, and that view is reasonable within the context of professionally held views, then a negligence action should fail if the test in *Hunter v Hanley*[2] is strictly followed, because what must be shown is that *no other* professional person of ordinary skill would have taken that particular course of action if acting with ordinary care[3]. Nevertheless, courts do not always follow this logic[4].

1 1992 SLT 849.
2 1955 SC 200, 1955 SLT 317.
3 For a general discussion of the difficulties posed by the *Hunter v Hanley* test in medical negligence and professional negligence in general, see Thomson *Delictual Liability* pp 131–133 and Stewart *Delict* para 5.8.
4 See para 2.08 above.

The historical standard of care in English law

2.12 As with Scots law, earlier English decisions tend to suggest that solicitors were only liable in cases where there had been gross negligence as opposed to a degree of lack of skill. In *Purves v Landell* Lord Brougham stated[1]:

'But it is of the very essence of this action for negligence of a crass description which we call *crassa neglentia* that there should be gross ignorance, that the man who has undertaken to perform the duty of an attorney . . . should have undertaken to discharge the duty professionally, for which he was very ill qualified, or, if not ill qualified to discharge it, which he had so negligently discharged as to damnify his employer, or deprive him of the benefit which he had a right to expect from the service.'

In that case, Lord Brougham drew a distinction between the giving of bad or erroneous advice which resulted in some sort of loss to the client and complete incompetence on the part of the solicitor. It was only the latter, apparently, which would found a negligence claim[2]. Like Scots law, English law has moved on from a situation where only *culpa lata* or gross negligence could found a claim against a solicitor. In the standard English text on professional negligence, the authors submit that the nineteenth-century authorities on the level of skill and care required of solicitors must be treated with caution except in cases where they have been expressly approved in more recent decisions[3].

1 (1845) 12 Cl & Fin 91 at 98–99.
2 For examples of other early English cases where this standard was adopted, see *Baikie v Chandless* (1811) 3 Camp 17; *Faithfull v Kesteven* (1910) 103 LT 56, CA.
3 Jackson and Powell *Professional Negligence* para 4–38.

The modern standard of care in English law

2.13 The modern standard of care in English law is broadly similar to the standard of care in Scots law. It is that standard to be expected of a reasonably competent solicitor acting with due care and attention. The English position, however, does tend to emphasise any specific instructions given[1]. In English law as in Scots law a distinction is drawn between negligence and an error of judgment in a particular matter. In the leading case of *Midland Bank Trust Co Ltd v Hett, Stubbs & Kemp* Oliver J described the general standard of care in the following terms[2]:

'Now no doubt the duties owed by a solicitor to his client are high, in the sense that he holds himself out as practising in a highly skilled and exacting profession, but I think that the court must beware of imposing upon solicitors . . . duties which go beyond the scope of the work they are requested and undertake to do. It may be that a particularly meticulous and conscientious practitioner would, in his client's general interest, take it upon himself to pursue a line of enquiry beyond the strict limits comprehended by his instructions. But that is not the test. The test is what the reasonably competent practitioner would do having regard to the standards normally adopted in his profession.'

Jackson and Powell sum up the content of the duty of care under English law by quoting the views of a judge in a Canadian case[3]. In that case Riley J stated that the implied obligations on a solicitor were:

'1 To be skilful and careful;
2 To advise his client in all matters relevant to his retainer, so far as may be reasonably necessary;
3 To protect the interest of his client;
4 To carry out his instructions by all proper means;
5 To consult with his client on all questions of doubt which do not fall within the express or implied discretion left to him;
6 To keep his client informed to such an extent as may be reasonably necessary, according to the same criteria.'

Again, it should be noted that this general description of the standard of care makes reference to the retainer and any instructions given, as well as the general standard to be expected of a reasonably competent solicitor.

1 Jackson and Powell *Professional Negligence*, para 4–40.
2 *Midland Bank Trust Co Ltd v Hett, Stubbs & Kemp* [1979] Ch 384 at 402–403, [1978] 3 All ER 571 at 583.
3 *Tiffin Holdings Ltd v Millican* (1991) 49 DLR (2d) 216.

Evidence of reasonable skill and care

2.14 One of the fundamental aspects of the standard of skill and care is that the solicitor's conduct has to be judged in accordance with the standards applicable at the time of the alleged negligence. The concept of professional negligence is a moving and not a static concept. The result of advice given or action taken by a solicitor may not be the desired or expected result nor a satisfactory result for the client, but that does not necessarily mean that there has been negligence. Hindsight alone is not something which can be used to found a claim of negligence. It has to be shown that the practice adopted by the solicitor at the time did not come up to the required standard of care at that time[1]. In

Cooke v Falconer's Reps[2] it was held that the court would look at the state of law as it stood at the time of the error and not as it had been elucidated by subsequent decisions. The Lord President stated[3]:

'The matter was not free from doubt. No doubt it is now a settled point; but we must draw ourselves back to the period when this alleged gross piece of ignorance was committed. It is plain . . . that this was a question of very considerable doubt.'

It must be accepted, however, that it is often very difficult to ascertain and apply the standards of bygone practice to the actions of solicitors in relation to a current claim. In negligence claims, evidence is often led from other solicitors who are regarded as experienced in the particular type of practice called into question. These experts should give evidence as to what the practice was among solicitors at the time of the conduct. It is often very difficult for an expert practitioner to place himself or herself in a different time. Practitioners are used to adjusting to changes in the law and practice and the main concern of a practitioner, expert or otherwise, is to keep up to date and not out of date.

1 *Bell v Strathearn & Blair* (1954) 104 LJ 618 (the Scottish report of this case deals with whether the pursuers required a mandate to bring the action); *Duchess of Argyll v Beuselinck* [1972] 2 Lloyd's Rep 172.
2 (1850) 13 D 157.
3 Ibid at 171.

Errors of judgment and law

2.15 Assuming that this hurdle can be overcome, there is a difference between making an error of judgment in a particular matter and failing to meet the required standard of care. If it can be shown that a solicitor has conformed to standard practice, then, provided he or she has not breached a particular contractual instruction, it is likely that there will be no negligence. It is accepted that there are points of law on which there can be differing opinions. In litigation matters there are always two opposing sides and no one would seriously suggest that the legal representatives of the losing litigant must be negligent. So far as the actual body of the law is concerned, older authorities suggest that theoretically solicitors are not expected to know every aspect of the law and be able to quote the correct chapter and verse for each and every situation[1].

Even earlier decisions do, however, draw a distinction between ignorance of statute or case which contains a clear rule and an error in interpretation of the law which might have been made by any practitioner. In *Lee v Walker*[2] a patent agent was held liable where loss occurred to his client as a result of the agent's ignorance of a particular decision which related to his field of expertise, namely, the law relating to patent applications. Where the law has been unclear the solicitor should not be liable if he or she adopts a particular interpretation which turns out to be wrong, provided the interpretation is one which some practitioners might have adopted. There are a number of older cases which illustrate this principle[3]. In *Maclean v Grant*[4] a writer was employed to enforce a testamentary provision against the testator's heritable estate. He did this by adjudication. Part of the estate was feudally vested in the testator, but part was still vested in his father. Because of the method used it was eventually held that the adjudication ranked only on parts of the estate and Mrs Maclean received no part of the provision in her favour. Several other agents for creditors had made the same mistake and raised fresh adjudications. Mrs Maclean's agent did not. The mistake arose because of a misinterpretation of a recent Act of Parliament. It was held that the agent was not liable because the interpretation of the particular statute had been open to some doubt. In *Cooke v Falconer's Reps*[5] there was an error in publishing an inhibition in 1804 which was set aside in 1815. The state of the law in 1804 was, however, unclear and the court held that the agent was not liable. The Lord President opined[6]:

'It is a case to which we must look narrowly; and we must inquire whether there was . . . any negligence so gross and culpable as rendered him liable for this neglect. Is it to be said that, with all these conflicting decisions, it was *luce clarius* what course should have been pursued? The matter was not free from doubt . . . It is plain from Mr Ross's lectures, and from the decisions, that this was a question of very considerable doubt . . .'

It is sometimes difficult, however, to see how this theory can operate. Even older Scottish authority seems to take the view that a solicitor is likely to escape liability only if the particular legal point is unclear or where there has been no definite ruling. In a modern context it is the author's view that an obvious error in law will render a solicitor liable in negligence, even though the law in question was tucked away in an obscure schedule to an Act of Parliament or a decision which, although not well known, could be looked up. A solicitor will be expected to know where to look for the law. A solicitor will be expected to keep up to date in his or her own area of practice and to know his or her own limitations. A solicitor will also be expected to know when to seek expert help from counsel or from another practising solicitor. It is unlikely to be a defence to a claim for damages that a solicitor was unaware of a particular statute or decision, although it will still be a defence if a reasonable interpretation of the law turns out to be incorrect[7].

1 *Montriou v Jefferys* (1825) 2 C & P 113 at 116, where the learned judge stated that no lawyer including a judge was bound to know all the law.
2 (1872) LR 7 CP 121.
3 *Grant v McLeay* (1791) Bell Oct Cas 319; *Maclean v Grant* 15 November 1805 FC 495; *Cooke v Falconer's Reps* (1850) 13 D 157.
4 15 November 1805 FC 495.
5 (1850) 13 D 157.
6 Ibid at 171.
7 For a discussion of the position in England, see Jackson and Powell *Professional Negligence*, paras 4–41 and 4–42.

Courts overruling general practice

2.16 It might be thought from the decision in *Hunter v Hanley*[1] that if a solicitor can establish that there is a general practice and that he or she did not deviate from it, there can be no question of a claim for negligence. It should always, however, be remembered that professional negligence is only a branch of the general law, whether a claim is brought under contract or delict, and that a contractual claim is still based on a duty of care. It is therefore always open to the courts to ignore a general practice and decide that there has been negligence even where the general practice has been followed. This occured in the important Privy Council case of *Edward Wong Finance Co Ltd v Johnson Stokes & Master*[2].

This case was an appeal to the Privy Council from the Court of Appeal in Hong Kong. The Court of Appeal in Hong Kong had held that solicitors were not negligent in circumstances where they allowed the proceeds of a loan to be paid over without obtaining a clear title and in turn a valid and effectual security for the lenders. The solicitors had conformed to what was described as 'Hong Kong practice' in allowing the funds to be released in exchange for an undertaking from the seller's solicitor to hand over a clear and unencumbered title. The seller's solicitor absconded with the funds.

Evidence was led in the case which showed that the solicitor had acted in accordance with the general practice of the profession in Hong Kong. The Privy Council held that the solicitor had been negligent because the general practice itself involved foreseeable risks. While the local law society of Hong Kong had not condemned the practice, a report had been issued by them which pointed out the risks involved in the practice. There was therefore an element of foreseeable risk which in the view of the Privy Council ought to have been foreseen. This is perhaps an unusual case but it may have implications for Scotland.

The English procedure for the settlement of conveyancing transactions is apparently different in that two cheques are routinely handed over, one of which is payable to any heritable creditors of the seller to discharge any secured debt. In the Hong Kong case, the heritable creditors of the seller were not paid because the solicitor absconded with the money and, accordingly, a clear title could not be delivered. It is sometimes the practice in Scottish transactions to accept a letter of obligation from the seller's solicitor undertaking to deliver a signed discharge together with an appropriate form instructing the recording or registration of the discharge. This can happen where the transaction is being settled very quickly after conclusion of missives or where an independent solicitor acts for the lender to the seller. One wonders what the decision of the court might be if a cheque were to be paid over to the seller's solicitor in exchange for such an undertaking and the seller's solicitor thereafter failed to implement the undertaking because the price was insufficient to pay off the seller's loan. The question may be academic because the seller's solicitor's obligation would normally be covered by the master policy, but there could conceivably be an argument that there was a responsibility on the purchaser's solicitor to assess the value and worth of the undertaking being given by the seller's solicitor and the risks involved in accepting the undertaking. There would, of course, be an alternative method of settling at a meeting involving the lender or the lender's agents at which the documents and cheques were all handed round.

One of the factors in the Privy Council's decision in the *Edward Wong* case was that the seller's solicitor was a recently established sole practitioner. The insurance cover in respect of letters of obligation of a non-classic kind has been altered recently, and the practice of solicitors in relation to letters of obligation and undertakings between firms is always the subject of discussion. In these circumstances, general practice among solicitors should perhaps be altered in circumstances where the risk may be greater than usual[3]. In general terms some judges will be more likely to accept evidence of practice as being the measure of the duty of care than others. In the leading English case of *Midland Bank Trust Co Ltd v Hett, Stubbs & Kemp*, Oliver J seemed less than impressed by the evidence of a number of experienced solicitors. He expressed himself in the following terms[4]:

'The extent of the legal duty in any given situation must, I think, be a question of law for the court. But evidence which really amounts to no more than an expression of opinion by a particular practitioner of what he thinks he would have done . . . in the position of the defendants is of little assistance to the court; whilst evidence of the witnesses' view of what, as a matter of law, the solicitor's duty was in the particular circumstances of the case is, I should have thought, inadmissible for that is the very question which it is the court's function to decide.'

1 1955 SC 200, 1955 SLT 213.
2 [1984] AC 296, [1984] 2 WLR 36.
3 For a discussion on letters of obligation, see Rennie 'Letters of Obligation' 1995 SLPQ 87.
4 [1979] Ch 384 at 402, [1978] 3 All ER 571 at 582; and see *Brown v Gould & Swayne* [1996] PNLR 130, where the court held that evidence of a conveyancing expert was inadmissible.

Disagreements as to general practice

2.17 In many negligence cases which come to court, expert witnesses are cited by the claimant and the solicitor. In these circumstances it is obvious that there may be a difference of opinion as to the practice generally employed by solicitors in relation to the particular point. One has, of course, to understand that the opinion given by an expert very often depends on the particular set of facts put before him or her. Any court practitioner will be able to testify to the fact that pursuer and defender in any litigation often have completely different versions of the facts in question. Nevertheless, there can be genuine differences of opinion even where the facts are agreed[1]. This difference of opinion can arise because there may be different practices in different areas but more often it arises because the two experts adopt differing standards of practice. It is often difficult to remember that the standard required under the *Hunter v Hanley* principle is ordinary practice not best practice. All that is required is that the solicitor come up to normal standard in the profession. Where experts give opposing views on the same set of facts, one might think that there would be no negligence, but a court is at liberty to assess the level of expertise and experience which each expert has and decide whose evidence is to be accepted[2]. In the author's view, where there has been an obvious loss as a result of a practice adopted, a court is more likely to find that there has been negligence than not in a case where there is a difference of opinion as to standard practice[3].

1 See *Gordon v Wilson* 1992 SLT 849.
2 *Peach v Iain G Chalmers & Co* 1992 SCLR 423.
3 See, for example, *G & K Ladenbau (UK) Ltd v Crawley and de Reya* [1978] 1 All ER 682, [1978] 1 WLR 266.

The effect of Law Society regulations and recommendations

2.18 The Law Society of Scotland is the professional body which controls the conduct of solicitors. It also has powers to decide that a solicitor has in a particular set of circumstances provided an inadequate professional service, to order that fees be reduced or waived and also to order that limited compensation be payable. The Law Society has promulgated various regulations, including a code of conduct and regulations dealing with professional practice where acting for both parties[1]. The Law Society also issues practice notes, guidelines and publications which are all designed to help solicitors in various aspects of practice[2]. If a solicitor breaches these rules, then this is likely to be adduced as evidence that the standard of care was not met. If, after all, a solicitor does not comply with the professional standards laid down by his or her own professional body, that solicitor can hardly argue that there has been no negligence if failure to comply with the professional rule in question can be said to have resulted in a loss to the client. This causal link may not be proved in every case, but there is no doubt that courts will have regard to the professional standards adopted by the solicitor concerned in the particular transaction or litigation.

Solicitors who act for both parties must comply with the regulations laid down. These regulations contain prohibitions on acting for both parties except in certain circumstances, and even in circumstances where dual representation is allowed there are safeguards set down to ensure that both clients are aware of the situation and of the fact that they would require to take independent advice should any conflict arise. If some of the formal requirements in the rules have not been carried out then this will tend to suggest to a court that there may have been an overall slackness in the handling of the transaction. The solicitors may then face an uphill struggle to prove that whatever has gone wrong has not gone wrong because of their own action or inaction. If, for example, a solicitor acts for both parties in a purchase and sale of a dwellinghouse and fails to advise both parties at the outset in writing that he or she is acting for both parties, and also fails to take account of the fact that since one of the parties is not an established client, he or she should not be acting for both parties, that solicitor will be very fortunate to defeat a claim for negligence if something goes wrong with the legal aspects of the conveyancing. In these circumstances the solicitor will almost certainly be caught in the middle of the argument, unable to give impartial advice to either side. In England, where acting for both parties has never been as common as in Scotland, courts have frequently found solicitors liable in negligence cases where they have acted for parties with potentially conflicting interests. The view which has been taken is that if a problem arises, the solicitor, if he continues to act, must be negligent so far as one party or the other party is concerned. As Jackson and Powell put it[3]:

> 'If he makes a mistake or omission to the detriment of either party, the court will more readily castigate the error as "negligent", since he ought not to have put himself in such a position in the first place.'

The same considerations apply in England where solicitors act for both borrower and lender[4]. The more recent English cases involving lack of disclosure of commercial matters to a lender also emphasise the risks involved in acting for borrower and lender, even where the terms of the loan appear to have been negotiated before the solicitor was ever instructed[5].

1 Code of Conduct (Scotland) Rules 1992; Solicitors (Scotland) Practice Rules 1986.
2 See, for example, Law Society Guidelines on Closing Dates 1991; Law Society Guidelines on Acting for Separated Spouses in the Sale of the Matrimonial Home 1994; Law Society Guidelines on Conflict of Interest in Commercial Security Transactions 1994.
3 *Professional Negligence* para 4–58.
4 See *Wills v Wood* (1984) Times, 24 March; *Anglia Hastings & Thanet Building Society v House & Son* (1981) 260 EG 1128.
5 See *Mortgage Express v Bowerman & Partners* (1995) Times, 1 August; *Target Holdings Ltd v Redferns* [1995] 3 All ER 785, [1995] 3 WLR 352; *Bank of East Asia Ltd v Shepherd & Wedderburn, WS* 1995 SCLR 598, 1995 SLT 1074.

The Law Society House Purchase and Sale Guide for Clients

2.19 One of the most recent publications to come from the Law Society of Scotland is the House Purchase and Sale Guide for Clients. This pamphlet is designed for clients, as opposed to solicitors, and it is assumed that solicitors will pass it on to clients.

The pamphlet does not have the force of law nor is it a practice rule or regulation. It is interesting, however, to examine this guide in some detail because it sets out the level of service which clients can expect from solicitors in a domestic conveyancing transaction. The introduction to the guide states that its purpose is to explain what happens in a conveyancing transaction and to give the client an idea of what he or she can expect from a competent and conscientious solicitor. Accordingly, one might expect that a solicitor who deviates from the level of service set out in the pamphlet would be hard pressed to show that there had not been negligence.

The pamphlet characterises good professional service as including good legal advice, prompt attention to business, availability to discuss matters and good communication. A solicitor is also expected to provide the purchasing client with an outline of the whole procedure in the transaction including all financial aspects such as the price, mortgage requirements, expenses and charges. The pamphlet envisages that in a purchase, the solicitor may well note interest and may also have to advise the client on the different types of surveys available and the costs involved. The pamphlet also envisages that the solicitor may give advice regarding the mortgage or loan, there being many different mortgage products available. It is suggested that before any offer is made, the terms of the offer should be discussed with the client, and after the offer has been made the client should receive a copy. It is also suggested that the solicitor should discuss the terms of any qualifications to the offer and give the client copies of all the documents which form the concluded bargain. As one would expect, the pamphlet indicates that the solicitor should examine the title and advise on the title extent and any burdens. In so far as the seller's side of the transaction is concerned, the solicitor should advise the seller as to the precise terms of any offer and any obligations being undertaken. The pamphlet also indicates that the solicitor should advise the seller if bridging will be required and should obtain a redemption statement from any lender. There is no doubt in the author's mind that a document of this type will be used in any negligence claim if it can be shown that a solicitor has not carried through the basic tasks which are set out[1].

1 Jackson and Powell *Professional Negligence*, paras 4–50, 4–51 (where the authors note a trend to uniform practice in England as a result of written standards and protocols issued by the Law Society).

Higher standards of care

2.20 It will always be possible for a client specifically to contract with a solicitor so as to impose higher duties than the normal standard of care. These obligations can, however, arise by implication. It is obvious that no one firm of solicitors is the same as another. A country practice of three partners may be perfectly capable of offering advice on general domestic and commercial conveyancing, court work and matrimonial matters. It might not, however, be in a position to offer advice on a multi-million pound company takeover. If a client consults a specialist in the field, then the standard of care will be that standard to be expected of those who specialise in that particular field[1].

1 See *Duchess of Argyll v Beuselinck* [1972] 2 Lloyd's Rep 172; Jackson and Powell *Professional Negligence*, para 4–52.

Conclusion

2.21 Anyone studying the test laid down by Lord President Clyde in *Hunter v Hanley* might be forgiven for thinking that it must take a brave man or woman with secure financial backing to bring any action against a solicitor for professional negligence. After all, as the Lord President himself points out, the onus is heavy and even where the case is based on an alleged deviation from normal practice there are three hurdles to overcome[1]. Nevertheless, it has to be accepted that claims against solicitors are on the increase and many of them are either successful or are settled before they come to proof. The *Hunter v Hanley* test is used in most occasions where there has not been a breach of a specific instruction and one must therefore wonder why the test appears to be so easily satisfied in so many cases. There are in the author's view several significant reasons for this:

(1) Although it is finally a matter for the court to decide what the standards should be, the court hears evidence from professional expert witnesses as to the appropriate professional practice in the particular area concerned. This evidence is normally taken from senior practitioners with a lengthy experience in the particular branch of law concerned. The practical problem is that in all claims made, there has been a loss of some sort. It is a lot easier for an expert witness to criticise and condemn a particular line of conduct which has resulted in loss than to uphold it. An expert witness who defends a solicitor's conduct has to be prepared to say that he

or she or others in the profession would or could have followed the same practice with the same potentially disastrous results. It is, not surprisingly, sometimes difficult to obtain expert evidence for the defending solicitor. In this respect defending a claim against a medical practitioner can be easier because the general public is sometimes more likely to accept that the doctor is always doing his or her best, that results are never certain and that different doctors even in the same practice often have different approaches to the same medical problem.

(2) A great many claims are brought by institutional lenders in circumstances where there are written instructions or some written code of practice. Very often, it is possible to bypass the general standard of care entirely and simply found on a breach of an actual instruction[2]. It may be, for example, that a solicitor need not report a dead inhibition to a lending client because it does not affect the security or the title. On the other hand, if a particular clause in the written instructions from the lender states that all adverse entries in the personal registers must be disclosed, then there may be a breach of that contractual term. The lender may then allege that had the inhibition been disclosed, no loan would have been made because there was a question mark over the debtor's financial status.

(3) Recent English cases have sought to expand the duty of care to cover general matters of disclosure. All solicitors would accept that they are liable if they fail to record or register a standard security. There may, however, be other matters of information which come to the solicitor's notice which have nothing to do with the validity of the security but which may suggest there is something wrong with the borrower or with the property secured. This type of case is difficult to fit into the test set out in *Hunter v Hanley*. There will be those in the profession who take the view that in the circumstances, there is no legal duty to disclose and that the only duty is to examine the title and prepare a valid security[3]. Nevertheless, courts may now be taking a more robust view of the overall nature of a solicitor's duty of care, especially where lenders are involved[4].

(4) There is always a good reason to settle any action and claims against solicitors are no exception. Few solicitors relish the thought of having to give evidence and defend their own conduct in circumstances where the client has suffered a loss and, of course, the outcome of litigation is never certain. The vast majority of negligence claims are settled without any decision from the court.

(5) There is a tendency in the solicitor profession to gravitate towards uniformity in matters of practice. Many solicitors who see some new clause in another solicitor's offer or lease immediately amend their own *pro forma* documentation to include the clause. The Law Society of Scotland is also keenly involved in questions of skill and general levels of competence and has issued guidance to the profession in many areas[5].

1 1955 SC 200 at 206, 1955 SLT 213 at 217: see para 2.07 above. The courts in England have also indicated that the onus on the claimant is a heavy one: see the discussion in Jackson and Powell *Professional Negligence*, para 4–60.
2 See Chapter 3 below.
3 See *Midland Bank plc v Cameron, Thom, Peterkins & Duncans* 1988 SCLR 209, 1988 SLT 611.
4 See Chapter 5 below.
5 The ill-fated standard missive clauses did not bring about uniform practice but other rules, codes, guidance notes and pamphlets may do so.

CHAPTER 3

The Contract Between Solicitors and Clients

The status of solicitors

3.01 The solicitors' branch of the profession is relatively modern. Law agents as such were first recognised as a nation-wide body by the Law Agents (Scotland) Act 1873. Prior to that there appeared to be a sub-division of law agents into clerks, Writers to the Signet and solicitors. The first recognised solicitors were the Society of Solicitors in the Supreme Courts, who were recognised in 1754[1]. Thereafter, many local societies were formed outwith Edinburgh notably in Aberdeen, Glasgow and Paisley. Various Acts of Sederunt sought to regulate the qualifications of solicitors or procurators[2]. The first attempt to regulate the profession by Act of Parliament came in 1865[3]. This Act effectively allowed procurators in any county or divisional county which did not have an existing society to form themselves into a society. Each society had to issue regulations for the examination of apprentices. In 1870 a Royal Commission recommended one general examination for law agents throughout Scotland and the abolition of the privileges enjoyed by the societies in Aberdeen, Glasgow, Edinburgh and Paisley. The Law Agents (Scotland) Act of 1873 was passed to carry through these recommendations. Nowadays, the solicitors' branch of the profession is regulated by statute[4] and by a host of subordinate legislation taking the form of rules promulgated by the Law Society of Scotland[5].

1 Act of Sederunt 10 August 1754.
2 Act of Sederunt 12 November 1825; Act of Sederunt 10 July 1839.
3 Procurators (Scotland) Act 1865.
4 See the Solicitors (Scotland) Act 1980.
5 For a full historical summary of the development of the solicitors' branch of the profession, see Begg *The Law of Scotland relating to Law Agents* Chapter 1.

The nature of the contract

3.02 The legal relationship between a solicitor and a client is essentially a contract of agency and, apart from claims under delict[1], the legal duties of a solicitor flow from that contract. Despite this it is unusual for the relationship between solicitor and client to be talked of in contractual terms. In some cases the first time that a solicitor realises that his relationship with a client is contractual is when he receives a writ claiming damages for breach of contract. Solicitors and clients tend to view their relationship as a professional relationship where individual instructions are given, received and carried through. One of the reasons for this view is, of course, that the contract between solicitor and client is rarely in writing. Like any contract of agency there is no requirement for the contract to be in writing. The nature of the legal relationship between solicitor and client was set out distinctly by Lord Justice Clerk Inglis in the leading case of *Bell v Ogilvie*. He said[2]:

'The relation of agent and client is in general constituted without any written contract, and without any special contract, either written or verbal. The mere acceptance of employment creates that relation – a relation carrying with it certain well-known consequences, without any necessity for expressing them. The agent, on the one hand, engages that he possesses the requisite skill, and will employ it with all due diligence in the client's service; and the client, on the other hand, becomes bound to supply funds for disbursements, and to pay the agent at the proper time reasonable remuneration for his services. These correlative obligations are all implied, unless any of them be expressly dispensed with.'

In a more recent text, the nature of the contract between solicitor and client has been described as the *fons et origo* of the solicitor's duties[3]. This tends to suggest that the duties of a solicitor may in some cases be limited by the contract[4]. However, the court is unlikely to infer a modification of the solicitor's general duty of care in a contract unless there is a clear written agreement to this effect, and exclusions of liability may fall foul of the provisions of the Unfair Contract Terms Act 1977[5].

1 See para 2.01 above.
2 (1863) 2 M 336 at 340.
3 Jackson and Powell *Professional Negligence* para 4–03.
4 See *Midland Bank Trust Co Ltd v Hett, Stubbs & Kemp* [1979] Ch 384 at 402, [1978] 3 All ER 571 at 582.
5 See para 3.08 below.

A contract to perform services

3.03 The legal relationship between solicitor and client, while essentially a contract of agency, is more than that. The solicitor does not simply act for the client, nor does the solicitor simply carry through instructions blindly. The contract is a contract to perform services to the required standard of care and in accordance with the instructions given. It is important to remember this when dealing with claims of professional negligence. A solicitor's duties may not be strictly confined to the bare instruction. A solicitor who is instructed to purchase heritable property will be bound not only to purchase the property, but also to obtain a good marketable title free from any onerous conditions. On the other hand, a solicitor who contravenes instructions but carries through work to the required standard of care, may still be liable in damages to his client for breach of contract. In essence the solicitor has failed to perform the services contracted for. This is an important point, especially in negligence claims by institutional lenders, where, in the vast majority of cases, the nature and content of the contract between solicitor and lender client is specified in a set of written instructions or mortgage procedures.

Solicitors still, however, owe contractual duties in circumstances where there is no set of written instructions. These contractual duties will be dependant on the nature and content of the instructions received and may from time to time exceed the duties owed under the general standard of care. A solicitor may be approached by a client who wishes to purchase a plot of ground for building. The site may be served by a private access road. It will be a matter of evidence as to whether the contract between solicitor and client extended to placing an obligation on the solicitor to ensure that adequate servitudes exist in respect of services for water, electricity, gas and drainage. On the one hand, the solicitor may argue that all he or she was instructed to do was to purchase a plot of land with access thereto, and that no mention was made of the possibility of the client building anything on the plot which would require services. On the other hand, the client may argue that the solicitor was made aware in general terms of the purpose for which the client wished to purchase the plot.

The difficulty here is that often there will be nothing in writing and it then becomes a question of trying to ascertain in the first place what the specifically agreed contractual duties were and in the second place, what the general duties were in terms of the standard of care. The solicitor may lose on either or both heads of liability. On the one hand, it may be implied that a solicitor purchasing a plot of ground which is obviously not of the size of an agricultural field, ought to have it in contemplation that his client may intend some form of development and therefore at the very least ought to inquire from the client what services and servitudes are required. If this were proved, there could be a breach of the general standard of care. On the other hand, the evidence may show that the client made the solicitor aware of the precise purpose of the purchase and the fact that certain ancillary rights would be necessary. If this were proved, the solicitor would be liable because of a breach of a contractual obligation contained in the instructions from the client.

Instruction notes and communication

3.04 In cases where there are no written instructions, it is important that the solicitor has at least some file note indicating the basic instruction from the client. This applies not just to general instructions given at the commencement of the relationship concerning a particular task, but also to additional instructions given during the continuing relationship on various matters which have arisen from time to time. A solicitor may be instructed to purchase a plot of ground for the erection of a single dwelling-house. It may be that the initial instruction includes a requirement to obtain a right of access along a private road. If the examination of title does not disclose a servitude right of access or a common right in the road, then this is certainly a matter which ought to be reported to the client. The client may be advised that there is evidence that a servitude right of access for foot and vehicular traffic has been exercised for the prescriptive period of twenty years. If the client accepts this position, then that ought to be recorded by a clear file note of the meeting or telephone conversation during which the question was discussed. It should also be followed up, in the opinion of the author, by a letter from the solicitor to the client in which the position is clearly stated and the client's acceptance of that position is clearly stated. The file note and letter should also reiterate any advice given by the solicitor concerning the risks involved in accepting the position where a client instructs a solicitor to do something which carries more than the normal element of risk or which is against advice already given by the solicitor.

It is important to note, however, that a solicitor will not avoid a claim for negligence simply by asking for instructions at every juncture. It is the responsibility of a solicitor to advise a client fully and adequately before asking for advice. Most offers for heritable property are met with qualified acceptances running to a number of clauses, many of which are purely technical in their nature. While a solicitor should send a copy of a qualified acceptance to the client, it is not normally enough to do this without comment and simply ask the client for instructions as to whether or not to conclude the bargain. If the qualified acceptance states that no permissions, warrants or completion certificates are to be produced in respect of a five-year-old dining-room extension, the solicitor must advise the client (including any lender) of the significance of this qualification and the risks which will be undertaken if it is accepted. A defence of following client's instructions will succeed if the client has had appropriate advice but may not succeed in other cases. A client may, for example, insist that missives are concluded for the purchase of a house even where no loan has been arranged, but the solicitor will have an obligation to advise the client that the missives will be legally binding whether or not a loan is obtained[1].

While writing is not necessary for the constitution of the contract between solicitor and client nor for the proof or verification of instructions, there is no doubt that in cases where this is a matter of dispute between solicitor and client, the court is more likely to believe the client if there are neither written communications nor file notes which support the solicitor's position. There are, in the author's view, two main reasons for this. In the first place, claims are very often brought against solicitors some years after the event. A court may well feel that it is more likely that a client will remember the detail of a particular transaction or litigation which has been an important event in the life of that client than a solicitor who has perhaps dealt with hundreds of other transactions or cases in the intervening period. In the second place, the solicitor's evidence is likely to be that while the precise events cannot be recollected, the invariable practice of the solicitor was to act in a particular way or to advise a client in a particular manner[2].

The experience of the insurers and the brokers who manage the master policy for the Law Society of Scotland is that in many cases solicitors have not communicated effectively with their clients, with the result that the client has been left confused or with the wrong impression. Recent examples of this type of genuine confusion include cases where solicitors have been instructed to convey the dwellinghouse of an ageing parent or parents to their children with a view to avoiding the payment of nursing home charges should the parents require nursing care in the future. Generally speaking, the family solicitor is employed to act for all parties in the preparation of the conveyance. The parents will have had a verbal assurance from their children that despite the gift of the house, they will be allowed to live in the house for as long as they require. There may well be an initial meeting between the solicitor and the whole family and the solicitor may well advise the parents at that meeting that there are certain risks involved in conveying the property. It is imperative that these risks are spelled out to the parents in writing. Preferably, the parents should be asked to confirm the instruction in writing so that there is no doubt that they understand the risks.

Problems can and do arise for solicitors in these circumstances where, some years after the conveyance, the children are sequestrated. If there is no reserved liferent or other protection for the parents, then the permanent trustee may simply take the house as an asset for the children's creditors. In a number of cases of this type, the solicitors have been prepared to state that they are sure they must have advised the parents of the risks. Despite this, difficulties arise where there is nothing in writing. Where the parents make a claim against the solicitor for negligence in looking after their interests, it is sometimes counter-productive for the solicitor to state that he or she was well aware of the risks which were being undertaken by the parents. If there is nothing in writing, that merely underlines the obvious risks and may go to help the parents in the negligence claim. To all intents it appears from the file at least that the solicitor knew of the risks but did not advise or do anything to protect the parents[3].

1 Contrast *Morris v Duke-Cohan & Co* (1975) 119 SJ 826 where solicitors were held liable after following instructions with *Okafor v Malcolm Slowe & Co* (1968) 207 EG 345 where they were not; see Ryder *Professional Conduct for Scottish Solicitors* p 96.

2 See Begg *Law Agents* p 74; *Goody v Baring* [1956] 2 All ER 11, [1956] 1 WLR 448; *Robins v Meadows & Moran* [1991] 29 EG 145.

3 See *Hopkinson v Williams* 1993 SLT 907, where solicitors took indirect instructions from a relation of the owner of the property.

Professional standards and codes

3.05 While breaches of Law Society regulations may not themselves amount to negligence, the fact that a solicitor is in breach of a regulation is likely to persuade a court that there may have been an overall slackness in the solicitor's approach. This will apply to help the client pursuing the claim, especially if there is nothing in writing as evidence of the solicitor's version of events. There are various regulations, practice notes and codes which apply to solicitors. While it would not be accurate to say that these amount to obligations which are implied into every contract between solicitor and client, they do set standards of practice which will be relevant in a negligence claim. Where, for example, a solicitor acts for both parties in breach of the professional rules[1], and one suffers a loss which is not obviously connected with the breach, it may still be difficult to convince a court that the solicitor devoted the appropriate amount of skill and care to that party's side of the transaction. What is clear is that there is no lessening of the duty of care to both parties[2], and the courts are likely to hold that there has been negligence if it appears that the solicitor was keen to push through a transaction with little or no regard to the interests of one of the parties[3]. The Law Society of Scotland has promulgated a Code of Conduct for solicitors[4]. Clause 5(a) of the Code states that solicitors must act on the basis of their clients' proper instructions or on the instructions of another solicitor who acts for the client. This proposition is further explained in the Code in the following terms[5]:

'Solicitors require to discuss with and advise their clients on the objectives of the work carried out on behalf of the clients and the means by which the objectives are to be pursued. With the agreement of the client, a solicitor may restrict the objectives and the steps to be taken consistent with the provision of adequate professional service. A solicitor may not accept an improper instruction, for example, to assist a client in a matter which the solicitor knows to be criminal or fraudulent, but a solicitor may advise on the legal consequences of any proposed course of conduct or assist a client in determining the validity, scope or application of the law.'

The Code of Conduct goes on to state that solicitors ought to communicate effectively with their clients and this general proposition includes the obligation to provide clients with relevant information regarding the matter in hand, the action taken on behalf of the client and any significant development in relation to the client's case or transaction. Solicitors are also under an obligation in terms of the Code to explain matters to the extent reasonably necessary to allow the client to take an informed decision regarding the instructions which ought to be given. The Code states that information should be clear and comprehensive and 'where necessary or appropriate, confirmed in writing'. The Code of Conduct merely serves to underline the need for clear, effective and well-evidenced communication between solicitor and client, especially in circumstances where the transaction involved or the step to be taken is unusual. If a solicitor is instructed to do or to accept something which he would not normally do without breaching the general standard of care, then there is no doubt that this ought to be recorded in writing between solicitor and client. Obvious examples of this are:

(1) The making of a gift or some other gratuitous transaction.

(2) The granting of a security in circumstances where the granter derives no benefit from any loan facilities made available, as where a wife signs a standard security as joint owner of a matrimonial home at the request of the husband's bankers in respect of a loan made to the husband's business[6].

(3) The acceptance of a title which is less than marketable or has some other defect, even where it is supported by an insurance indemnity.

(4) The acceptance of a settlement in a court case in terms which might be regarded as unfavourable to the client in circumstances where there is a reasonable prospect of success.

(5) Where the disclosure of some matter has come to the notice of the solicitor and the solicitor feels this must be disclosed to the client, either because of the solicitor's general duty to act in the client's best interests or because of some specific instruction to disclose all matters adversely affecting the client's position[7].

(6) Generally, where solicitors are acting for both parties to a transaction.

(7) Generally, where a solicitor acts on an instruction which is contrary to advice given by the solicitor.

The list above is not, of course, exhaustive and there will be other situations where solicitors may feel that it is necessary to confirm an instruction in writing. The author does not mean to suggest that in each and every case enumerated above where there is no file note or letter confirming the position, the solicitor will be negligent. The problem will be that the solicitor will find it more difficult to prove that the client has been properly advised and was well aware of the situation. It seems to the author that the onus is always likely to be on the solicitor to show that the client was aware of the situation and understood the implications in circumstances where there are no written notes or other communication setting out the position clearly.

1 Solicitors (Scotland) Practice Rules 1986.
2 *Sim v Clark* (1831) 10 S 85.
3 See, for example, *Anglia Hastings & Thanet Building Society v House & Son* (1981) 260 EG 1128.
4 Code of Conduct (Scotland) Rules 1992.
5 Ibid, Clause 5(e).
6 See *Mumford v Bank of Scotland, Smith v Bank of Scotland* 1995 SCLR 839, 1996 SLT 392.

7 See *Mortgage Express v Bowerman & Partners*, (1995) Times, 1 August; *Target Holdings Ltd v Redferns* [1995] 3 All ER 785, [1995] 3 WLR 352; *Bank of East Asia v Shepherd & Wedderburn, WS* 1995 SCLR 598, 1995 SLT 1074.

Implied contractual duties

3.06 Apart from any duties expressly undertaken by the solicitor in the contract with the client, there remains the question as to whether the general nature of the task entrusted to the solicitor results in certain obligations to do specific things being implied into the contract. For the most part, implied duties of this kind are dealt with in the context of the overall general duty of care, but there has been some attempt, at least in England, to imply specific duties arising out of particular contracts or retainers between solicitor and client. One of the leading English cases in relation to this matter and in relation to negligence claims against solicitors in general is *Midland Bank Trust Co Ltd v Hett, Stubbs & Kemp*[1].

The facts of the case were that in March 1961 a father agreed to grant to his son an option to purchase from him a 300-acre farm, which at the time was let to the son by the father. Father and son went to a firm of solicitors who drew up a document which was signed by the father and dated 24 March 1961. The document granted an option to the son to purchase the farm at £75.00 per acre, provided that the option was exercised within a period of 10 years. A nominal option fee of £1.00 was paid, but the solicitors forgot to register the option as an estate contract under the Land Charges Act 1925. The son discussed the possible exercise of the option with the firm of solicitors on a number of occasions. On 17 August 1967 the father, having consulted other solicitors and having discovered that the option had not been registered, sold the farm and conveyed it to his wife with the sole object of defeating the option. After the sale the solicitors registered the option and on 6 October 1967 the son served notice purporting to exercise the option. Neither the father nor his wife complied with the notice. The wife died and the son sued his father and his mother's executors seeking a declarator that the option was binding. On 8 February 1972, the father died and on 11 May 1973 the son died. The son's executors continued the action which was not successful except for an award of damages against the father's estate. Before he died, the son had commenced an action against the solicitors for negligence and his executors continued the action. The solicitors were found liable and it was held that the case was not time-barred.

The judge (Oliver J) analysed the potential liability of the solicitors in delict and in contract and in an exhaustive judgment, citing a wealth of English authority, attemped to analyse the particular contractual obligations undertaken by the solicitors in the transaction. In this analysis the judge attempted to move away from the general duty to perform a professional contract to the basic professional standard. The judge stated that a contract between a solicitor and a client gave rise to a complex series of rights and duties of which the duty to exercise reasonable care and skill was only one. He compared the duties of a solicitor to the duties of a carpenter employed to supply and construct oak shelving. He indicated that such a contract involved several contractual duties. The carpenter had to supply oak wood of adequate quality and to fix the shelf with reasonable care and skill. In the case before him, Oliver J held that the obligations undertaken by the solicitors were specifically to draw up and have completed an enforceable option which would bind the parties, to take such steps as were necessary and practicable to ensure that the obligation was real and ran with the lands no matter who owned the lands, and to carry out the work in accordance with the general standard of care normally expected of a competent practitioner. In the case before him it was perhaps reasonably easy to break down the general duties owed by the solicitors into specific duties in the particular case. It might also be relatively easy to do this in a straightforward domestic conveyancing transaction where acting for the purchaser and lender. There one might say that the specific duties are:

(1) To conclude a legally binding contract for the purchase.
(2) To ensure that the title of the seller to the subjects purchased is properly conveyed to the purchaser and recorded or registered.
(3) To ensure that the purchaser and any lender for whom the solicitors also act has a valid and marketable title to or security over the subjects purchased.
(4) To ensure that any lender for whom the solicitors act has a valid and unenforceable recorded or registered security over the subjects.

It is, of course, not so easy to break down every legal task into individual contractual obligations. It has been pointed out, for example, that it is difficult to do this in the context of a solicitor instructed to conduct litigation[2]. In most cases where claims are brought against solicitors, the pleadings will aver some particular aspect of the solicitor's conduct which fails to come up to the general standard of care, rather than a specific breach or breaches of the contract in individual respects. In many ways, this is a less risky way of conducting a negligence claim from the client's point of view, because it can sometimes avoid tricky evidential questions as to what was or was not actually instructed.

1 [1979] Ch 384, [1978] 3 All ER 571.
2 Jackson and Powell *Professional Negligence*, para 4–05.

Written contracts and instructions

3.07 There is no requirement for the contract between a solicitor and a client to be reduced to writing. Nevertheless, especially where institutional lenders are concerned, it is normal for the lenders' requirements to be set out in written instructions or procedure notes. In some cases lending institutions issue a booklet of standing instructions from time to time, in addition to the individual instructions issued with each lending transaction. Solicitors must bear in mind that acceptance of instructions on this basis implies a contractual obligation on their part to carry out the instructions. Generally speaking, the more specific the obligation, the greater the risk that the solicitor may be liable for failure to comply.

The general duty of care is, of course, based on a standard of reasonableness. There is no absolute duty on a solicitor to ensure that everything turns out exactly as the client wishes. The problem which arises in relation to written instructions is whether or not a specific instruction to achieve a certain result is to be treated as an absolute obligation on the part of the solicitor, or merely an obligation to use reasonable skill and care to try to ensure that the result is achieved. Most written instructions from lenders or lending institutions state that the solicitors are to obtain a valid security. In some cases this will be stated to be a valid first-ranking security. The question has arisen as to whether this is an absolute obligation or simply an obligation to take reasonable care to ensure that a first-ranking security is obtained. The problem was more acute prior to the introduction of the computerised presentment book in the Register of Sasines, when securities could, of course, be recorded in the so-called 'blind period' not covered by the interim report. Where there was a simple purchase, or where separate solicitors acted for lender and borrower, the problem was generally resolved by the implementation of a letter of obligation; but in re-mortgage cases, where the same solicitor acted for borrower and lender, there was no letter of obligation and the question arose as to whether the solicitor was liable to the lender if another security appeared on the record and took precedence in circumstances where the solicitor had done all that any solicitor could reasonably have done exercising skill and care. Much, of course, would depend in such a case on the actual wording of the instructions. If the instructions were worded in such a fashion that the solicitor had to *take all normal steps* to ensure a first-ranking security, then, in the opinion of the author, there would be no liability. If, on the other hand, the instructions were simply *to ensure* that the lender had a first-ranking security, then the author's view is that the position might be different and the solicitor might well have undertaken an obligation which was akin to a guarantee or letter of obligation.

A similar problem can be envisaged in relation to servitudes. There is no doubt that the general standard of care would imply an obligation on a solicitor to take all usual and normal steps to ensure that a title to a property is not burdened with an unduly onerous servitude. Servitudes can, however, be constituted by prescription or indeed by unrecorded or unregistered deed. A solicitor could therefore carry out a normal title examination and be completely unaware of the existence of a servitude constituted by these means. If there were no facts placed before the solicitor which put the solicitor on his or her guard, then it is submitted the solicitor would not have been negligent in these circumstances. If, however, the written instructions from the lending institution stated specifically and unequivocally that the solicitor was *to ensure that the property is not burdened* by any servitude, then that may be interpreted by the courts as an obligation which was not just an obligation to take reasonable care.

The position is perhaps more acute when one considers the question of building warrants, planning permissions, completion certificates and superiors' consents in respect of alterations to property. Where such alterations exist, then it is normal practice, at least in respect of reasonably recent alterations, to request planning permissions, building warrants, completion certificates and superiors' consents. Where local authority consents are not available, the practice has grown up of accepting a letter of comfort from the local authority. These take various forms but basically they tend to indicate that although there may not be the requisite permission, warrant or completion certificate, the local authority proposes to take no action in respect of the alteration. It is always a matter of judgment for the solicitor as to whether or not this letter should be accepted. Generally speaking, the older the alteration is, the more likely it is that the letter of comfort can be accepted. The instructions from the lender, however, may stipulate that the solicitor must obtain planning permissions, building warrants, completion certificates and superiors' consents in respect of any alteration to the property. In these circumstances, a solicitor who accepts a letter of comfort for an old alteration may well come up to the general standard of care required by the law but still be liable to a lending institution because of a breach of a specific contractual duty. It has been held that where missives provide that a completion certificate is to be produced, the purchaser need not accept a letter of comfort and can rescind[1].

It must always be remembered that even in relation to the general standard of care, a court can hold that a solicitor has been negligent in circumstances where that solicitor has faithfully followed general standard practice. In the unusual case of *Edward Wong Finance Co Ltd v Johnson Stokes & Master*[2] the Privy Council, in a Hong Kong appeal, refused to accept that the fact that a solicitor for a lender had released money to a vendor's solicitor in return for an undertaking from that solicitor to hand over a clear title unencumbered by existing securities was in accordance with accepted practice among Hong Kong solicitors exculpated the solicitor in a negligence action. The Privy Council took the view that it might have been foreseen that the other solicitors would embezzle the funds and not implement the undertaking. This is, of course, a decision of the Privy Council in a Hong Kong case relative to a particular practice which clearly involved some risk and in respect of which a warning had been issued by the Hong Kong Law Society. Nevertheless, it emphasises that the general standard of care is not necessarily the only standard by which it is decided whether implied contractual obligations can be said to exist.

1 *Hawke v Mathers* 1995 SCLR (Notes) 1004.
2 [1984] AC 296, [1984] 2 WLR 36.

Exemptions and exclusion clauses

3.08 It has been suggested in an age where competition has driven fees down that clients should not be entitled to expect the same standard of care as they might expect if paying a full fee. This argument has been articulated especially in relation to domestic conveyancing transactions. The abolition of scale fees by the Law Society of Scotland at the behest of the government some years ago has resulted in conveyancing fees being reduced by a considerable amount. There are those who are of the view that the level of fees charged by some firms must mean that clients are not obtaining a proper service. It has been suggested that in these circumstances, solicitors should be deprived of the benefit of cover under the master policy or, alternatively, that clients should be deprived of the right to claim should a mistake occur[1]. It has also been suggested that where work is being done for less than a full fee, a solicitor should be entitled to enter into a specific contract with a client whereby the normal standard of care to be expected of the solicitor is excluded or reduced.

While there may be some commercial justification in these arguments, it is likely that any attempt to reduce or exclude liability on the part of a solicitor for a breach of the general standard of care will fall foul of the Unfair Contract Terms Act 1977, which imposes restrictions on the contractual exclusion or restriction of liability for breach of duty in a number of cases. Where any term of a contract which can be deemed to be a consumer contract attempts to exclude or restrict liability to the consumer or customer, or attempts to provide that a party renders no performance or renders a performance substantially different from that which the consumer or customer has reasonably expected, such a term shall have no effect unless it was fair and reasonable to incorporate the term in the contract[2]. A 'consumer contract' is defined as a contract in which one party to the contract deals and the other party to the contract (the consumer) does not deal or hold himself out as dealing in the course of business[3].

These provisions also apply to what are described in the Act as 'standard form contracts'. There is no definition of a standard form contract in the Act. In so far as solicitors are concerned, it seems to the author that a written contract with a domestic conveyancing client which attempted to exclude liability would be a consumer contract which would require to satisfy the fair and reasonable test. It is hard to imagine a court holding that it would be fair and reasonable to exclude liability for negligence in circumstances where the solicitor is offering to carry out services for a lay person. Similarly, in cases where solicitors routinely carry out conveyancing at low fees and at the same time issue a standard form of contract to customers which purports to exclude liability for negligence, it seems likely that such a contract would be regarded as a standard form contract in terms of the Act and, again, would require to satisfy the fair and reasonable test. For the reasons stated above, it is unlikely that a court would hold that it was fair and reasonable in such a standard form contract to exclude or reduce liability for negligence. It is the view of the author that a court would hold that a solicitor was in a position to know what the exclusion meant, whereas a lay person would be at a commercial disadvantage in such circumstances.

So far as contractual terms and conditions of engagement are concerned, therefore, it seems clear that although clients and especially lending institutions may be able to increase the contractual burden on solicitors, it will be difficult if not impossible for solicitors to reduce the general obligations imposed on them by the general standard of care. The experience of surveyors who have attempted to exclude liability in respect of mortgage valuations suggests that such clauses will fall foul of the 1977 Act[4].

1 A double deductible has now been introduced as an additional excess in the master policy in such cases.
2 Unfair Contract Terms Act 1977, s 17.
3 Unfair Contract Terms Act 1977, s 25(1).
4 *Smith v Eric S Bush* [1990] 1 AC 831, [1989] 2 All ER 514.

CHAPTER 4

Obligations Owed to Third Parties

Introduction

4.01 The basic duty of care owed by a solicitor is to his or her client. Similarly any specific contractual obligations are, generally speaking, owed to the client who instructs the legal task concerned. There have been English cases where solicitors have been held to be liable in delict to third parties with whom they have no contract. This is a somewhat difficult area of law and, at least in the case of disappointed beneficiaries, the law of England and the law of Scotland may not be the same. Historically, solicitors have been bound only to advance the interests of their own clients, irrespective of the interests of any third parties[1]. In the English case of *Fish v Kelly*[2] an employee consulted the solicitor of his employer concerning notice. The solicitor gave incorrect advice in relation to the employee's rights. The court held that no claim for damages lay against the solicitor because there was no relationship of solicitor and client. It is also fair to say that the court took into account the fact that the advice was given in answer to a casual inquiry and not in circumstances where the employee had, for example, made an appointment to see the solicitor on the point in question.

In *Robertson v Fleming*[3] a client instructed a solicitor to prepare a bond of relief and an assignation in security of a lease in favour of parties who had agreed to become cautioners for that party in a completely separate obligation. The cautioners had agreed to become cautioners only on condition that they obtained this security. The solicitor did not intimate the assignation nor register the deed. His client, who had instructed the preparation of the deed, became insolvent and the cautioners had no security in respect of their guarantees. They sued the solicitor, and the Court of Session held that the solicitor was liable. The solicitor appealed to the House of Lords on the grounds that there was never any legal relationship between the cautioners and himself and there was, therefore, no legal basis for the claim. The House of Lords reversed the decision of the Court of Session. In the leading judgment the Lord Chancellor, Lord Campbell, stated[4]:

'I never had any doubt of the unsoundness of the doctrine . . . that A employing B, a professional lawyer, to do any act for the benefit of C, A having to pay B, and there being no intercourse of any sort between B and C – if through the gross negligence or ignorance of B in transacting the business, C loses the benefit intended for him by A, C may maintain an action against B and recover damages for the loss sustained.'

The decision in *Robertson v Fleming* was confidently stated by the Lord Chancellor to be the law of England as well as the law of Scotland. It is fair to say that it has not been followed in England in cases involving disappointed legatees who do not receive benefits intended by a testator due to the negligence of the solicitor in drawing up the will[5]. So far as the development of the law is concerned, it is now accepted that there may be liability to a third party in delict where the third party has relied on a statement or a representation made. One might think that this would be bound to apply in all cases even where there has been no reliance on the solicitor, but the Outer House of the Court of Session has refused to accept this proposition in circumstances where there has been no real reliance by the claimant on the advice or actions of the solicitor[6]. Accordingly, the law has developed in different strands.

1 Begg *The Law of Scotland relating to Law Agents* pp 259, 260, 265; *Parker v Rolls* (1854) 14 CB 691; *Fish v Kelly* (1864) 17 CBNS 194; *Robertson v Fleming* (1861) 23 D (HL) 8, (1861) 4 Macq 167.
2 (1864) 17 CBNS 194.
3 (1861) 23 D (HL) 8, (1861) 4 Macq 167.
4 (1861) 23 D (HL) 8 at 10, (1861) 4 Macq 167 at 177.
5 *Ross v Caunters* [1980] Ch 297, [1979] 3 All ER 580; *White v Jones* [1995] 2 AC 207, [1995] 1 All ER 691.
6 See para 4.10 below.

Liability to third parties for deliberate wrongdoing

4.02 There is no reason why a solicitor cannot be held liable in delict to a non-client in circumstances where the solicitor deliberately commits a wrongful act which results in loss to a third party. In some circumstances, if a solicitor conspires with his client to commit a wrongful act which damages a third party the solicitor may be liable jointly and severally with the client[1]. Similarly, a solicitor who fraudulently misrepresents the position to third parties may also be liable in delict. A solicitor who was acting solely for a borrower and deliberately misrepresented the nature of the security being offered by the client to a lender for whom he did not act was held to be liable[2]. A solicitor may also be liable to a third party where a debt is recovered in circumstances where the solicitor was aware that the debt had been fully paid[3].

This does not mean that a solicitor is liable to the client of another firm where that other client is sued and it turns out that the legal basis for the case is unfounded. A solicitor is entitled to advance his client's interests and to put the best case. There may be liability for wrongful use of diligence, but only where the solicitor has been involved in a serious irregularity which is of his or her own making[4]. In *Henderson v Rollo*[5] a woman obtained a decree for aliment against the father of her illegitimate child. A few days after the decree the child died. Two years later the woman instructed a solicitor to issue a charge on the decree which would have been a warrant to imprison the father for non-payment to the dead child. The solicitor was unaware of the fact that the child had died. The father was charged on the decree and imprisoned. The father raised an action against the mother of the child, the solicitor and the messenger-at-arms. The court found that neither the solicitor nor the messenger-at-arms was liable, on the grounds that they were ignorant of the true state of affairs. In *Smith & Taylor*[6] however, solicitors were held liable when they charged a debtor on an induciae of six days when the appropriate period was fifteen days and on the expiry of the six-day period presented a bankruptcy petition alleging notour bankruptcy.

1 *Paterson v Walker* (1848) 11 D 167.
2 *Haldane v Donaldson* (1840) 1 Robin 226.
3 *Keith v Taylors* (1821) 1 S 56. The decision was reversed by the House of Lords for technical reasons.
4 *Pollock v Clark* (1829) 8 S 1; *Smith v Taylor & Co* (1882) 10 R 291.
5 (1871) 10 M 104.
6 (1882) 10 R 291.

Liability to third parties for negligent misrepresentation relied on

4.03 The notion that a party could not be liable for a negligent misrepresentation relied upon by a third party was overturned by the decision in *Hedley Byrne & Co Ltd v Heller & Partners Ltd*[1]. In that case Hedley Byrne asked the bankers Heller & Partners whether one of their customers was of respectable standing. Heller & Partners responded positively in relation to the customer. Relying on this representation, Hedley Byrne entered into a contract with the customer. The customer went into liquidation and Hedley Byrne suffered loss. There was, of course, no contract between Hedley Byrne and Heller & Partners so there was no contractual remedy available. The House of Lords held that Heller & Partners were liable to Hedley Byrne in delict because they owed a duty of care to Hedley Byrne where they had undertaken responsibility for the accuracy of the representation which they had made, and either knew or ought to have known that Hedley Byrne would be relying on the accuracy of that representation.

The law relating to liability for negligent misrepresentation was further developed in the case of *Caparo Industries plc v Dickman*[2]. The *Caparo* case involved a firm of accountants who had carried out the audit of a company. The audit showed that the company was in a reasonable financial state. In reliance on the audit certain parties, including existing shareholders, acquired shares. The audit was inaccurate and the company's financial position was not as good as had been disclosed. There was no doubt that the investors had relied on the audit, but the House of Lords held that the relationship between the auditors and the shareholders or potential investors was too remote. The auditor did not owe a duty of care to the general public who might wish to acquire shares in reliance on the audit. Leading judgments were delivered by Lord Bridge and Lord Oliver in the House of Lords. The *Hedley Byrne* principle, if principle it was, was restricted in its application. Lord Bridge opined that[3]:

> 'The salient feature of all these cases is that the defendant giving evidence or information was fully aware of the transaction which the plaintiff had in contemplation, knew that the advice or information would be communicated to him directly or indirectly, and knew that it was very likely that the plaintiff would rely on that advice or information in deciding whether or not to engage in the transaction in contemplation.'

The *Hedley Byrne* principle has been accepted by the Scottish courts. In particular, it has been accepted in the case of a professional surveyor instructed by a building society in circumstances where a purchaser suffers pure economic loss as a result of a negligent survey[4]. In these circumstances the surveyor is employed by the building society and there is no contractual remedy available to the purchaser. The court held that the surveyor owed a duty of care in delict to the purchaser where the surveyor knew or must be held to have known that the report would be relied on by the purchaser before concluding missives.

Solicitors have been held liable for negligent misrepresentation in a number of cases. A solicitor was held liable when he gave a reference for a client which negligently failed to disclose that the client had been charged with criminal offences involving dishonesty[5]. Where solicitors advised a party charged with a motor offence that he could either defend himself or pay them to represent him without advising that Legal Aid might be available, they were held to be liable[6]. The solicitors had not accepted the motorist as a client so there was no contractual relationship. The basis of liability was that although the solicitors had not accepted the motorist as a client, they had given some sort of advice and had omitted to advise an obvious and alternative course of action, namely, to claim Legal Aid or seek indemnification for legal costs from the insurance company involved.

1 [1964] AC 465, [1963] 2 All ER 575.
2 [1990] 2 AC 605, [1990] 1 All ER 568.
3 [1990] 2 AC 605 at 620, [1990] 1 All ER 568 at 576.
4 *Martin v Bell-Ingram* 1986 SLT 575.
5 *Edwards v Lee* (1991) 141 NLJ 1517.
6 *Crossman v Ward Bracewell & Co* (1989) 5 PN 103.

Answers to observations

4.04 Solicitors acting for sellers in conveyancing transactions will be familiar with the lists of observations on title and other matters which are submitted by the solicitors acting for the purchasers. Generally speaking, the purchaser's solicitors require satisfactory answers to these observations before the transaction can be settled. The seller's solicitors may be able to answer some of these observations themselves and in other cases will require to obtain information either from the seller or from another source. Where an answer to an observation involves the production of another document, such as a search report or a planning permission or a building warrant, then the purchaser will, of course, be deemed to rely on whatever is produced rather than any representation by the seller or the seller's solicitor.

In other cases, however, the position may be less clear, as where the seller's solicitors are asked to confirm that a particular state of affairs exists. It is common, for example, for a seller's solicitor to be asked to confirm that none of the moveable items included in the sale is the subject of any hire purchase agreement or other charge. It is also common for the seller's solicitor to be asked to confirm that there are no outstanding obligations in relation to the maintenance of private roads, boundary walls, common parts and the like. Solicitors are also familiar with general requests to confirm that the feuing conditions have been implemented. Some solicitors respond to inquiries of this nature simply by confirming the position or, alternatively, confirming the statement 'in so far as they are aware'.

A solicitor should always check these matters out with his or her client or an appropriate authority or body before responding.

There is some doubt as to whether a solicitor may be liable if an answer to an observation turns out to be incorrect. The matter was raised in an English case and the court refused to hold that no duty of care existed in the answering of observations[1]. In a later case it was held that in a routine transaction the sellers' solicitors did not owe a duty of care to a prospective purchaser in answering an observation[2]. In that case, however, the sellers themselves were found liable in circumstances where the incorrect reply from the sellers' solicitors was 'not to the lessor's knowledge'. In *Clelland v Morton Fraser & Milligan*[3] a purchaser tried to sue the seller's solicitors in respect of an alleged misrepresentation to the effect that a building warrant existed for the subdivision of a flat. The sheriff principal dismissed the claim because there was no contract between the purchaser and the solicitor and the action had not been raised under delict. The sheriff principal did indicate, however, that a case based on the *Hedley Byrne*[4] principle might have been relevant. The position might obviously be different if the evidence showed clearly that the solicitor was aware that the answer to the observation was wholly incorrect.

1 *Wilson v Bloomfield* (1979) 123 SJ 860.
2 *Gran Gelato Ltd v Richcliff (Group) Ltd* [1992] Ch 560, [1992] 1 All ER 865.
3 1996 GWD 31–1833.
4 *Hedley Byrne & Co Ltd v Heller & Partners Ltd* [1964] AC 465, [1963] 2 All ER 575.

Duties to third parties in contentious matters

4.05 It is extremely difficult to see how a solicitor can owe a duty of care to another solicitor's client where there is a dispute between the two clients. In these circumstances each solicitor is bound to protect his or her own client's interests and may even have a positive duty to take steps which are likely to injure the interests of the opposing client. There may be circumstances where instructions are given by a client which are professionally unacceptable or conflict with the solicitor's duties to the court. In these circumstances the appropriate course of action is to withdraw from acting in good time and on giving adequate notice to the client and any court involved.

Formal obligations to third parties: certificates and reports on title

4.06 Solicitors have been used to granting reports on title and certificates of title to building societies and other lenders in circumstances where they act not only for the borrower but also for the lender. In these circumstances the lender is, of course, a client and not a third party. For some time, however, solicitors have also granted reports or certificates to parties who are not their clients. In a typical corporate take-over the assets of the company to be acquired may include a number of heritable properties. If the solicitor acting for the acquiring company has to examine all the titles there may be substantial delay and expense. Accordingly, in these circumstances it is quite common for the solicitors acting for the company being acquired to grant a certificate of title to the acquiring company. The terms of these certificates vary and they may, of course, be heavily qualified in certain circumstances. This practice has now been extended to cover situations where, because of conflict of interest, banks and other lending institutions instruct their own solicitors to deal with a loan transaction rather than the purchaser's solicitors.

Where there is separate representation there can, of course, be delays in the conveyancing because there will be three solicitors involved. Lenders have therefore adopted the practice of asking the purchaser/borrower's solicitor to grant a certificate of title in which certain matters are warranted. It is clear that this creates a contractual relationship between the purchaser's solicitor and the lender which is quite different from the normal solicitor/client relationship. There is also likely to be a delictual duty of care where the third party relies on the statements in the certificate[1]. A solicitor will be liable for any breach of warranty or undertaking contained in the certificate. In a case decided in New Zealand the Court of Appeal held that solicitors could be liable in just these circumstances[2]. Solicitors should obviously be careful that they do not warrant or undertake matters in a certificate of title which may not be capable of fulfilment[3].

There appears to be a difference, in Scots law at any rate, between a formal certificate granted by a solicitor and the informal passing on of information from client to bank or other third party. The leading case in Scotland is *Midland Bank plc v Cameron, Thom, Peterkins & Duncans*[4]. In that case the solicitors were instructed to act for a borrower and also for a bank which was lending. Strictly speaking, therefore, the case does not exactly fit into the category of cases where solicitors are alleged to have made representations to third parties, although Lord Jauncey appears to have treated the bank as a third party rather than a client. The actual instructions to the solicitors from the bank were to prepare standard securities over properties. In the course of the transaction the solicitors wrote a letter to the bank setting out certain commercial matters relating to their clients. The information which was contained in the letter was supplied by the client, but it was in fact inaccurate in several respects. There was no question of the solicitors being aware of the inaccuracy. The bank sued the solicitors, alleging breach of duty. In the Outer House Lord Jauncey held that there was no duty of care in respect of the inaccurate statements and that the only duties which the solicitors owed to the bank were in terms of their instructions from the bank, namely, to prepare valid securities. These duties had been fulfilled. In the course of giving judgment Lord Jauncey considered the circumstances in which a solicitor might owe a duty of care to a third party. He treated the bank as a third party for the purposes of the information given in the letter, if not for the purposes of the preparation of the security. He stated that for a solicitor to be liable to a third party the following conditions must be met[5]:

'(1) The solicitor must assume responsibility for the advice or information furnished to the third party;
(2) The solicitor must let it be known to the third party expressly or impliedly that he claims, by reason of his calling, to have the requisite skill or knowledge to give the advice or furnish the information;
(3) The third party must have relied upon that advice or information as matter for which the solicitor has assumed personal responsibility;
(4) The solicitor must have been aware that the third party was likely so to rely.'

Lord Jauncey was content to accept that in the context of the transaction the solicitors' only duty was to carry out strictly legal duties in the examination of the title and preparation of the security documentation. Lord Jauncey did not accept that the solicitors had a wider duty to verify the accuracy or otherwise of the statements made by the borrowers which were passed on in the letter. Lord Jauncey was also of the view that there was no duty on the solicitors to analyse the statements or come to a view as to the value of the security being offered to the bank in the light of the accuracy or otherwise of the statements made. This case will be considered in greater detail when the duty of care of solicitors in relation to commercial advice and disclosure is considered[6].

1 *Hedley Byrne & Co Ltd v Heller & Partners Ltd* [1964] AC 465, [1963] 2 All ER 575.
2 *Allied Finance & Investments Ltd v Haddow & Co Ltd* [1983] NZLR 22, where solicitors were liable where they granted a certificate in relation to the effect of a security over a yacht which turned out to be inaccurate because the client did not own the yacht.
3 See Rennie 'Certificates of Title – legal context' (1995) 48 JLSS 377.

4 1988 SCLR 209, 1988 SLT 611.
5 1988 SCLR 200 at 216, 1988 SLT 611 at 616.
6 See Chapter 5 below.

Duties to disappointed beneficiaries

4.07 The position in Scots law relating to the liability of a solicitor to a disappointed beneficiary under a will which has not been executed, or which has been found to be defective, has already been noted[1]. At the moment there is a clear difference between Scots law and English law in this respect. The Scottish position has been criticised as being unjust and anomalous[2]. The Scottish position is based on the House of Lords case of *Robertson v Fleming*[3]. Accordingly, a decision of the House of Lords in a Scottish appeal is likely to be necessary before the position can be reversed and Scots law brought into line with English law. It seems likely to the author that if the House of Lords come to consider this question they will reverse *Robertson v Fleming* as a matter of policy, whatever the academic arguments may be.

1 See para 1.09 above; *Robertson v Fleming* (1861) 23 D (HL) 8, (1861) 4 Macq 167; *Weir v J M Hodge & Son* 1990 SLT 266; *MacDougall v Clydesdale Bank Trustees* 1993 SCLR 832.
2 Smith *A Short Commentary on the Law of Scotland* (1962) p 683; Thomson *Delictual Liability* pp 135, 136; Blaikie 'Professional Negligence: The Dilatory Solicitor and the Disappointed Legatee' 1996 SLPQ 245.
3 (1861) 23 D (HL) 8, (1861) 4 Macq 167.

The academic debate

4.08 The question which arises is whether or not there can be a liability to beneficiaries where these beneficiaries have not relied on the solicitor to carry out his duties to the required standard of care. The House of Lords in *Robertson v Fleming* and the Lord Chancellor in particular had no doubt in 1861 that no such duty of care existed. The Lord Chancellor took the view that this was as much the law of Scotland as the law of England[1]. Other judges took a similar view. Lord Carnworth said[2]:

> 'Such a doctrine would, as is pointed out by my noble friend, lead to the result that a disappointed legatee might sue the testator's solicitor for negligence in not causing the will to be duly signed and attested though he might be an entire stranger both to the solicitor and to the testator.'

Lord Wensleydale was of the same opinion. He said[3]:

'It is said, however, that by the law of Scotland, quite independently of the question who the contracting parties are, whenever an attorney or agent is employed by anyone to do any act which when done will be beneficial to a third person, and that act is negligently done, an action for negligence may be maintained by the third person against the attorney or agent. I cannot think that any such proposition is made out to be part of the law of Scotland.'

English law took a different position from Scots law in the case of *Ross v Caunters*[4]. In that case the court considered the judgment in *Robertson v Fleming*, but took the view that the reasoning behind the judgment could no longer be supported in the light of the cases of *Donoghue v Stevenson*[5] and *Hedley Byrne & Co Ltd v Heller & Partners Ltd*[6]. The court held that a solicitor who was instructed to carry out some transaction which would result in a benefit to an identified third party owed a duty to that third party to use proper care in carrying out the instructions. Liability was in delict rather than contract and there was, according to the court, a sufficient degree of proximity between the solicitor and the identified third party for whose benefit the solicitor was instructed to carry out the transaction for it to be within the solicitor's reasonable contemplation that his acts or omissions in carrying out the instructions would be likely to injure the third party. The court also held that there was no policy reason to limit the ambit of the duty of care of a solicitor to the actual client.

The decision in *Ross v Caunters* relies heavily on the notion of the general duty of care laid down by Lord Atkins in *Donoghue v Stevenson*[7]. That principle is often referred to as 'the neighbourhood principle'[8]. Although the *Hedley Byrne* case was referred to in *Ross v Caunters*, it is not strictly relevant, because in *Hedley Byrne* it was vital to the decision that the negligent misrepresentation had actually been relied upon by the party who suffered the loss. In *Ross v Caunters* and in all the disappointed beneficiary cases it cannot normally be said that the beneficiary relied on the solicitor to perform the task. In most cases the solicitor will not have made any representation to the third party and the beneficiary will not even have been aware that the solicitor has been instructed to carry out the task to the benefit of that third party[9].

Despite all the arguments which have surrounded *Ross v Caunters*, the position may now be said to be beyond doubt in England as a result of the decision in *White v Jones*[10]. In that case the testator instructed his solicitors to prepare a new will, including bequests to two of his daughters. The instructions were received on 17 July, 1986 but nothing was done for a month. On 16 August, the managing clerk in the firm instructed the probate department to draw up a will or codicil incorporating the new legacies. The managing clerk went on holiday and on his return made arrangements to visit the testator on 17 September. The testator had, however, died on 14 September without signing any new will or codicil. The two daughters brought an action against the solicitors for damages. At first instance the judge in the High Court held that there was no duty of care and dismissed the action. The daughters appealed to the Court of Appeal and the appeal was allowed, on the grounds that a solicitor was liable in damages to a prospective beneficiary in these circumstances.

The solicitors appealed to the House of Lords. The argument adduced for the solicitors was that there was no duty of care owed by solicitors to anyone other than the client, since the relationship between solicitor and client was contractual in nature. The case was heard before five Law Lords. By a majority of 3 to 2, the House of Lords held that where a solicitor accepted instructions to draw up a will and as a result of his negligence an intended beneficiary under the will was deprived of a legacy the solicitor was liable for the loss of the legacy. The reasons given by the three Law Lords who refused the appeal were varied. Lords Goff and Nolan justified the decision on the grounds that it must be reasonably foreseeable that the negligence would result in the beneficiary being deprived of an intended legacy. They also pointed out that the testator being dead and the estate having suffered no loss as such there was no other remedy available for the loss caused by the negligence unless the beneficiary could claim. Lord Browne-Wilkinson justified the decision by holding that a solicitor in these circumstances must be held to be in a special relationship with those intended to benefit under it, so that a duty of care must be owed to the intended beneficiary to act with due expedition and care in relation to the task.

1 (1861) 4 Macq 167 at 177.
2 Ibid at 185.
3 Ibid at 199, 200.
4 [1980] Ch 297, [1979] 3 All ER 580.
5 1932 SC (HL) 31, 1932 SLT 317.
6 [1964] AC 465, [1963] 2 All ER 575.
7 1932 SC (HL) 31 at 44, 1932 SLT 317 at 323.
8 Thomson *Delictual Liability* pp 54–60.
9 For a general discussion on *Ross v Caunters*, see Jackson and Powell *Professional Negligence* paras 4–19 to 4–27.
10 [1995] 2 AC 207, [1995] 1 All ER 691.

Principle or policy?

4.09 In the view of the author the decision in *White v Jones* is as much a decision of policy as one of principle. In a wide-ranging judgment (involving discussion of the position in other countries) Lord Goff laid emphasis on the basic justice of allowing the claim. He stated[1]:

'For the reasons I have already given, an ordinary action in tortious negligence on the lines proposed by Megarry VC in *Ross v Caunters* must, with the greatest respect, be regarded as inappropriate, because it does not meet any of the conceptual problems which have been raised. Furthermore, for the reasons I have previously given, the *Hedley Byrne* principle cannot, in the absence of special circumstances, give rise on ordinary principles to an assumption of responsibility by the testator's solicitor towards an intended beneficiary. Even so, it seems to me that it is open to your Lordships' House . . . to fashion a remedy to fill a lacuna in the law and so prevent the injustice which would otherwise occur on the facts of cases such as the present . . . If the solicitors were negligent and their negligence did not come to light until after the death of the testator, there would be no remedy for the ensuing loss unless the intended beneficiary could claim. In my opinion, therefore, your Lordships' House should in cases such as these extend to the intended beneficiary a remedy under the *Hedley Byrne* principle by holding that the assumption of responsibility by the solicitor towards his client should be held in law to extend to the intended beneficiary who (as the solicitor can reasonably foresee) may, as a result of the solicitor's negligence, be deprived of his intended legacy in circumstances in which neither the testator nor his estate will have a remedy against the solicitor.'

1 [1995] 2 AC 207 at 267, [1995] 1 All ER 691 at 710.

The current Scottish position

4.10 The position of the disappointed beneficiary has been considered directly in the case of *Weir v J M Hodge & Son*[1]. In that case a solicitor was alleged to have given advice to a client to the effect that her nieces and nephews would become entitled under her husband's settlement to certain estate, which included a one half share in heritable property which was held under a survivorship destination between husband and wife. This being the wife's understanding, she excluded the pursuers in the case from any benefit under her own will. The special destination in the title had never been evacuated by the husband's settlement, so that on his death it became the absolute property of his wife and did not fall into his estate. In the circumstances the pursuers, as the residuary beneficiaries in the husband's estate, were not entitled to any share in the heritable property. It was accepted by the solicitors that any advice which had been given to the effect that the special destination had been evacuated by the husband's testamentary settlements was negligently given.

The residuary beneficiaries under the husband's testamentary settlements raised an action against the solicitors. The solicitors contended that they were not liable to make reparation to third parties who might be injured by their negligent acts or omissions in the course of acting for a client. The pursuers maintained that *Robertson v Fleming*[2] was out of date and out of step with the overall development of the law of negligence. The court held that a Lord Ordinary was bound by the decision of the House of Lords in *Robertson v Fleming*, notwithstanding that the decision might be at variance with subsequent developments of the English common law. Lord Weir in the Outer House dismissed the action on this basis. In the course of argument before the Lord Ordinary reference was made to the case of *Robertson v Bannigan*[3]. In that case Lord Hunter referred to *Robertson v Fleming* as an anomalous decision which might not have survived the *Hedley Byrne* decision[4]. Lord Weir also made reference to *Bolton v Jameson & Mackay*[5], where *Robertson v Fleming* was referred to but the action was dismissed on other grounds. While Lord Weir felt bound by the decision in *Robertson v Fleming*, he did make the following statement[6]:

> 'The situation has now been reached when, in my view, the decision in *Robertson v Fleming* is to be regarded as out of sympathy with the modern law of negligence . . . It may well be that the House of Lords would depart from *Robertson v Fleming* but I was asked to anticipate such a step on my own initiative . . . I have given careful consideration to this submission, and although the course urged upon me is not without its temptations, on reflection, I do not consider that it is within my power to hold that the case of *Robertson v Fleming* is no longer binding.'

More recently, in *MacDougall v Clydesdale Bank Trustees*[7], Lord Cameron similarly refused to accept the existence of this type of duty of care. In this case, however, the disappointed legatee had died and it was in fact a beneficiary of the legatee who was claiming. It might well be that such a claim would have been held to be too remote in any event. There is no doubt that there are many conceptual difficulties surrounding the application of the law of delict to this particular situation. One cannot simply regard *Robertson v Fleming* as a decision taken to protect the legal profession and wholly unfounded in principle, and at least two of the judges in the House of Lords in *White v Jones*[8] were of the view that the conceptual problems were too difficult to overcome. However that may be, there is no doubt that *White v Jones* is the law of England. It will be interesting to see what happens if this question is ever taken to the House of Lords in a Scottish appeal. For what it is worth, it is the author's view that *Robertson v Fleming* will be overturned and the court will adopt the principle or policy that a solicitor is liable to a disappointed beneficiary in circumstances where the negligence of the solicitor has resulted in a loss of benefit to that beneficiary.

1 1990 SLT 266.
2 (1861) 23 D (HL) 8, (1861) 4 Macq 167.
3 1965 SC 20, 1965 SLT 66.
4 1965 SLT 66 at 67.
5 1989 SLT 222.
6 1990 SLT 266 at 270.
7 1993 SCLR 832.
8 [1995] 2 AC 207, [1995] 1 All ER 691.

CHAPTER 5

Duties Relating to Commercial Advice and Disclosure

Introduction

5.01 Until recently most Scottish lawyers would have held to the view that their main obligation in a conveyancing transaction was to obtain a valid marketable title for the purchaser or a valid and enforceable security for the lender, and that commercial considerations regarding the prudence of a particular transaction or the value of a particular security were properly matters for the client. This restricted view of the ambit of the standard of care was largely based on practice and the case of *Midland Bank plc v Cameron, Thom, Peterkins & Duncans*[1].

In that case the solicitors sent a letter to the lenders containing certain statements which concerned the borrowers' financial affairs. The solicitors were acting for the borrowers and they were also acting for the bank as lender in the preparation of standard securities. The bank averred that the letter contained two material inaccuracies and sought to hold the solicitors liable on the basis that it had lent money on the strength of the information contained in the letter. The securities which had been prepared were perfectly valid and enforceable. The bank took the view that its loss did not stem from any matter relating to the validity or enforceability of the securities but from its own original decision to lend, which had been influenced by the information contained in the solicitors' letter. In the Outer House Lord Jauncey adopted a restrictive interpretation of a solicitor's duty of care in these circumstances. He took the view that the instruction was to do no more than prepare valid standard securities over particular properties. He stated[2]:

> 'It is not averred that the defenders were instructed to do anything other than prepare these securities, but in carrying out their instructions it is said that they were under a duty to verify the value of the pursuers' securities and to verify the accuracy of the contents of the letter of 6th December 1979 . . . At the stage when a lender instructs the preparation of standard securities, it is reasonable to assume that he has agreed to make a loan and has satisfied himself as to the sufficiency of the security therefor. Is it then

to be taken that the solicitor charged with the preparation of the security documents is, at his own hand, to undertake independent verification of the value of the security subjects? I do not consider that a simple instruction to prepare security documents can import so far-reaching a duty and the general averment of practice does not remedy the deficiency.'

Lord Jauncey also considered whether or not the letter might amount to some sort of representation by the solicitors themselves. It is interesting to note that in this part of his judgment Lord Jauncey appears to treat the bank as a third party, rather than as a client of the solicitors. He appears to have treated the bank as a client only for the restricted purpose of the preparation of the securities. Lord Jauncey was of the view that before a solicitor could be liable to a third party, circumstances akin to those which arose in *Hedley Byrne & Co Ltd v Heller & Partners Ltd*[3] would require to exist[4].

The *Midland Bank* case was decided in 1988 at a time when solicitors involved in purchase and loan transactions tended to treat the purchaser as the real client and the lender as an institution having the character of an interested third party. That view of the relationship between solicitor and lender client would not be supported today and certainly was never accurate in a legal sense. The peripheral duties of care in relation to commercial matters and disclosure tend to overlap with one another, but can conveniently be separated into three distinct categories:

(1) Questions relating to the value of the security.
(2) Questions relating to the giving of commercial, as opposed to legal, advice.
(3) Questions relating to disclosure and to the passing of information which the solicitor obtains in the course of the transaction and which may not be directly related to the main legal task but which might give rise to commercial concern on the part of the client.

Questions of this type have arisen most frequently in relation to so-called 'back-to-back' sales and purchases, where a loss is made by a lender who bases a commercial decision to lend on the ultimate purchase price, being unaware of an immediately preceding sale at a lower price. In a situation of this type, all three categories of peripheral duty may be involved. In the first place, the value of the lender's security may be far less than the lender assumed it to be; in the second place, the solicitor acting for the lender, having had access to evidence of previous sales, may have had an opportunity to comment on the commercial wisdom of the transaction; and thirdly, the solicitor may have been in a position to pass on information to the lender relating to the nature of previous transactions which might conceivably have affected the lender's original decision to advance funds. While there is considerable overlap in these duties, it is important to look at them separately.

1 1988 SCLR 209, 1988 SLT 611.
2 1988 SCLR 209 at 218, 1988 SLT 611 at 618.
3 [1964] AC 465, [1963] 2 All ER 575.
4 For a discussion of this aspect of the decision, see para 4.06 above.

The value of the security

5.02 It is a long-established principle of the law of professional negligence that a solicitor engaged in the preparation of a security for a lender is not *prima facie* liable if the security turns out to be less valuable than the lender supposed it to be. It seems to be clear that this has been the law in England for some time[1]. So far as Scots law is concerned, the old case of *Ronaldson v Drummond & Reid*[2] suggests that the only situation in which a solicitor can be liable for a deficiency in the value of the security is where that solicitor has some other higher or fiduciary duty, such as that of a trustee. In that case the solicitor concerned was the agent of the borrower as well as the lender and the lender was a body of trustees. The solicitor was one of the trustees and no valuation of the security was obtained. The borrower was in occupation of the actual property and accordingly there was no rent by which the value could be gauged. Added to this was the fact that the title was leasehold and not feudal. The case therefore turned very much on its own facts.

Begg states[3] that a solicitor who has been guilty of no misconduct, gross negligence or want of professional skill will not be responsible for the deficiency of a security, unless his position is one of trust as well as agency, or unless he has been specifically instructed to see to the sufficiency of the security.

Begg also points out that it had been held in England that a solicitor lending clients' money on mortgages was not liable for a loss if the solicitor's advice on the sufficiency of the mortgages was founded on the opinions of competent surveyors where these valuations had been submitted to the lender[4]. More recently, Lord Jauncey in the case of *Midland Bank plc v Cameron, Thom, Peterkins & Duncans* reaffirmed the principle that instructions to solicitors to prepare a standard security do not import any duty to verify the value of that security[5]. There will be cases where a solicitor may specifically undertake a liability in relation to the value of a security, but it is the author's view that these cases will be few and far between and a solicitor should not in any circumstances undertake so onerous a liability[6]. Where there are no other factors relating to disclosure of facts which might suggest an inadequate value, then it is unlikely that the solicitor will be liable.

1 *Hayne v Rhodes* (1846) 8 Ad & El 342; *Rae v Meek* (1889) 14 App Cas 558.
2 (1881) 8 R 767.
3 Begg *The Law of Scotland relating to Law Agents* p 243.
4 *Chapman v Chapman* (1870) LR 9 Eq 276.
5 1988 SCLR 209, 1988 SLT 611: see para 5.01 above.
6 For an analysis of cases of this type, see *Dooby v Watson* (1888) 39 ChD 178 at 182–183.

The giving of commercial or business advice

5.03 The motto of the Law Society of Scotland is *humani nihil alienum*. A rough translation of this is that nothing which is connected with humanity is foreign to a Scottish solicitor. Scottish solicitors have in the past been regarded as general men and women of business, taking a wide interest in their clients' affairs. The author suspects that this view of the Scottish solicitor is no longer justified and may carry with it certain dangers for the practitioner. Many clients base their choice of solicitor on cost alone, and may instruct many different solicitors over a period of time. There is not, therefore, the same opportunity as in the past for a solicitor to become well acquainted with a client and his or her business. Solicitors should always be aware that the distinction between legal advice and commercial advice is often very difficult to draw. In the *Midland Bank* case Lord Jauncey took the view that the fact that the solicitors passed on information of a commercial nature did not of itself imply that they were making representations or giving commercial advice on which the bank was entitled to rely. Jackson and Powell, in their modern treatise on professional negligence, put it in this way[1]:

> 'A solicitor is not a general adviser on matters of business (unless he specifically agrees to act in that capacity). Thus he is not generally under a duty to advise whether, legal considerations apart, the transaction which he is instructed to carry out is a prudent one.'

Solicitors are often asked for an opinion on matters of a commercial nature. Where, for example, there is a closing date for the purchase of property, a solicitor may be asked to advise on the level of offer to be made. In cases like this it is best to restrict the advice to generalities and to advise the client to work out the highest offer which can be afforded and then simply to make that offer. Solicitors would be extremely unwise to give any view in relation to the prudence of a commercial transaction, even though they may feel that it might be helpful to do so. Where, however, a client takes a commercial decision which is unusual and gives rise to a greater than normal element of risk, it seems clear that the solicitor should not simply stand back, but should issue a warning. If a client, for example, instructs a solicitor to lodge an offer for property without the benefit of a survey then, although this may be ultimately a matter for the client, a solicitor should warn of the risks involved and ensure that the client clearly understands that any offer signed by the solicitor will be binding.

There are a number of English cases which deal with the question of commercial advice[2]. It is worthwhile looking at some of the cases in greater detail. In *Bowdage v Harold Michelmore & Co*[3] a client granted an option to another party over a heritable property. The option was for a fee of £400 and was to last for six months. As is often the case, the holder of the option requested an extension and the option was extended on two separate occasions. The owner of the property agreed to grant these extensions, but before the expiry of the second extended period another offer was received for the property from a different party at a significantly higher price than was provided for in the option agreement. Because the option was still in force the owner of the property could not accept that offer and the option was then exercised at the lower price. The owner sued her solicitors for negligence claiming first, that they had not given her advice to the effect that the original option fee was too low and, secondly, that they had not advised her to consult a surveyor in relation to the option fee to be charged. The court dismissed the claim, taking the view that it was not for the solicitors to give advice as to the reasonableness or otherwise of the proposed price, nor to recommend that she should consult an independent valuer.

Similar views were expressed in the leading English case of *Yager v Fishman & Co*[4]. In that case a client claimed damages for negligence against two firms of solicitors in relation to certain leasehold premises. The client was a businessman who had various interests in the timber and plywood trades. The lease in question contained a break clause which entitled the tenant to terminate the lease provided the right to break was exercised on certain dates. The complaint of the client was that the solicitor had allowed one of these dates to go by without reminding the client of his right to terminate the lease. When the complaint was originally made to the solicitors they responded by stating that it was no part of their duty to keep a record of when a client had to give notice to determine a lease. The client was aware of the terms of the lease and the court held that it was no part of the solicitor's duty to remind the client of the date for exercising the option, unless the solicitors had specific instructions to that effect. Some of the statements from the judges are illuminating. Scott LJ said[5]:

'But at any rate until at least October 1940 I am satisfied that as a business choice he [the client] was still wanting to get a tenant and not to get the under-lease brought to an end. Indeed, from first to last, I infer from the correspondence that he was a businessman who took his own business decisions, and did not ask advice on them from his lawyers. He was quite well able to decide for himself whether it was better policy to get rid of the under-lease and cut his loss, or to get hold of it for himself, and recoup himself by sub-letting. It was only on legal questions that he turned to his lawyers.'

Again, the same judge stated[6]:

'There is no allegation in the statement of claim against either firm of any request by the respondent for advice upon any question of business as distinct from law – in particular upon the question whether it would be better business for the respondent on the one hand to try and get out of the under-lease liability even at the expense of paying all arrears of rent, and accepting liability for dilapidations, or, on the other hand to maintain the under-lease and find a tenant whose rent would cover his current and future financial liability to the landlord. To impose on a solicitor the legal responsibility of answering such a business question would require both unequivocal instruction and unqualified acceptance; for it is no part of a solicitor's normal duty to profess the skill and experience for giving such advice.'

There were indications in the judgments in the *Yager* case that the position might be different if the client were wholly inexperienced and about to walk into some sort of commercial trap. Goddard LJ said[7]:

'But it does seem to me that, when solicitors are charged with negligence, it is material to know a great deal about the extent of the client's knowledge and experience. He seems to have been a director of the London Plywood and Timber Co and of the H Yager Investment Trust; and must at some time have had an interest in or connection with the Euston

Furniture Co, for whom he was guarantor; so I infer that he was a man of considerable business experience. The nature and amount of advice which, in a matter of this sort, a solicitor would be expected to give to a person wholly unacquainted with business may differ very materially from what he would offer to an experienced businessman, who would naturally decide for himself the course he thought it in his interest to take. Whether, for instance, it was desirable to arrange to take advantage of an opportunity to get a lease determined, or whether to get a new tenant to take over the remainder of the term, was a matter of business on which, I should think, Yager would desire to follow his own opinion.'

In a rather cynical passage du Parcq LJ said[8]:

'He was then left with the argument that at least the respondent ought to have been reminded of the date when such a notice ought to be given. The answer to that is that the respondent's solicitors were not bound to supply deficiencies in their client's memory unless they were clearly requested to do so. I am by no means sure that Yager would have welcomed a bill of costs which included charges for reminding him, unasked, of dates which he might be assumed to have in mind.'

What has always to be borne in mind in relation to the law of professional negligence is that standards change from time to time. Even as early as 1944, judges in the *Yager* case were hinting that a higher standard might apply if the client were inexperienced in business matters. This approach is illustrated in the more recent case of *Neushul v Mellish & Harkavy*[9]. In that case solicitors who had previously acted for a client and had some knowledge of his financial affairs stood back and allowed another client, who was a widow, to lend a substantial sum of money to the first client in contemplation of marriage. The solicitors were involved in arranging finance for this transaction. The Court of Appeal held by a majority that the solicitors were negligent because they failed to warn the widow against the commercial wisdom of making the loan. The basis of the decision was really that it should have been obvious that the lady might be about to make a serious business error or, in the words of one judge, 'was rushing into an unwise not to say disastrous adventure'.

In modern times the legal consequences and the financial implications of any particular course of action may become hopelessly intertwined. One judge has expressed the view that the significance of the legal consequences may often lie in the financial implications[10]. While it is difficult to draw general conclusions in relation to a solicitor's liability for the giving of commercial advice it is the author's view that the following is reasonably clear:

1 That in the normal course of events a solicitor has no duty to give commercial or business advice, unless the solicitor undertakes to do so.
2 A solicitor should not stand by and allow a client, especially an inexperienced client, to pursue a course of action which has obvious commercial dangers.
3 Where a client, even an experienced client, intends to pursue some unusual or risky course of action, such as to acquire property without a survey, it is wise for the solicitor to confirm that the client is acting on his or her own initiative and, where appropriate, against advice.
4 A solicitor may have a duty in certain circumstances to comment on the wisdom of a course of action if the solicitor is aware of certain facts and circumstances which might make that course of action imprudent.

1 Jackson and Powell *Professional Negligence* para 4–108.
2 See ibid para 4–108 et seq.
3 (1962) 106 SJ 512.
4 [1944] 1 All ER 552.
5 Ibid at 554.
6 Ibid at 555.
7 Ibid at 556.
8 Ibid at 558.
9 (1967) 111 SJ 399.
10 *County Personnel (Employment Agency) Ltd v Alan R Pulver & Co* [1987] 1 All ER 289, [1987] 1 WLR 916; see also *Reeves v Thrings & Long* [1996] PNLR 265.

The duty to disclose information

5.04 It has always been the case that a solicitor is under a general obligation to act in his or her client's best interests. That obligation is now enshrined in the Code of Conduct promulgated by the Law Society of Scotland. Paragraph 2 of the Code states:

'Solicitors must always act in the best interests of their clients subject to preserving their independence as solicitors and to the due observance of the law, professional practice rules and the principles of good professional conduct.'

Paragraph 3 of the Code states that solicitors shall not act for two or more clients in matters where there is a conflict of interest, and paragraph 4 states that the observance of client confidentiality is a fundamental duty of all solicitors. There are, of course, separate rules in relation to conflict of interest[1]. These three principles from the Code of Conduct contain some very fundamental statements concerning the role of solicitors in society. It is, perhaps, unfortunate that in pertinent cases solicitors are pointed in different directions as a result of the combined effect of these principles.

Nowhere is this tension more acute than when a solicitor acts for a borrower and a lender and discovers a piece of information concerning the borrower or the secured subjects which, although it has no effect on the validity of any security to be granted, might influence the original decision to lend. In cases of this type a solicitor may feel that he or she owes an overriding duty of confidentiality to the borrower, and that no disclosure should therefore be made to the lender. On the other hand, the lender is as much a client as the borrower and entitled to the same professional standard of care in all circumstances. Where a solicitor examines a set of titles and discovers that the property has only recently been purchased for a sum which is significantly less than the price now to be paid by his client, there may be a clear conflict of interest. On the one hand, the solicitor may feel that his sole duty to the lender is to prepare a valid and effectual security. On the other hand, the solicitor may feel that the valuation which the lender has obtained cannot be accurate. In these circumstances it is the author's view that the only appropriate course of action is to request instructions from the borrower to disclose such matters to the lender, and in the event that these instructions are not forthcoming to cease to act for both parties.

That is not to say that there will be an absolute duty of disclosure in each and every set of circumstances. It is appropriate to trace the development of the law in relation to the duty of disclosure. One of the earliest cases is the case of *Scholes v Brook*[2]. In that case solicitors discovered, in the course of a title examination, that the valuation obtained by the lenders might be seriously wrong. This information was gleaned from a comparison of recent prices. The solicitors concerned did not advise the lenders but instead invited the valuers to reconsider their valuation. The valuers took the view that their original valuation was correct and no one advised the lenders. The court held that the solicitors had done all that they were required to do by bringing the matter to the attention of the other professionals most closely involved. The valuers were held to be negligent. *Scholes v Brook* was decided in 1891 at a time, no doubt, when complicated mortgage fraud and money-laundering schemes were less prevalent and it is fair to say that the law has moved on since that time. There are a number of English cases which deal with a solicitor's responsibility to pass on information which may be outwith the specific ambit of the task for which the solicitor has been instructed[3]. Each case is decided very much on its own facts. In the leading case of *Midland*

Bank Trust Co Ltd v Hett, Stubbs & Kemp[4], the court tied the solicitor's duties very closely to the specific instructions. In that case Oliver J said[5]:

'The court must beware of imposing on solicitors . . . duties which go beyond the scope of what they are requested and undertake to do. It may be that a particularly meticulous and conscientious practitioner would, in his client's general interests, take it on himself to pursue a line of enquiry beyond the strict limits comprehended by his instructions. But that is not the test. The test is what the reasonably competent practitioner would do having regard to the standards normally adopted in his profession and cases . . . demonstrate that the duty is directly related to the confines of the retainer.'

Oliver J's words suggest that a bank which simply instructs the preparation of a standard security cannot expect a solicitor to undertake wider duties to warn of specific risks which do not affect the validity of the security. On the other hand, in the case of *Boyce v Rendells*[6] the court held that if, in the course of taking instructions, a professional such as a solicitor obtained information which might have an effect on a client, that solicitor should not simply advise within the confines of his or her instructions but should call attention to the risks and, if necessary, advise accordingly.

A solicitor will still be entitled to exercise judgment in relation to what should or should not be disclosed. There is and always has been a difference between negligence and a *bona fide* error of judgment. In *Central Land Investment Ltd v Wynn*[7] a client failed in a negligence action against a solicitor in relation to a conveyancing transaction. There was redevelopment being carried out in the neighbourhood of a shop, and the solicitor advised that as a result of this the flow of pedestrian traffic might be affected. The solicitor, however, did not advise the clients of a closing order which affected a neighbouring road. The solicitor's judgment was that the closure of the road would not be relevant to the shop or to the business to be carried on in the shop. The court held that this was a *bona fide* exercise of judgment and was not negligence.

In some cases courts have been prepared to hold solicitors liable where various circumstances in a transaction give rise to suspicions that everything may not be genuine, even where the solicitor has carried out his basic instructions in a legal sense. A good example of this type of case is *Anglia Hastings & Thanet Building Society v House & Son*[8]. In that case a building society sued a firm of surveyors after suffering a serious shortfall following a repossession and sale of two flats. The surveyors brought the solicitors who had acted in the preparation of the securities into the action as third parties, because they were of the view that certain facts had come to light in the course of the transaction which the solicitors had not passed on to the lenders and which might have persuaded the lenders not to lend. In the transactions the solicitors had acted for the borrowers and the building society in the preparation of the securities over the two flats.

The solicitors in the case accepted some fault, so the case cannot be regarded as a precedent for all purposes. The solicitor involved was a director of the development company which was selling the flats, and the solicitor's firm was still acting for these developers at the time of the transaction in another capacity, although not in the sale of the flats concerned. In addition, one of the purchasers was described in the case as a somewhat shadowy figure who had never appeared in person nor responded to letters, and it was clear that the judge was in some doubt as to whether that purchaser actually existed. The other purchaser had stated that he was a barrister at the outset of the transactions, but it was known to the solicitor concerned that he had ceased to be a barrister at some stage before the loan was drawn and, accordingly, the solicitor might have had some concern as to whether that particular purchaser would have any income to repay the loan. Moreover, the solicitors did not disclose to the building society that second mortgages were being obtained to pay the balances of the prices, despite the fact that the loan instructions indicated that the borrowers were each providing a deposit. As if these facts did not produce enough conflict, the solicitor's firm was also acting for the second mortgagees.

These facts were sufficient for the court to hold that the major liability should fall on the solicitors, despite the fact that the lenders had clearly relied on valuations when taking the commercial decision to lend. The court did not like the smell of the transaction and felt that the solicitors ought to have had a wider view of the lenders' best interests. The court apportioned 70% of the liability to the solicitors and 30% to the surveyors. There were various elements of dubious practice in the case. The court had regard, first of all, to the question of conflict of interest. The solicitors were acting not only for the borrowers but also for the lenders and for the second mortgagees, and were also acting in other matters for the sellers. The solicitors had also failed to disclose that one of the conditions of the mortgage in relation to the deposits to be paid by the purchasers was not being implemented. Generally speaking, it appeared that the solicitors had looked after everyone's interests except the interests of the first lenders.

1 See the Solicitors (Scotland) Practice Rules 1986.
2 (1891) 63 LT 837.
3 For a discussion of the English cases, see *Jackson and Powell* paras 4–95 to 4–101.
4 1979 Ch 384, [1978] 3 All ER 571.
5 [1978] 3 All ER 571 at 583.
6 (1983) 268 EG 268.
7 (1972) 223 EG 2334.
8 (1981) 260 EG 1128.

5.05 The three recent leading cases dealing with the question of disclosure are *Mortgage Express v Bowerman & Partners*[1], *Target Holdings Ltd v Redferns*[2] and *Bank of East Asia Ltd v Shepherd & Wedderburn, WS*[3]. The *Mortgage Express* case is a decision of the Court of Appeal, the *Target* case is a decision of the House of Lords and the *Bank of East Asia* case is a decision of the Inner House of the Court of Session. All three cases deal with the question of what a solicitor ought to disclose to a client in the course of a transaction.

The *Mortgage Express* and *Target Holdings* cases related to back-to-back sales, where financial institutions were lending on the strength of a valuation and the highest price, in circumstances where the previous price was significantly lower. In the transactions there was doubt concerning the accuracy of the valuations obtained and, possibly, the genuineness of the ultimate purchase transactions. Both English cases are authority for the view that, in the circumstances of a sub-sale of this nature, there is now a duty of disclosure on the solicitor acting for the lender. In the *Target* case there was another issue in relation to duties arising from trust. Where a negligence claim exists, the amount of the claim can be reduced by factors such as contributory negligence (possibly in delict cases only), or a failure to mitigate loss. In the *Target* case the instructions were to use the funds provided by the lender for the ultimate purchase of the property by the borrower. There were back-to-back sales at lower prices preceding the ultimate purchase. In effect the solicitors (who were acting for everyone, including the lender and the sub-purchasers in the sub-sales) used the funds received from the lender to settle the previous sub-sales even before contracts were exchanged for the last purchase.

The Court of Appeal held by a majority that this was not so much negligence as breach of trust, since the solicitors had been given the loan funds in trust for the particular purpose of funding the ultimate purchase. Since the solicitors had used the funds to fund previous purchases, they were held to be in breach of trust and were therefore absolutely liable to refund the whole of the moneys lent under deduction only of such sums as were eventually recovered by the lenders on realisation of the security. There were, accordingly, no questions of contributory negligence or failure to mitigate loss to be discussed. The argument based on breach of trust was overturned in the House of Lords, but without affecting any question of the duty of disclosure.

The *Mortgage Express* case is the one which has the most direct relevance to the duty of disclosure. In that case solicitors acted both for the purchaser and for the lender. It was plain that the solicitor regarded the purchaser as his 'direct' client. Neither the purchaser nor the lender asked the solicitor to give any advice about the commercial merits of the transaction. A valuation of £199,000 had been obtained from surveyors. The purchase price on the last purchase was £220,000 and the loan being provided was £180,000. Accordingly, on the face of it, the security should have been adequate. During the course of the transaction, the solicitor became aware of a simultaneous sub-sale at a price of £150,000, some £70,000 below the price being paid by his 'direct' client, the ultimate purchaser. The solicitor (who was not involved in the prior sub-sale) advised the purchaser, and the purchaser indicated that he still wished to proceed. This was not information which was in any way confidential to the purchaser. It affected a party further down the chain of transactions, so there was no duty of confidentiality which would have barred the solicitor from advising the lender of the situation. Nevertheless, the solicitor did not advise the lender. Eventually the property was repossessed and the lender suffered a loss. The lender sued the surveyors and the solicitors. The court concluded that if a solicitor discovered facts which a reasonably competent solicitor would realise might have a material bearing on the value of the lender's security, or on some ingredient of the lending decision, then the solicitor had a duty to point that out to the lender.

The judgments in the case make it clear, however, that the question of disclosure is still a matter for the judgment of the individual solicitor concerned. The *Mortgage Express* case is not authority for the view that a solicitor must disclose everything in every transaction which might conceivably have some sort of bearing, however small, on the lender's original decision to lend. In the *Mortgage Express* case the solicitor had thought it important enough to tell the purchaser about the prior sub-sale. The solicitor was, therefore, to some extent caught on the point of his own disclosure, because the lender was as much a client as the purchaser. If the solicitor had thought it necessary to pass the information on to the purchaser as one of the clients interested in the transaction, then that same solicitor ought to have thought it important enough to pass the information on to the lending client who was, after all, the client making the bigger investment. In the *Mortgage Express* case the lender's standing instructions asked for details of any information which was relevant and that, no doubt, was a factor in the decision, but the court also came to its decision based on a judgment of the ordinary practice of solicitors, as opposed to any contractual instructions voluntarily undertaken. The court concluded that a lender would be bound to be greatly concerned to learn of a simultaneous sale at a figure of £50,000 below the valuation on which they were relying and £30,000 less than their proposed advance.

1 (1995) Times, 1 August.
2 [1995] 3 All ER 785, [1995] 3 WLR 352.
3 1995 SLT 1074.

5.06 The English cases contradict to a great extent the view of Lord Jauncey in *Midland Bank plc v Cameron, Thom, Peterkins & Duncans*[1], where he held that a solicitor who was merely instructed to prepare mortgage documents need not concern himself with the commercial decision to lend. The recent Scottish case of *Bank of East Asia Ltd v Shepherd & Wedderburn, WS*[2] casts some doubts as to the applicability of the *Midland Bank* decision even in Scotland. The *Bank of East Asia* case has been debated on the Procedure Roll and been the subject of an appeal to the Inner House of the Court of Session. The matter will not be going to proof.

In the case a construction company unsuccessfully attempted to obtain funding from its own bankers to complete a construction project. The Bank of East Asia was then approached and agreed to lend. The bank instructed the company's own solicitors to act on its behalf in the drawing up of an assignation of the sums due to the company by the client in terms of the construction contract. An assignation in ordinary form was drawn up and was intimated to the client in the construction contract. The intention was that the bank should have the full benefit of all sums due under that contract. The bank then advanced the money. At the time, various sums had been certified under the building contract as being due. A few days after the execution of the assignation the company entered into a minute of agreement with the client under the building contract whereby payments were deferred. Later on in that year the company went into receivership. The bank then sought to recover from the client in terms of the assignation and raised an action against the client in England.

The client argued that it was entitled to deduct from the sums due losses incurred in respect of bad workmanship and delay. The bank took the view that its security ought to have provided it with an absolute right to payment of the balance of the sums due under the contract, and it raised an action against the solicitors claiming that the solicitors had failed to ensure that all sums due would be paid to it without deduction. The bank argued that had it been properly advised as to its entitlement under the assignation, it would never have advanced the money on that type of security. The bank also argued that the solicitors had acted in a situation where there was a clear conflict of interest, since the solicitors had acted both for the bank and for the company in the preparation of the assignation.

The Lord Ordinary allowed a proof before answer and the solicitors reclaimed to the Inner House on the grounds first, that the instructions were simply to complete the mechanics of a loan and security transaction, the terms of which had been agreed, and, secondly, that the bank's pleadings contained no averment of a contractual term involving a duty on them to give advice as to the actual value of the security. The solicitors also argued that there was no averment which set out how a security of this type could be prepared which would in all circumstances be exempt from the ordinary law of retention or set-off. The solicitors argued that it was general knowledge that retentions were common in the final settlement of sums due under building contracts. The bank argued that information in the hands of the solicitors ought to have been passed to it to indicate the possibility of retentions being made. In the course of the argument various cases were referred to, including the *Midland Bank*[3] case and *Rae v Meek*[4]. The solicitors' argument was based mainly on the fact that they were not employed to give any advice on the value of the security. As a general statement this is, of course, an accepted principle of the law of professional negligence[5].

The case was taken to an Extra Division of the Inner House, where it was held that if a solicitor acting for a potential lender was in possession of information of which the potential lender was ignorant and which tended to show that the proposed security was worth significantly less than the lender seemed to believe, the solicitors might well require to advise the lender of the risk prior to acting upon instructions, and the duty was no less incumbent on the solicitor by virtue of the fact that he or she was already acting for the borrower. It was argued for the solicitors that all relevant facts concerning the construction contract were already in the possession of the bank and that the solicitors knew nothing which the bank did not already know. The court took the view that while it was not difficult to read this into the bank's pleadings, the possibility that the bank's knowledge was imperfect could not be excluded. Accordingly, the case was sent for proof before answer. The judgment of the court was delivered by Lord McCluskey. He said[6]:

'In the debate before us parties were hardly at issue as to the relevant law: if a solicitor is instructed by a potential lender simply to prepare a security document for signature by the borrower, those instructions do not impose upon him any duty to enquire into and advise about the underlying or future value of the security. On the other hand, if the solicitor is already acting for the potential borrower and by reason of so acting is in possession of information of which the potential lender is ignorant, being information which shows or tends to show that the security which he has been instructed to prepare is valueless or of significantly less value than the potential lender appears to think, then if he accepts the potential lender's instructions he may well, before acting upon the instructions, require to advise the potential lender of the risk of which he is aware.'

1 1988 SCLR 209, 1988 SLT 611.
2 1995 SCLR 598, 1995 SLT 1074.
3 See note 1 above.
4 (1889) 14 App Cas 558.
5 Begg *Law Agents* pp 242–243 and 337; *Jackson and Powell* para 4–143.
6 1995 SLT 1074 at 1079.

5.07 The English authorities appear to suggest that, in relation to the disclosure of matters which may suggest that the value of a security is less than the lender thinks or which may call into question the prudence of the transaction, the following is now the law:

1 The duty of disclosure is not a new or extended duty but simply an aspect of the ordinary duty of care owed by a solicitor.
2 Contractual instructions may contain undertakings in relation to the disclosure of specific matters or generally in relation to the disclosure of matters which might adversely affect the interests of a lender, and a breach of any such undertaking will result in liability under contract.

3 Whether there are contractual instructions or not, there is likely to be some sort of duty of disclosure under the general standard of care in certain cases.
4 Each individual case will still require to be treated on its own merits, and what may require to be disclosed in one case may not require disclosure in another.
5 Where a solicitor acts for a borrower and a lender there may be cases where something which is disclosed to the borrower need not be disclosed to the lender, but if this is a matter which has a potential effect on the value of the property being taken in security it ought to be disclosed to the lender.
6 There still seems to be scope for a solicitor to exercise judgment on the need to disclose depending on the surrounding circumstances, and if a solicitor makes inquiry which reveals facts or information which justify, for example, a sudden increase in price, then there may be no need to disclose, provided the information obtained by the solicitor is credible. Thus, in the case of a sub-sale at a higher price, a solicitor may be in a position to exercise judgment if it is shown that substantial renovation work has been carried out to the property which has obviously had an effect on its value.
7 Questions of contributory negligence, failure to mitigate loss or shared liability may arise in cases of this type, especially where lenders have relied on valuations provided by surveyors. However, it ought to be noted that contributory negligence tends to be a defence only in the case of a breach of the general duty of care and not in the case of a breach of a specific contractual instruction[1]. Similarly, it is unlikely that contributory negligence will be a defence where any form of fraud or deceit is involved[2].
8 There may be an unfortunate difference between cases involving surveyors and those involving solicitors. A surveyor will normally be entitled to deduct a natural fall in the property values from the amount of a negligence claim. In the *Mortgage Express v Bowerman* case[3], it was held that although the surveyors involved would be entitled to make such a deduction the solicitors would not, because their lack of disclosure was a factor in the original decision to lend. The view was taken that had the solicitors disclosed, the lenders might not have lent at all so they would have lost nothing. Accordingly, any natural fall in the value of the property was irrelevant[4].
9 Even where a duty of disclosure is found to exist, questions of causation, remoteness and contributory negligence will be relevant to the question of liability[5].

10 Although certain facts may require disclosure, there is no positive duty on a solicitor to investigate the financial position of a client for the benefit of a lender[6].

1 *Bristol & West Building Society v A Kramer & Co* (1995) Times, 6 February.
2 *Alliance & Leicester Building Society v Edgestop Ltd* [1994] 2 All ER 38, [1993] 1 WLR 1462.
3 (1995) Times, 1 August.
4 This proposition may now be doubtful: see para 9.10 below and *South Australia Asset Corporation v York Montague Ltd* [1996] 3 All ER 365.
5 See paras 9.02–9.04 below.
6 *Birmingham Midshires Mortgage Services Ltd v David Parry* [1996] PNLR 494.

Matters which may now require disclosure

5.08 The cases relating to non-disclosure have tended to revolve around back-to-back sales and purchases, but that is not the only type of information which might now require to be disclosed. Generally speaking, if a solicitor has information which might affect the value of a security or which might reflect on the prudence of a particular transaction (whether a loan or a purchase), then, unless there is a plausible explanation backed up with evidence on which the solicitor can exercise a *bona fide* judgment, it seems likely that a court will hold that there is some duty to disclose. Obvious examples of this might be matters which come to the notice of a solicitor concerning the financial solvency of a client who is proposing to take out a loan. A search may disclose various inhibitions or attempts to sequestrate the borrower. It may be that none of these entries has any legal effect on the grant of a security because of prescription, discharge or some other factor. Nevertheless, entries of this type, particularly if they are recent, will indicate clearly that the borrower may be a bad financial risk. Given the fact that most lenders' application forms require the borrower to state whether they have any decrees or diligences against them, such entries may also indicate the possibility of a mis-statement in the application form. It has been held in England that solicitors have a duty to warn lenders of facts which suggest that clients may not be able to repay a mortgage[1]. Other matters which may affect the value of a security are cash-back or discount schemes, whereby builders pay back part of the price to a purchaser of a new house, the loan being based on the full price.

While most cases involving disclosure will arise where a solicitor acts for a borrower and a lender, the duty to disclose is not restricted to that situation. Solicitors acting solely for lenders will only have duties to the lender and, of course, they will not have any problem of confidentiality. Where a solicitor does act for lender and purchaser and a question of disclosure arises, the best test, in the submission of the author, is whether or not the solicitor would have had no hesitation in disclosing the matter to the lender if the solicitor had been acting for the lender alone. If the answer to that question is 'yes' then it seems likely that there will be a duty of disclosure.

1 *National Home Loans Corporation v Giffen Couch & Archer* (1996) Times, 7 December.

Historical failures to disclose

5.09 The standard of care against which a solicitor's conduct is judged is the standard of practice applicable at the time of the alleged negligence and not the standard applicable at the time of the loss or indeed the making of the claim. Accordingly, although recent cases[1] indicate that there may now be a duty of disclosure in certain circumstances, there may be room for an argument that in historical cases general practice among solicitors at the time of a particular non-disclosure would not have suggested a duty to disclose at that time in the particular circumstances of an individual case.

1 Many of the English cases relate to loans made in the boom years of 1989 and 1990, and English courts have generally but not always found against the solicitors concerned. See *Perry v Edwin Coe* (1994) Independent, 1 April; *Bristol & West Building Society v A Kramer & Co* (1995) Times, 6 February; *Johnson v Bingley* (1995) Times, 28 February; *Halifax Mortgage Services v Stepsky* (1995) Times, 1 December; *Mortgage Express Ltd v Bowerman & Partners* (1995) Times, 1 August, [1996] PNLR 62; *Hypo Mortgage Services Ltd v David Parry & Co* (1996) EGCS 39; *Bristol & West Building Society v Mothew (Stapley & Co)* (1996) Times, 2 August, (1996) EGCS 136; *Bristol & West Building Society v May, May & Merrimans* (1996) Times, 25 April, [1996] PNLR 138; *Birmingham Midshires Mortgage Services Ltd v David Parry* [1996] PNLR 494; *Mortgage Express Ltd v Newman & Co* [1996] PNLR 603; *National Home Loans Corporation v Giffen Couch & Archer* (1996) Times, 7 December.

CHAPTER 6

Negligence in Conveyancing and Related Non-Litigation Matters

Introduction

6.01 It is often said that the buying of a house is the single most important purchase any individual ever makes. For most people that is undoubtedly true and for that reason it might be said that the main duty of a solicitor acting for a purchaser in a conveyancing transaction is to obtain a valid marketable title, so that the purchaser is not only secure in his or her ownership and possession but will be able to sell the property and realise the investment at a later date. Nowadays, however, the duties of a solicitor in a purchase transaction extend to far more than just matters of title. With the advent of registration of title questions of validity cease to be as prominent as they were, given the fact that the Keeper of the Registers guarantees the title sheet unless indemnity has been excluded.

It is fair to say that most disputes in conveyancing transactions tend to relate to the missives or peripheral matters, such as the lack of building warrants or completion certificates, the sufficiency of mineral reports and the like. The absence or content of such additional documentation is just as likely to frustrate a subsequent sale as a title problem. Indeed, many title problems can be solved more easily than problems relating to ancillary matters. If it turns out that a title does not cover the whole of the garden, the matter may be rectified either by the use of a section 19 agreement between neighbours[1] or by the acquisition of an additional strip, even at some cost. If, however, a property is less than ten years old, and for some reason does not have a National House Builders Council (NHBC) guarantee or a suitable architect's certificate, it may be impossible to solve this problem retrospectively. Jackson and Powell, in their standard work on professional negligence, state that the greater part of the solicitor's duty in a conveyancing transaction is directed towards protecting the client against possible future risks[2]. It is certainly true that there is always a feeling of something having come home to roost when a solicitor is faced with a claim arising from a five-year-old transaction.

Much has been said recently concerning the relationship between low conveyancing fees and slack conveyancing procedure. Unfortunately, it is not always easy to find reliable statistics. The author has no doubt, however, that the pressure on solicitors to carry out routine domestic conveyancing as cheaply as possible has led to some lowering of standards. This is especially true in regard to the standard of reporting to the client in relation to the title and other important aspects of the transaction. When the author was an apprentice in 1967, conveyancing transactions were conducted at a somewhat leisurely pace and indeed it was common for the transaction to settle after the date of entry simply because the title examination was not complete. In these circumstances, purchasers often took entry on consignation of the price or where there was a loan, on payment of a deposit. Solicitors were not keen finally to settle a transaction until they had seen each and every prior writ and raised as many observations as were necessary. In addition to the normal reporting to a client in the course of a transaction, a formal written report in a stiff binding was sent to the client at the conclusion of the transaction, along with the solicitors' cash statement. The report contained a description of the property taken from the title deeds with a copy plan and a summary of the important burdens in the title. The status of the road footpath and sewer was also noted.

The author doubts whether such a high standard of reporting pertains today in an ordinary domestic conveyancing transaction. In commercial transactions, it is still quite common to provide a written report on the title especially where a number of properties are being acquired as an investment portfolio, but it has to be said that commercial clients are usually prepared to pay appropriately for good service.

1 Land Registration (Scotland) Act 1979, s 19.
2 Jackson and Powell *Professional Negligence* para 4–134.

The conveyancing transaction

6.02 An ordinary conveyancing transaction can be said to be split into several distinct phases:
(1) The instruction phase.
(2) The missive phase.
(3) The title phase.
(4) The settlement and post-settlement phase.
There is no doubt that over the years there has been a change in emphasis in the overall transaction. Initially, the solicitor's main

duties lay in the title phase. The instruction phase consisted of taking details of the property and, in some cases, in instructing a survey and obtaining a loan. The missive phase consisted of an offer of perhaps six or seven clauses and a straight acceptance. The settlement phase consisted of handing over a cheque in return for the signed disposition, titles, letter of obligation and receipted state for settlement, with no attendant problems relating to non-supersession or deeds of trust. The main work of the solicitor was in the title phase, which involved a careful and detailed examination of the titles, the raising of appropriate observations and the preparation of a disposition and loan documents.

It is a feature of modern conveyancing that a great deal of work (and sometimes the vast majority of the work) now takes place during the missive phase of the transaction. Missives are now infinitely more complicated than they were and contain a wide variety of clauses, some of which have little or no connection with the title to the property. Where the seller sends the titles with the qualified acceptance and invites the purchaser to accept the title as it stands or at least with the burdens applicable thereto, the title phase and the missive phase are thrown together. In this type of case the time for reporting to the client may be shortened but the duties of the solicitor remain the same, despite the fact that there may be no scope for raising title queries later on in the transaction. Where missives are concluded in this way the purchaser may be contractually bound to accept the title no matter what it contains.

Even the settlement phase of the transaction has become more complicated. The decision in *Sharp v Thomson*[1] makes it clear that no property right accrues to the purchaser on delivery of the disposition. Where the seller is a limited company, there is a risk that the purchaser's title may be defeated. At the settlement phase it is also important to ensure that the missives are kept alive in respect of obligations which have yet to be fulfilled[2]. The vast majority of purchases involve secured loans and where the purchase is of domestic property the same solicitor normally acts for the purchaser and for the lender. There has been a tendency in the legal profession in the past to regard the purchaser as the 'primary' or 'real' client and the lender as some sort of third party simply there to provide funds once standard security forms have been signed and a report on title submitted. Many of the claims made by lenders against solicitors arise solely from the fact that the solicitor has failed to take account of the interests of the lender as a client, or has failed to acknowledge the lender as a client at all[3]. Solicitors owe duties of care to their clients, be they purchaser or lender, at every phase of the conveyancing transaction and it is appropriate to look at these duties as they arise in each phase[4].

1 1995 SC 455, 1995 SCLR 683.
2 See Cusine and Rennie *Missives* (1993) para 5.06 et seq; *Winston v Patrick* 1980 SC 246, 1981 SLT 41; Reid 'Prior Communings and Conveyancing Practice' (1981) 26 JLSS 414; Reid 'Avoiding *Winston v Patrick*' (1983) 28 JLSS (Workshop) 330; Cusine '*Winston v Patrick* Revisited Briefly' (1986) 31 JLSS 16; Cusine '*Winston v Patrick* and their heirs and assignees' (1988) 33 JLSS 102.
3 See the remarks made in *Mortgage Express v Bowerman & Partners* (1995) Times, 1 August; Rennie 'Negligence, Instructions and the Lender's Need to Know' (1994) 39 JLSS 135; Rennie 'Negligence, Securities and the Expanding Duty of Care' (1995) 40 JLSS 58.
4 For a general discussion on the nature of a conveyancing transaction, see *Cusine and Rennie*; Halliday *Conveyancing Law and Practice in Scotland* vol II (1986), Chs 15 and 22; Gretton and Reid *Conveyancing* (1993) Ch 1; Sinclair *Handbook of Conveyancing Practice in Scotland* (1986).

The instruction phase: purchase

6.03 As has already been stated, a solicitor is bound to act in accordance with the instructions which he or she receives. It is important, therefore, for the solicitor to ensure that appropriate instructions are given and that these are carefully noted[1]. It is the solicitor's duty to ensure that he or she asks the right questions in order to obtain proper instructions. The instructions required will, of course, vary depending on the type of property, so it is unwise to generalise on the type of questions which the solicitor should ask or the information which he or she should obtain. Obviously, the solicitor should obtain clear instructions or information in relation to the description of the property to be purchased, the price to be paid, the date of entry, the moveable items to be included, any extensions or alterations to the property and if the property is situated in a rural area, information concerning services such as roads, water supplies, drainage and sewage discharge. If the property is new or relatively new, then the solicitor should consider what information he or she will require in relation to NHBC guarantees, architect's certificates, planning permissions, building warrants and completion certificates. The solicitor should ensure that any pro forma offer which he or she customarily uses adequately caters for all of these matters.

It is often the case that the solicitor is in possession of a schedule of particulars or a survey report relative to the property to be purchased. A solicitor should take careful note of anything contained in the schedule or the survey report. If the schedule indicates that the property comes with a garden of half an acre and the survey report indicates that the grounds pertaining to the dwellinghouse are only a quarter of an acre, this is a matter which should be sorted out before any offer is lodged. General words of description in an offer such as 'with the ground pertaining thereto' may carry only the ground which is physically possessed. Similarly, if the schedule of particulars, survey or some other documentation clearly indicates that the property has recently been extended or altered, the solicitor should ensure that any offer lodged provides for the production of appropriate permissions and consents, including completion certificates where applicable. It is up to the solicitor to make appropriate inquiries and to use whatever information is to hand to ensure that any offer which is lodged adequately protects the purchaser. Similarly, while it is not generally a solicitor's duty to give advice on the prudence of a particular transaction, it would be negligent for a solicitor to fail to point out something in an initial survey report which suggested that the property might be a poor investment[2]. The solicitor should ensure that instructions are taken from the appropriate party[3] and that he or she knows the name of the party who is to take title[4].

1 See paras 3.02–3.04 above.
2 See para 5.03 above.
3 *Hopkinson v Williams* 1993 SLT 907.
4 *Glasper v Rodger* 1996 SLT 44.

Description of domestic property

6.04 Domestic property comes in various shapes and sizes. A property is normally either detached, semi-detached, end-terraced, mid-terraced, flatted as part of a block or tenement, or flatted as part of a conversion of a previously self-contained dwellinghouse. It is of vital importance that the solicitor ascertains just what type of dwellinghouse is involved. Fewer problems surround detached and semi-detached properties than the rest. Nevertheless, even in a well-defined property it is important to inquire whether there are ancillary buildings such as garages, greenhouses, sheds and the like. While these items may normally be regarded as heritable, they need not be so, depending on the actual degree of attachment[1].

It is often useful even in suburban properties to inquire whether the garden is delineated by a fence or some other physical boundary. In the case of rural properties this can be particularly important where a less than precise description may be found in the title deeds. It must always be borne in mind by the solicitor that although a client is entitled to a disposition covering all that has been seen by the client as physically possessed by the seller[2], there is still scope for argument where what has been seen is not clearly fenced off. Where there is some doubt as to the extent of ground, then consideration ought to be given as to whether a plan is required for annexation to the offer. In the case of mid-terraced or end-terraced properties, it is important to ascertain whether there is a rear lane which serves the property, especially where there is a garage. If this is the case, then the offer should stipulate for a servitude right of access. Information should also be sought from the client as to whether there are any common paths which run along the front or rear of the terrace.

In the case of flatted property in tenements or blocks, it is vital to ascertain whether or not the flat has its own exclusive address or whether the postal number attached to the flat also applies to all the other flats in the tenement. It is also important to ascertain the precise location of the flat in the tenement or block so that the description in the offer can be framed appropriately. In this connection it is better to avoid terms like 'right-hand', 'middle', 'left-hand' or 'first right'. These expressions are confusing, especially where the common stair turns back on itself within the tenement. The question can then arise as to whether it is the right-hand flat viewed from the street or the right-hand flat viewed from the landing. If the internal stair turns back on itself then a flat can be the right- or left-hand flat depending on the position from which the flat is viewed. It is safer to describe a flat by reference to a compass point, such as 'the northmost flat on the first floor above the ground floor', although it is appreciated that such directional points are not often available at the time of instruction.

In the case of top-floor flats, care should be taken to inquire whether any attic or garret is included. Titles to top-floor flats with attic conversions are notoriously difficult. In the absence of any provision in the title deeds, the air space between the top flat and the roof is in the ownership of the top flat but that may not include ownership of a dormer which has been thrown out of a common roof[3]. If the description in the offer simply refers to the top flat right at 359 Smith Street, Glasgow, then there may be a question as to whether that description also includes any attic conversion. If there is a subsequent title problem and the purchaser wishes to rescind the contract because there is no title to the whole or part of the attic conversion, the seller may argue that the attic part of the top flat was never actually purchased in terms of the missives.

Care should also be taken to ascertain whether or not there are any other rights to any other areas of ground or outhouses. If there are areas of exclusive garden ground or coal cellars, lockups or sheds pertaining to the flat, then information should be obtained so that these are mentioned specifically in the offer. If no proper instruction is taken then the purchaser may have to rely on whatever words of general description are contained in the offer and also on whether the offer contains a clause of pertinents. The law of pertinents is notoriously confusing and a client should not have to rely on it to ensure that everything he or she intends to purchase has been included in the offer which is lodged[4].

Flatted conversions present special problems of their own. Detailed instruction is necessary before any offer is lodged, and in some cases it will be useful to see the titles in advance so that a proper description of all that is to be purchased is inserted in the offer. In particular, the solicitor should ascertain what areas of ground pertain exclusively to the flat to be purchased and what areas of ground are common to both flats in the conversion. The solicitor should also ascertain the status of any driveways and accesses which may serve one or both flats. In a transaction of this type it will usually be necessary to meet the client before the offer is lodged and go over the schedule of particulars and any plan which is available. It may also be necessary to make a site visit and to annex a plan to any offer.

So far as the question of negligence is concerned, it is the duty of the solicitor to frame the offer in such a way as it include everything that the client thinks is being purchased. While to a certain extent it is up to the client to give appropriate instructions in this regard, there is also an obligation on the solicitor to make appropriate inquiries of the client and of any other party who may hold information to enable the solicitor to describe the property in an adequate manner. It would be extremely risky, for example, to lodge an offer for a lower flat conversion of a former self-contained villa with a description in the following terms:

'The upper flatted dwellinghouse known as 58b Nithswood Road, Glasgow, with the ground pertaining thereto, common rights and others and the pertinents.'

In the case of flatted property, most pro forma offers contain a clause which states that the share of maintenance of common parts is on an equitable basis. While that clause may pass muster for a flat in a tenement of eight flats of the same size, it may not be good enough in the case of a flatted conversion where one flat is significantly larger than the other. In the case of a flatted conversion, it is safer to ascertain in advance the precise shares of maintenance so far as common parts are concerned. The same applies in connection with common rights. It should always be borne in mind that if the titles are silent, then the roof, and with it the obligation to maintain the roof, will pertain to the upper flat[5].

1 See *Christie v Smith's Executrix* 1949 SC 572.
2 *Houldsworth v Gordon Cumming* 1910 SC (HL) 49.
3 See *Taylor v Dunlop* (1872) 11 M 25; *Sanderson's Trustees v Yule* (1897) 25 R 211.
4 For a general discusssion of the law of pertinents, see *Halliday* vol II para 18–38.
5 *Taylor v Dunlop* (1872) 11 M 25; *Sanderson's Trustees v Yule* (1897) 25 R 211.

Description of commercial property

6.05 Different considerations apply when considering the description to be inserted in an offer for commercial property. An offer does not need to contain a full conveyancing description of the property. In the case of a commercial property, however, a much more detailed description of the subject matter is often required than in the case of a domestic property. In the case of a commercial property, it is often essential to visit the site. Some time ago the author acted for a client who wished to buy a shop. The client was inexperienced and simply described the shop as a grocery store in a small terrace of shops. The author inquired whether the shop had any exclusive ground and the client replied that there was nothing apart from a common yard at the rear. An offer was drawn up which specified the property by postal address and provided that it would include a common right to the rear ground. A qualified acceptance was received which indicated the possibility of a boundary problem. The author then visited the site and was horrified to find that there was a private service road at the front of the property over which an access right would be required, that the shop was not just a grocer's shop but a licensed grocer's shop and that the shop contained a sub-post office. None of these facts had been gleaned from the client at the initial interview and, of course, all were vital to the transaction.

A solicitor dealing with the purchase of a commercial property must ascertain precisely what is being purchased and also ascertain the nature of the business, because in a commercial transaction a business is being acquired as well as heritable property. Where the commercial property is a yard or an open field to be used as a development, a plan will be essential[1]. It is vital that any such plan be approved by the client before it is annexed to the offer. It is often a good idea to use an up-to-date ordnance survey map, if the property can be identified from that map, especially where the property is situated in an operational area for land registration purposes.

Greater care must be taken over the question of heritable fittings and fixtures in the case of commercial property. Where important items of plant and machinery are to be included in the price, then these should be listed individually or in an attached inventory. It may be that such items of plant and machinery might be regarded as heritable, but this should not be left to chance nor in a general clause including all the fittings and fixtures used in connection with the business.

Stock may also be an important item to be purchased with a commercial property. Provision should be made for the acquisition of the stock in the missives, and instruction should be taken from the client as to whether the stock is to be kept at a certain level or run down. In a commercial business, many of the moveable items may be on loan, lease or hire purchase. It is important that the missives cater for this situation and that the client is kept fully informed. It is advisable to obtain information in relation to this before the offer is lodged so that the client will be aware of what liabilities are to be taken on in this regard. Solicitors can sometimes become too involved in the conveyancing, forgetting that a client may not wish to take on a leasing liability for an old alarm system in circumstances where the leasing agreement can be terminated only on payment of a substantial penalty.

1 See *McManus Developments Ltd v Barbridge Properties Ltd* [1996] PNLR 431.

The price

6.06 In a domestic conveyancing transaction the price ought to be a relatively straightforward item. It goes without saying that the solicitor ought to obtain clear instructions from the client as to what price is to be offered. Generally speaking, it is not a good idea to take an instruction which leaves the fixing of the price to the solicitor even where there is a closing date. The scope for argument is too obvious. Either the solicitor will pitch the price too low, in which case the client will lose the house, or the solicitor will pitch the price too high, in which case the client will pay over the odds. In a closing-date situation, the best advice is to tell the client to work out his or her top price and offer that price on the basis that no second chance will be given[1].

In some cases there may be a question of apportionment of the price between heritable and moveable property. This can become a critical matter where the price is close to the stamp duty limit. Solicitors should bear in mind that they have a professional duty to act properly and reasonably in any such apportionment. The position of the lender must also be catered for here. The lender will be basing the decision to lend on the price and on any valuation received. If a substantial reduction in the price of the heritable property is to be made, the lender should be advised. If, after all, the apportionment is genuine then it reflects not only on the value of the moveable items but on the value of the heritage. In the case of commercial properties the question of apportionment can be more critical. Capital gains tax liabilities can be increased if the apportionment is not handled correctly. Where there is doubt as to the correct apportionment, the solicitor should suggest to the client that appropriate advice be taken from an accountant.

Of more importance in commercial property is the question of Value Added Tax. Where a property is new (as defined in the VAT legislation), VAT must be charged on the price. This rule does not simply apply to property which is being sold new for the first time. It applies to property less than three years' old. Apart from this, commercial property is normally exempt from VAT, but it is possible for the seller to waive the exemption and opt to charge VAT. It is important, whether acting for seller or purchaser, to clarify whether VAT is to be charged. Again, if there is any doubt, the client ought to be referred to an accountant for expert advice.

In some cases, the price of commercial property is not fixed but may be subject to increases or decreases depending on a suspensive condition. An obvious example of this is where property is acquired for development purposes subject to a suspensive condition that planning permission be granted. In a number of cases, a base price will be stated in the missives, subject to certain increases in the event that subsequent planning permissions are obtained which allow for a greater density of development. Great care must be taken in relation to the instructions to be obtained for such clauses and when the missives are framed, the purchaser's solicitor must ensure that the missives are kept alive for as long as it will take to ascertain whether any further money is due. It must always be remembered that a non-supersession clause with a two-year time limit can be a double-edged weapon in this regard[2].

1 On closing dates in general and the Law Society guidelines in connection therewith, see *Cusine and Rennie* paras 1.35–1.37.
2 See *Pena v Ray* 1987 SLT 609.

The date of entry

6.07 In the case of normal domestic property, the date of entry will be a straightforward matter. Instructions should be taken and advice given in relation to the possible need for bridging loans, where it is not possible to synchronise a date of entry for a sale with a date of entry for a purchase. In the case of a commercial purchase of investment property which is already leased, appropriate instructions ought to be taken in relation to the nature of the leased property and whether vacant possession of any part of the development is required, since it has been held that the existence of a lease on a property purchased is not necessarily a breach of a warrandice clause[1]. If vacant possession is required, then it is necessary to stipulate for this in the missives. It has been held that it is not essential to the validity of a set of missives that there is an actual date of entry[2]. However, it is unwise to rely on that decision because it involves a degree of uncertainty for the purchaser as to when he or she will obtain entry.

Where commercial property is being purchased subject to a suspensive condition in relation to the obtaining of planning permission or the transfer of a licence, care must be taken to obtain proper instructions in relation to any time limits which are to be imposed, and it is often useful at this point to inquire of the purchaser whether he or she wishes the right to waive any suspensive conditions and proceed on an unconditional basis. If this is what the purchaser wants, then an appropriate clause must be inserted in the offer[3]. Sometimes clients ask for built-in flexibility in relation to the date of entry, especially where they are buying without having sold. It is not appropriate to frame a clause which says that the date of entry will be on a certain date or such other date as may be mutually agreed, because the question will then arise as to what is to happen if the parties fail to agree upon a date[4]. It is appropriate in such a case to provide that the date of entry shall be such date as the parties may agree but no later than a certain fixed date. The client should be advised in such a situation that the other contracting party cannot be forced to alter the date from the end date.

1 *Lothian and Border Farmers Ltd v McCutchion* 1952 SLT 450.
2 *Gordon District Council v Wimpey Homes Holdings Ltd* 1988 SCLR 545, 1988 SLT 481.
3 See *Cusine and Rennie* para 4.88; *Manheath Ltd v H J Banks & Co Ltd* 1996 GWD 1–50.
4 See *Sloans Dairies Ltd v Glasgow Corporation* 1977 SC 223, 1977 SLT 17.

Fittings and fixtures

6.08 In the case of a domestic purchase the solicitor should ascertain what moveable items are included in the price. In some cases, the purchasers will simply respond to such an inquiry by referring to everything that is included in the selling agent's schedule. It should always be borne in mind that schedules are updated from time to time and that the seller may have agreed to a particular price based on the fact that none or some of the moveable items are to be excluded. If the moveable items are to be described in this manner then it is preferable for the schedule concerned to be annexed to the offer.

It is, however, generally better to take direct instruction from the purchaser as to the individual items to be purchased and simply to list these in the offer. That way a solicitor is less likely to be accused of submitting an offer which has excluded some important item. Where a commercial business is being acquired along with heritable property, it is more likely that an inventory will be required, especially where the moveable items are important for the running of the business. It is not sufficient to offer for commercial heritable property such as a public house together with 'all fittings and fixtures heritable and moveable presently in the premises and necessary for the running of the business'. A provision of this type is not easily interpreted in connection, for example, with pictures which are stated by the seller to be his or her personal property, but which the purchaser thinks are necessary for the general ambience of the hotel or public house premises.

Pertinents and necessary servitude rights

6.09 It is important to ascertain from the client whether there are any incorporeal heritable rights which are necessary for the convenient use and enjoyment of the main subjects being purchased. The most obvious example is a right of access over a private road or a right to connect pipes to or from a septic tank which may be situated in someone else's ground. As with all matters in the instruction phase, the obtaining of clear instructions and good information can prevent catastrophe during the title phase when observations are raised.

There is a tendency in modern conveyancing practice to submit an offer with as many catch-all clauses as possible, the idea being that if proper instructions have for some reason not been taken, there is bound to be a clause in the schedule attached to the offer which will protect the purchaser. Obvious examples of this type of practice are alternative clauses relating to roads, footpaths and sewers. The author has seen missives which contained two clauses in the schedule to the offer which faced in opposite directions. The first clause provided that evidence would be exhibited to the effect that the road, footpath and sewer were public and that there were no outstanding liabilities in this connection. The second clause provided that in the event of the road being private, the title deeds would contain servitude rights of access, and in the event of the subjects not being served by a public sewer, the title deeds would contain appropriate servitude rights to connect to a septic tank. The author has never been sure of the combined effect of these two clauses. If the seller accepted both clauses, then it might be that all the seller had to do was implement the less onerous of the two and, if the road were private and the subjects were not served by a public sewer, provide titles with the appropriate servitude rights. However, depending on the precise wording of the two clauses and of any qualifications pertaining thereto, the matter may be far from clear.

It behoves the purchaser's solicitor, therefore, to try to ascertain beforehand which of the two alternatives is likely to apply. In the vast majority of ordinary city or suburban properties there will be no question of a private road or a septic tank. In rural properties in remote areas a private road and a septic tank may be the norm and appropriate information should be obtained and instruction taken. At this stage, the purchaser should be advised by the solicitor of any continuing liabilities for maintenance. It should always be borne in mind that various permissions are required before discharge from a septic tank can be allowed to enter any stream, river or water course; and if a property is served by a septic tank, some information ought to be sought concerning the direction of the outfall and the existence of any permissions from the Scottish Environmental Protection Agency or other appropriate authority.

Apart from these obvious examples, it is appropriate to ascertain in advance whether there are any other ancillary rights which ought to be included. It is good practice when describing property in an offer to add the words 'together with the pertinents'. The law of pertinents is somewhat confusing and there are differing judicial dicta on whether the addition of the word 'pertinent' actually adds anything to what is being purchased or conveyed. Nevertheless, a clause of pertinents can be useful as a catch-all if some specific right has been omitted in the description[1].

1 See *Halliday* vol II paras 15–41, 18–38 and 19–39; *Cusine and Rennie* para 4.06; *Cooper's Trustees v Stark's Trustees* (1898) 25 R 1160; *Meacher v Blair-Oliphant* 1913 SC 417.

Alterations and extensions

6.10 Most pro forma offers submitted by solicitors contain a clause providing that appropriate permissions, warrants, completion certificates and consents or waivers will be delivered in respect of any alterations or extensions to the property. However, it is useful to inquire during the instruction phase whether or not there are any specific alterations. Similarly, if the solicitor is in possession of a surveyor's report, this should be scrutinised to see if mention is made of any such alterations or extensions. The reason for this is that sellers are often quite unaware of the legal significance of an alteration or extension which may have been carried out by a previous owner. A seller ought to be aware of a kitchen extension which is clearly sited in the former back garden, but the same cannot be said of an attic conversion to a bungalow carried out by a previous owner some twenty years ago. Such an extension, if properly done, will simply appear to the seller as part of the dwellinghouse. In any event, there is no guarantee that the selling solicitor, in going over the offer with the seller, will actually ask the appropriate questions in relation to each and every clause in the missives, including the alterations and extension clause. Accordingly, if the purchasing solicitor is aware of a particular alteration or extension, then careful note of that should be taken during the instruction phase and the offer should be amended to include specific reference to that particular alteration and extension[1].

1 For an example of a claim in relation to alterations, see *McAllister-Hall v Anderson Shaw & Gilbert* 1995 GWD 25-1334.

Services

6.11 As has already been noted, it is often important to take appropriate instructions in relation to the nature of any services such as roads, footpaths, water supplies, drainage and sewage outfall at the time instructions are taken, especially in the case of rural property.

Surveys

6.12 While a client is entitled to take whatever risks he or she wishes, a solicitor should always point out to a purchaser that it is important to obtain a survey before lodging an offer. Generally speaking, the more inexperienced the client, the higher the duty to point this out. Where a client insists on proceeding without a survey and the offer is not made subject to obtaining a satisfactory survey, the solicitor ought to obtain instructions in writing to this effect[1]. It is doubtful whether the acceptance of a straightforward instruction to lodge an offer without advising on the need for a survey is negligence per se. Jackson and Powell suggest that it may not be[2]. The case which they quote, however, relies on the fact that local practice did not require this[3]. The same authors suggest, however, that where a client is inexperienced and the property in question is old, there may be negligence if a solicitor fails to give appropriate advice on the need for a survey[4]. Undoubtedly, the safest course is to advise a survey and to note carefully any instruction to proceed without a survey, confirming such instruction in writing and, if possible, obtaining such instruction in writing.

So far as commercial properties are concerned, the same rules apply in theory, although an experienced businessman may be supposed to know more about the risks involved than an inexperienced first-time house purchaser. In many cases, a survey will have been instructed or carried out prior to any contact being made with the solicitor. There are, of course, different types of survey[5]. If a solicitor is actively involved in the obtaining of the finance for the purchase or the instruction of the survey, then the solicitor should advise the client as to the types of survey available and the rights which the purchaser may or may not have against the surveyor in each case. An ordinary mortgage valuation is not a survey but merely a valuation for a lender which may indicate certain obvious defects. A house purchase survey should point out ordinary defects in the dwellinghouse provided they are visible. A structural survey goes a step further, and is not normally advised unless a previous survey has raised the possibility of significant structural defects. Where a client requires a structural survey, some guidance should be given as to the likely cost.

1 See *Cusine and Rennie* para 1.02.
2 *Jackson and Powell* para 4–112.
3 *Brenner v Gregory* (1972) 30 DLR (3d) 672.
4 See *Buckland v Mackesy* (1968) 208 EG 969.
5 See *Cusine and Rennie* paras 1.02–1.07.

Finance for the purchase

6.13 It has been said that there is no duty on a solicitor to ensure that finance is available before an offer is submitted, although it is good practice to advise the client of the risks involved in concluding missives without being certain that finance is available[1]. The position appears to be slightly different in England, although it must always be remembered that the two conveyancing sytems are radically different. In England a purchaser can withdraw at any time before contracts are exchanged. In these circumstances, there may be a fairly lengthy time period during which it should be obvious whether or not finance is available. Jackson and Powell are clear[2] that in a situation where a client needs a loan to complete the transaction, the solicitor ought to warn the client of the risks involved in exchanging contracts before the mortgage has been approved[3]. Where the solicitor is actively involved in the arranging of the finance, he or she will have different obligations under the financial services legislation and regulations. It will be necessary for the solicitor to give best advice on which loan is the most appropriate for the client[4].

1 Ryder *Professional Conduct for Scottish Solicitors* (1995) p 96; Decision of the Professional Practice Committee, 7 July 1994.
2 *Jackson and Powell* paras 4–112 and 4–140.
3 See *Buckland v Mackesy* (1968) 208 EG 969.
4 For a general discussion of the types of loan available, see *Cusine and Rennie* paras 1.09–1.16.

The nature of the solicitor's authority

6.14 A solicitor acting in the purchase of property should always bear in mind the law of agency. Quite apart from any questions of negligence, the question of authority, actual or ostensible, may arise if the purchasing client states that the solicitor has acted without authority in lodging the offer or in respect of some particular clause in the offer. A solicitor is one of those professionals who enjoys an ostensible authority as well as an actual authority, and this may result in a client being bound to a certain provision in circumstances where no instructions were given. Despite this, however, a solicitor does not have ostensible authority to conclude a contract such as missives without the authority of the client[1]. In a situation where a purchaser instructs a solicitor to lodge an offer at a certain price, then the purchaser is likely to be bound by each and every provision of the offer. It is likely that ostensible authority would extend to peripheral matters, such as the acceptance of a letter of comfort instead of a completion certificate, or a servitude based on usage rather than on an express provision of the deeds. Solicitors should also remember that if they act without any instruction at all, the client may not be liable under the contract but the solicitor may be liable for breach of warranty of his or her warranty of own authority.

1 *Danish Dairy Co Ltd v Gillespie* 1922 SC 656; *Cusine and Rennie* para 3.08.

The parties

6.15 It is the duty of the solicitor to ensure that he or she knows the identity of the parties for whom any offer is being submitted. In most cases of a joint purchase the instructions will come from one of the parties. It is the author's view that where the parties are married or partners (legal or personal) in these circumstances the solicitor is entitled to treat that party as agent for the other party or parties in any instructions which are given. However, care should be taken where other relations give instructions[1] and over other matters such as survivorship destinations and matrimonial homes' consents and affidavits. Where the title is to be taken in joint names, many solicitors seem to insert a survivorship clause as a matter of course, believing that that is what the parties are bound to want. There is no doubt in the author's mind that to do this without instruction is negligent. The effect of a survivorship destination can be catastrophic, especially in cicumstances where the parties subsequently separate. It has been held that even where one party conveys a half share to the other as part of a divorce settlement, the survivorship destination is not evacuated if it is contractual, so that, on the death of the disponee spouse, the original one half of the title held by him or her will then revert to the disponer spouse[2]. The effect of a survivorship destination in such a case is, of course, to defeat entirely the matrimonial settlement.

Where title is being taken in the sole name of one party, the solicitor should ascertain whether that person is single or married. If the latter, the solicitor should ask the purchaser whether or not a matrimonial consent will be signed by his or her spouse in relation to any loan documents. The intending purchaser should also be warned by the solicitor that in the event of the purchaser wishing to sell or otherwise deal with the heritable property in the future, a consent may be required from the spouse. If the spouses are separated at the time of the transaction, then it may be possible for an affidavit to be granted by the purchaser to the effect that the subjects being purchased are not a matrimonial home so far as the spouse is concerned, but the purchaser should be warned that the property could become a matrimonial home in the future should there ever be a reconciliation and the estranged spouse come to live in the property.

Where a solicitor is acting in the purchase of a commercial property and the purchaser is a partnership or a limited company or some other juristic person, the solicitor should ensure at the outset that the name of the entity is accurate so that any offer is lodged in name of an entity which exists[3]. Similarly, it is important when acting for a corporate entity to ensure that the party giving instructions has appropriate authority to do so. Solicitors ought to be wary of situations which can arise where two or more parties are involved in a transaction which is purely for the benefit of one of them. Such a situation can arise where title to a property is in joint names of a husband and a wife and a bank proposes to take a security over the property in respect of moneys advanced or to be advanced solely for the benefit of the husband or, more usually, the husband's business. In these circumstances it is now appropriate for the solicitor to advise the disadvantaged spouse that she has no obligation to grant the security and that she will be putting her interest in the heritable property at risk by so doing. In these circumstances the disadvantaged spouse should be advised to take separate legal advice. It has been held in Scotland that a security granted in such circumstances will be valid and cannot be reduced on the grounds that the disadvantaged spouse was not aware that she was actually granting a security which put her share of the heritable property at risk[4].

There is no doubt in the author's mind that to act for all parties in a security transaction of this type without ensuring that the disadvantaged spouse has had the clearest possible advice and has given the clearest possible instruction of his or her wish to proceed to his or her own disadvantage would be negligence.

1 *Hopkinson v Williams* 1993 SLT 907.
2 See *Steele v Caldwell* 1979 SLT 228; *Smith v Mackintosh* 1988 SC 453, 1989 SCLR 83.
3 For a discussion on the problems which can arise where the wrong company name is used, see Halliday *Conveyancing Law and Practice in Scotland* vol I (1985) para 4–04.
4 *Mumford v Bank of Scotland, Smith v Bank of Scotland* 1995 SCLR 839, 1996 SLT 392.

The instruction phase: sale

6.16 In some ways a sale should present fewer risks for the solicitor than a purchase. All that is required is that the contract be concluded and the sale price paid on the due date. There are, however, various matters which can arise in the context of a sale and which may result in a negligence claim. Obviously, if the selling solicitor has acted in the original purchase and the title turns out to be defective, there is a claim. However, there are other matters which are worthy of consideration from the selling solicitor's point of view[1]. It is preferable for the selling solicitor to be well prepared for any offer. The degree of preparedness, however, depends on the timing of the instructions given to that solicitor. If the solicitor is advised that the property is going on the market at an early date, he or she will be in a position to apply for the seller's title deeds from any secured lender and to bring down any pre-sale reports which are necessary. The selling solicitor will also be in a position to apply for local authority reports and searches, although the client ought to be advised that if the property does not sell within a reasonable time, there may be added expense in updating these reports.

The selling solicitor should generally bear in mind that any information which he or she obtains from the seller prior to conclusion of missives ought to be taken on board, irrespective of the fact that errors in the previous transactions may not be his or her fault. An obvious example of this type of situation is where a seller advises a selling solicitor prior to conclusion of missives that no building warrant or planning permission exists in respect of an alteration or extension. If the selling solicitor did not act previously, then this omission cannot be laid at his or her door. However, the selling solicitor must use that information and ensure that any offer is met with a qualified acceptance which does not bind the seller to produce any such warrants or permissions.

It is good practice when taking instructions for a sale to ask the seller certain obvious questions. If, for example, the property is a relatively modern dwellinghouse, it would be sensible to ask whether or not it is covered by an NHBC guarantee or an architect's certificate. If the seller indicates that the property was constructed on his or her instructions, then the selling solicitor should ask for the appropriate planning permission, building warrant and completion certificate and give appropriate advice if some or all of these are lacking. If no advice is given on these matters, then a selling solicitor can be negligent if an offer is lodged and missives are not concluded because a completion certificate is missing and no steps have been taken in good time to obtain a duplicate. Things which are not in the first instance the selling solicitor's fault can still result in negligence claims if appropriate advice is not given at the appropriate time.

It has been said that it is the selling solicitor's duty to obtain the title deeds in advance of any sale and carry out a title examination to ensure that the seller has a title to sell and that there are no onerous burdens or conditions which would be likely to frustrate any sale. The author does not hold with this view. Unless information comes to the notice of the solicitor which indicates that there may be something wrong with the title, it is the author's view that the selling solicitor is entitled to assume that any preceding solicitor carried out his or her task properly and obtained a valid marketable title. The same might not be true in special circumstances, such as where one solicitor acts for a builder in acquiring a development and a second solicitor is to act in the selling or feuing off of plots in that development. In such a case, the second solicitor would have some duty to examine the title to ensure that it was suitable in all respects for future sales. The second solicitor would be likely to be held to be negligent if missives for the sales of plots were concluded and the transactions could not be settled because of some obvious defect in the title.

Where a seller is selling part of a property and retaining the remainder, appropriate servitudes for access, pipes and others should be reserved in the missives and the subsequent conveyance[2].

1 For a general discussion of the procedure to be adopted by the selling solicitor, see *Cusine and Rennie* paras 1.26–1.35.
2 *Moffat v Milne* 1993 GWD 8–572.

Loans, redemptions and secured creditors

6.17 Problems have arisen in conveyancing transactions where properties have been sold in a negative equity situation where the price does not cover the amount required to redeem existing secured loans. Again, the selling solicitor must take care in concluding missives. The author does not hold to the view that a selling solicitor will automatically be negligent if he or she concludes a bargain for the sale of property and it turns out that there are insufficient funds. The seller, after all, ought to know what has been borrowed and what is still outstanding on the property. However, there may be obvious pointers which a solicitor would be unwise to ignore, and clients cannot always be guaranteed to know the effect of loan documents which they have signed, especially in relation to second loans. If the client indicates in advance that the property is being sold purely to ease a financial burden, then the solicitor ought to be put on his or her guard and make inquiry as to the extent of any secured loans.

Similarly, if titles are received from a building society and included with the deeds are one or more notices of second charge, some inquiry as to the amounts to be repaid is warranted. Similarly, if a client indicates that he or she has been served with various writs for debt, the selling solicitor would be well advised to bring down a search in the personal register or inquire as to the existence of any inhibition. It is not that the selling solicitor is negligent because of the existence of inhibitions or undischarged securities; the negligence would arise only if the selling solicitor concluded missives on behalf of the seller in circumstances where any reasonable solicitor would have formed the view that the seller would be wholly unable to implement the obligation to hand over a good title and clear searches.

The selling solicitor should also bear in mind that in most cases he or she will be instructed by the secured lenders in respect of the discharge transaction or transactions. As with a purchase, the solicitor must remember that the lender's interests are distinct from the interests of the seller and that the duties of care are owed to both clients. In this connection, a selling solicitor should not make glib assumptions about the attitude of a lender. It may be that a property has been on the market for over a year and the only offer to be received is insufficient to repay the secured loan. Commercial logic dictates that the lender should allow the sale to go through and grant a discharge for a reduced amount, while retaining the personal obligation of the seller for the balance. After all, the alternative is to call up, repossess and sell an empty house on the open market. The commercial reality is that the building society's debt will increase and the price may go down, thus putting the lender in a worse position. The selling solicitor acting for the secured lender in the discharge should not take the attitude of the lender for granted. If it is clear that the sale price is insufficient to discharge the secured loan or loans, then the solicitor acting for the lender must take specific instructions before concluding missives. To do otherwise would be negligent both in relation to the lending client and in relation to the selling client, who would then be bound by a bargain which he or she could not implement. In such circumstances, a conflict of interest is likely to arise and the selling solicitor might require to ask the lending client to take independent advice. The selling solicitor should always bear in mind that he or she is not there to solve everyone's financial problems. The solicitor's role in such a situation is to take instruction and not to conclude any form of binding contract until such time as he or she is clear that everyone will sign the necessary documents (discharge, disposition or whatever) to allow the transaction to go through.

Delays in production of deeds

6.18 If it becomes clear to the selling solicitor that titles cannot be made available because they are still at the Land Register, then steps ought to be taken to obtain copies either from the previous solicitor or directly from the Land Register and this should not be left until an offer actually comes in. Sale transactions which go off the rails at the start because of a delay in production of deeds often stay off the rails. If a solicitor fails to react to a situation where deeds are missing and a purchaser eventually resiles from missives because deeds cannot be produced, then there may be liability, if a reasonable solicitor acting with due skill and care would have attempted to obtain copies of the deeds at an earlier date.

Property enquiry certificates

6.19 Where time has permitted the selling solicitor to obtain property enquiry certificates, there is an obligation on the selling solicitor to read them when they arrive and not simply put them at the front of the file to await an offer. If the property enquiry certificates disclose something adverse to the property then this is a matter which the selling solicitor ought to take up with the seller immediately, and not just when the offer arrives. It may be that a property enquiry certificate shows that the property has been the subject of a statutory notice for repairs. Such a notice may result in a liability on the seller. It is often the case, however, that these liabilities go back to previous sellers and there may be provision in previous missives which allow the present seller some relief from a previous owner. In some cases sums of money will have been retained from sale prices to meet the eventual liability. In a case of this type it can sometimes take a long time to resolve the question of liability and discharge it. If a selling solicitor fails to read a property enquiry certificate and merely submits it with a qualified acceptance, there is a risk that the purchaser will not accept the position or that the problem will not be resolved by the date of entry. If this is the case, then, depending on the terms of the missives, the purchaser may be entitled to rescind the contract with no penalty on the basis that the property enquiry certificate discloses something materially adverse. If it can be shown that the matter could have been sorted out at no expense to the seller had the selling solicitor noticed the statutory notice and taken steps jointly with the seller to resolve the position, then there may well be negligence.

Similarly, a selling solicitor should not simply sit back and hope that a purchaser or a purchaser's solicitor will accept an unusual situation without advising the seller of the possibilities. If the seller indicates that he or she has carried out alterations but has been unable to obtain a completion certificate, then it would be unwise to leave matters until an offer comes in and then attempt to conclude missives on the basis that the purchaser will take matters as they stand. The seller should be advised of the potential problem and attempts should be made to resolve it by the obtaining of a completion certificate or a letter of comfort, even though this may involve the seller in carrying out some work. If the seller refuses to accept the advice then the solicitor will have no blame attached to him or her if the missives eventually collapse. If no advice has been given in the face of the information, then the selling solicitor may have a liability if it can be shown that the problem was capable of resolution prior to receipt of the offer.

Land Register reports and boundary comparisons

6.20 It is normal practice in land registration cases to apply for the appropriate Land Register reports (forms 10 or 12), and in the case of a sale which will induce a first registration, for a boundary comparison report (form P16) prior to the receipt of any offer. When these reports are received it is the duty of the selling solicitor to read them and to communicate to the seller any problems which they disclose. If the form 10 or 12 discloses an inhibition against the seller then the seller must be advised of the legal effect of this inhibition in preventing any sale, and steps should be taken to ascertain whether or not it can be discharged from the sale proceeds. If the P16 report discloses that the ordnance survey boundaries coincide with the title boundaries then there should be no problem. Similarly, if the P16 report discloses that the seller's title covers a greater area than that which is being possessed then there should be no problem, because the purchaser will conclude missives for the lesser area as possessed.

If, however, the P16 report discloses that the seller is possessing more than is in his or her title, then there is an obvious problem which may have an effect on the sale. It is the selling solicitor's duty to bring this problem to the attention of the seller and to give advice as to how it may be resolved prior to concluding missives. It may be that in these circumstances an approach to a neighbour will require to be made and a section 19 agreement[1] or other conveyance executed. It is normally easier to persuade a neighbour to sign such a document before missives are actually being concluded. At this early stage a neighbour does not have the same bargaining power as he or she might have when an offer has been received at an attractive price. A selling solicitor who fails to advise a selling client as to the effect of an adverse P16 report and the need to try to rectify this prior to missives being concluded could be negligent.

1 See the Land Registration (Scotland) Act 1979, s 19.

The question of timing

6.21 So far as the selling solicitor is concerned, the possibilities for negligence claims outlined above in relation to various pieces of information which may come to the notice of the solicitor depend very much on the timing of the transaction. The situations envisaged above could result in a negligence claim only if the selling solicitor had information or time to get information prior to conclusion of missives, and, in addition, sufficient time to give advice and take whatever action may be necessary to resolve the problems. If a seller does not instruct his or her solicitor until an offer has been received then there may be no claim in relation to these matters unless, of course, the solicitor acted in the original purchase and the negligence arose at the time of the purchase. Accordingly, if a selling solicitor receives an offer out of the blue, he or she can take instructions only in relation to any acceptance to be granted. If it subsequently turns out that there are problems with the P16 report, local authority enquiry reports or warrants for alterations or extensions, then there will be no claim for negligence, provided that the selling solicitor has been through the offer clause by clause with the seller and asked for confirmation that the seller is in a position to implement all the obligations.

Selling for a commercial entity

6.22 Where the seller is a limited company or some other juristic person, the selling solicitor might be well advised to bring down appropriate searches to ensure that the company is still in existence and that the company name is accurate. The selling solicitor should also ensure that he or she is taking instructions from the appropriate person and determine whether or not board approval is required before any offer is accepted. The selling solicitor should make it clear, especially where the company is an English company, that under Scots law missives can be concluded without the company or any officer of the company having to sign any contractual document. This is not to say that a solicitor would necessarily be negligent for failing to carry out these precautions in a question with the company. There could, however, be problems with the other contracting party if it could be shown that the solicitor acted without appropriate authority or in respect of a company which had been struck off and therefore did not exist.

The missive phase: purchase

6.23 The duty of the purchaser's solicitor at the missive stage of the transaction is to translate the instructions into an offer and to submit the same to the selling solicitor or other agent. Prior to 1 August 1995 the offer required to be in probative or privileged writing. Since the passing of the Requirements of Writing (Scotland) Act 1995 there is no requirement for probative or self-proving writing, and privileged writing is abolished. The only requirement is that any offer be in writing[1]. All that is required is that the document is subscribed and no attestation is necessary[2]. Although some solicitors prefer to have missives which are attested and therefore self-proving[3], there is no legal requirement to this effect and a solicitor who concludes missives in subscribed but unattested writing will not be negligent[4].

In theory, a solicitor should have his or her client's instructions in relation to all the terms and conditions of the offer. In practice, instructions are taken on the main points of the offer such as the price, the date of entry, the moveable items included and any special features. The client relies on the solicitor to incorporate such other terms and conditions as are necessary for the protection of the client in a modern-day purchase. Modern offers take the form of a few introductory clauses which deal with the specifics of the transaction followed by a schedule containing a number of pro forma conditions which the solicitor applies to every transaction. As far as the standard of care is concerned, a solicitor will be expected to include such clauses as would normally be inserted by a solicitor of ordinary competence exercising due skill and care. The purpose of the conditions in the offer is to protect the purchaser against unforeseen risks and pitfalls. Accordingly, a modern offer would certainly require to contain clauses relating to the following:

(1) The matrimonial homes legislation, to ensure that entry can be taken free of any occupancy rights.
(2) Planning proposals, redevelopment proposals, notices and orders and the like.
(3) The status of the road, footpath and sewer (which will normally be public unless the property is in a rural area).
(4) The minerals, including a provision at least in the first instance that there will be no rights to enter the surface and that there will compensation payable for surface damage.
(5) The ground burdens, including a provision that these have been or will be redeemed except perhaps in tenemental property where an unallocated feuduty is still normal.
(6) The production of planning permissions, building warrants, completion certificates and superior's consents in respect of alterations or additions.
(7) The common parts of any tenemental or flatted property (especially the roof) and the maintenance costs referrable thereto.
(8) The delivery of a validly executed disposition or other conveyance and the exhibition of a valid marketable title with clear searches or, in the case of land registration transactions, appropriate reports and all other deeds and documents necessary for the Keeper to issue a land certificate without exclusion of indemnity.

(9) In the case of acquisitions from limited companies, the production of clear searches in the register of charges and in the companies register for a period of twenty-two days after the date of recording or registration of the purchaser's title.
(10) In the case of acquisition from limited companies, a provision requiring the holder of any floating charge to grant an appropriate letter of non-crystallisation or release.
(11) In the case of acquisition from limited companies, a provision to the effect that the directors will grant some form of warranty or indemnity if the letter of obligation from the selling solicitors is to be on behalf of the selling company.
(12) The risk of accidental destruction which will not normally pass to the purchaser until the date of entry and specification of rights to rescind the contract in the event of destruction or material damage prior to the date of entry.
(13) The title to any moveable items included in the sale.
(14) Vacant possession in addition to entry.
(15) Onerous burdens or conditions or overriding interests and the implementation of continuing conditions of the title.
(16) NHBC guarantees if the property is less than ten years old or, in cases of property not covered by the NHBC guarantees, appropriate certificates from a qualified architect including a duty of care in favour of the purchaser and his or her successors or, alternatively, the grant of a collateral warranty.
(17) The non-supersession of the missives for an appropriate period of time. The period is normally two years, but a purchasing solicitor will be negligent if he or she does not consider whether the two-year period is appropriate for each and every obligation undertaken[5].
(18) The availability of the *actio quanti minoris* to the purchaser.
(19) The condition of the central heating system and possibly any other working mechanisms in the property.
(20) Guarantees and surveys in respect of specialist work such as woodworm, dry rot, wet rot or rising damp.

The provisions outlined above might be regarded as the minimum requirements nowadays. There will, of course, be offers which contain more than this and the practice of solicitors may in the future dictate a higher standard. It must always be borne in mind that the test for negligence is often dependent on the normal practice of solicitors, which varies from time to time.

1 Requirements of Writing (Scotland) Act 1995, s 1(2)(a)(i).
2 Ibid s 2(1).
3 Self-proving status is acquired under s 3 of the Requirements of Writing (Scotland) Act 1995 by the attestation of one witness.

4 For a discussion of the practice in connection with the subscription of missives, see Rennie 'Setting Missives up and Apart' Greens Property Law Bulletin Issue 19, February 1996 p 2; Rennie 'Requirements of Writing: Problems in Practice' 1996 SLPQ 187.
5 See *Pena v Ray* 1987 SLT 609.

Commercial missives

6.24 In addition to the matters outlined above, other conditions will be appropriate for the acquisition of specific subjects and, in particular, commercial or agricultural subjects. Again, the standard or care will be linked to normal practice among solicitors engaged in this type of work. The basic duty of the solicitor is to translate the instructions and information obtained at the pre-missive stage into an offer which provides the appropriate safeguards[1]. Particular attention should be devoted to suspensive conditions in the case of acquisition of certain commercial subjects. It is clear that a solicitor who lodges an offer for a public house or a post office or an agricultural site for development purposes must include a suspensive condition in relation to the transfer of any licence, the appointment of the purchaser as postmaster or postmistress or the grant of appropriate planning permission for the development[2]. Basically, a solicitor engaged in offering for commercial or agricultural or industrial premises must remember that the interest of the purchasing client is not just in the heritable property but in the business carried on or to be carried on in that property. The solicitor must therefore ensure not only that the title is valid and marketable, but also that the proposed business can be carried on in the heritable property. Greater attention, therefore, is required to planning and licensing matters and indeed to prohibitions of certain uses in the title deeds.

1 For a general discussion of the content of commercial and agricultural missives, see *Cusine and Rennie* Ch 7.
2 For a discussion on suspensive conditions in missives, see *Cusine and Rennie* para 4.88.

Reporting on the offer

6.25 It is now normal practice for solicitors to send a copy of any offer to the purchaser. It should always, however, be borne in mind that it is never sufficient for a solicitor simply to send a copy of a complicated legal document to a client and blandly ask for approval. If the offer does not contain the normal protections for the client in respect of the particular type of transaction, then the fact that the solicitor has sent a copy to the client will not save the solicitor from a negligence claim. It is for the solicitor to provide the appropriate advice and safeguards. This does not mean, however, that a solicitor must explain every clause in the schedule attached to the offer. It is enough if the solicitor explains particular clauses having a particular reference to the transaction to the client to ensure that the client understands the meaning and import thereof. The matter was put in this way in an old English case[1]:

> 'An attorney . . . is bound to take care, that his client does not enter into any covenant or stipulation that may expose him to a greater degree of responsibility than is ordinarily attached to the business in hand, or, at all events, that he does not do so until all the consequences have been explained to him.'

The use of standard forms and schedules has been recognised in England where it has been held that although a solicitor may have a duty to advise a client about an abnormal or unusual term in an offer or a contract, the solicitor does not require to explain every standard condition[2].

1 *Stannard v Ullithorne* (1834) 10 Bing 491.
2 *Walker v Boyle, Boyle v Walker* [1982] 1 All ER 634, [1982] 1 WLR 495.

Standardisation and uniformity

6.26 It is now commonplace for professional bodies such as the Law Society and the Law Society of Scotland to issue guidelines, codes and practice notes in relation to various aspects of legal transactions. A client care manual has been issued by the Law Society of Scotland, as has a pamphlet outlining what a purchaser and seller in a conveyancing transaction ought to expect from his or her solicitor. There is no doubt that documents of this type will have an effect on the level of care required from each and every solicitor. It may well be that it will be difficult for a solicitor to defend a negligence claim if the practice adopted by that solicitor does not conform with good practice as laid down by the professional body[1]. Not all suggestions of a professional body will necessarily attain the status of holy writ so far as the standard of care is concerned. The Law Society of Scotland recommended a standard missive form in an attempt to speed up the conclusion of missives. The profession did not take up the standard form and accordingly it could hardly be said that a failure to incorporate each and every clause in the Law Society approved style would be negligence[2].

1 See *Jackson and Powell* para 4–50.
2 For a discussion of the clauses in the standard form of missive recommended by the Law Society of Scotland, and for the content of missives in general, see *Cusine and Rennie* Ch 4.

The qualified acceptance

6.27 Except in cases where the final offer is the result of a travelling draft, few offers meet with a straight acceptance nowadays. An offer containing over thirty clauses is likely to be met with a qualified acceptance containing twenty qualifications. It is the duty of the purchaser's solicitor to ensure that the purchaser is made aware of the nature of the qualifications and how they affect the protections and safeguards contained in the original offer. It is not sufficient for the purchaser's solicitor simply to send a copy of the qualified acceptance to the purchaser and ask for instructions. The solicitor must give advice on the nature of the qualifications and, where a view has to be taken by the purchaser, invite instructions. Where a safeguard is being removed or reduced the nature of the risk must be explained to the client. It is not enough, for example, to state that the seller cannot produce a building warrant and completion certificate for an attic conversion but has offered to produce a letter of comfort; the nature and effect of the letter of comfort must be explained to the client so that the client can properly assess the risk. If there is doubt, then it may be necessary to involve the surveyor or valuer and the lender in the decision.

Similarly, it is not sufficient simply to advise a client that although the title deeds contain no servitude in respect of the use of an access road, a servitude may be constituted in time by prescription. The nature of a servitude and the rules relating to prescription must be explained to the client so that the client can assess the risk of interruption to possession. A solicitor should also bear in mind that in most cases he or she will be acting not only for the purchaser but also for a lender. In these circumstances the solicitor must consider whether the lender's interests are likely to be affected by the acceptance of any qualification.

It has become common practice to send title deeds or other documents with the qualified acceptance. The object of this exercise is to force the purchaser to accept whatever burdens, conditions or limitations are contained in the title deeds or other documents. The purchaser's solicitor must be wary of falling into a trap. Very often the processes of examination of title and conclusion of missives are joined together. In these circumstances it will be necessary for the solicitor to explain fully the nature of the qualifications to the purchaser and also the nature of anything disclosed in the title and any other documents. If a solicitor accepts a title on behalf of a purchaser at the missives stage, then the purchaser will be bound to accept that title and there will be no room for any arguments at a later stage. If it turns out that the solicitor has accepted something which is adverse to the purchaser's interests, then unless there are clear instructions to accept the title as it stands, the solicitor is likely to be negligent. The problems for the purchasing solicitor are the time factor and the pressure to conclude missives. The solicitor must remember that any lender is also a client and that any title peculiarities which the purchaser wishes to accept may also require to be put to the lender. There is little point in putting title problems to the lender after missives have been concluded and the title has been accepted.

There is no doubt that a solicitor who has reported the terms of a qualified acceptance with appropriate explanations to the client in writing will be in a better position. If the qualified acceptance is discussed at a meeting then full notes of the meeting and any instructions given at the meeting ought to be kept on the file. If the purchaser gives instructions on the telephone after having received a copy of the qualified acceptance, the solicitor's advice and the instructions given should be noted on the file so that there is no doubt that the client confirmed that the bargain was to be concluded on the terms of the qualified acceptance. If the bargain is concluded then a copy of the letter concluding the bargain should be sent to the client, so that the client has a complete record of all the missives. In many cases a qualified acceptance will be followed by further modifications on behalf of the purchaser and the process of conclusion of missives may take some time. It is important that the purchaser is kept fully informed and that copies with the appropriate explanations are sent and instructions taken on any counter-offers or further qualifying letters. When the bargain is eventually concluded the client should be informed that there is a legally binding contract.

Withdrawals and time limits

6.28 In some cases a purchasing client will decide to withdraw. This may simply be the result of a change of mind or a change of circumstances, or it may be as a result of the nature of the qualifications received in respect of the offer. Although it has been held that an oral withdrawal is sufficient to prevent consensus[1], there is no doubt that any withdrawal should be evidenced by writing. Care should also be taken to ensure that any time limits for accepting any letter forming part of the missives are met according to their terms.

1 *McMillan v Caldwell* 1990 SC 389, 1991 SCLR 73.

The missive phase: sale

6.29 When an offer is received it is the duty of the selling solicitor to explain the terms of the offer to the seller and to take appropriate instructions. Given the fact that a modern offer may contain thirty or more clauses, it is not sufficient for the selling solicitor to send a copy of the offer to the seller and ask for instructions. The seller will decide whether or not to accept the price, the date of entry and the moveable fittings to be included, but will not be able to assimilate the plethora of legal clauses. The selling solicitor should go over the offer clause by clause, offer advice and explanation where required, and then take instructions.

The selling solicitor's duty is then to qualify the offer where necessary so as to protect the seller. Where, for example, an up-to-date property enquiry certificate is not available it is now normal practice for the selling solicitor to provide in the qualified acceptance that a property enquiry certificate will be provided, and that if this discloses anything materially adverse to the subjects the purchaser's only remedy shall be to rescind the contract without damages being due to or by either party. In such a qualification it is also normal practice to provide that the purchaser will have a certain number of days within which to respond to the property enquiry certificate, failing which the purchaser shall be bound to proceed. If a property enquiry certificate is available at the time the offer is received, the normal practice is for the selling solicitor to delete the appropriate clause in the missives and simply send the property enquiry certificate.

It is standard practice for a penalty clause to be inserted in all qualified acceptances. It would be negligent of a selling solicitor to fail to incorporate such a clause. If no such clause is inserted, the seller may have no right to charge interest if the purchaser fails to pay the price unless possession is taken, and will not have the right to rescind and resell until a reasonable time can be said to have elapsed[1]. Following the decision in *Lloyds Bank plc v Bamberger*[2] it is necessary for the penalty clause to stipulate that interest will continue to run after rescission until such time as the seller's loss can be quantified on resale.

The selling solicitor must take care that the seller is not bound to implement an obligation which cannot be implemented. It is sometimes tempting to accept a provision so as to conclude a bargain, in the hope that the purchaser or the purchaser's solicitor will accept something less. It must be borne in mind, however, that parties to missives sometimes look for technicalities which will release them from the contract. It may be that in the vast majority of cases a purchaser will accept a letter of comfort in place of a building warrant or completion certificate, especially where the alteration or extension is of some antiquity. However, there will always be the case where the purchaser wishes to be released from the bargain for a completely different reason. If the selling solicitor has bound the seller to produce a building warrant and completion certificate in circumstances where that solicitor knew that the seller could produce only a letter of comfort, then the purchaser will be able to rescind the contract and the selling solicitor may well be liable in negligence to the seller for failing to provide in the qualified acceptance that only a letter of comfort would be made available. Any time limit expressed in the offer should, where possible, be complied with.

1 *Rodger (Builders) Ltd v Fawdry* 1950 SC 483.
2 1993 SC 570, 1993 SCLR 727.

Title examination phase

6.30 It is the basic duty of the purchaser's solicitor to ensure that the purchaser has a good, valid and marketable title to the subjects of purchase. What the purchaser has acquired is the property as seen by the purchaser and as offered for sale by the seller. This should be the same as that contained in the seller's title, but in some cases the seller's title falls short of what has actually been purchased. In such cases it is clear that the purchaser is entitled to demand a title to the whole subjects and not just the subjects as contained in the seller's titles[1]. The purchaser's solicitor can, of course, examine only the deeds presented to him by the seller's solicitor. It may well be that the deeds disclose that the seller does have a valid marketable title. The purchasing solicitor, however, is not normally in a position to compare these deeds or the description of the property contained therein with the actual physical position of the ground as seen by the purchaser prior to the making of the offer. There is a school of thought which says that a solicitor should visit every property which is to be purchased by a client. It is the view of the author that this is not part of a solicitor's normal duty of care, unless the deeds disclose some sort of boundary discrepancy, or some information comes to the notice of the solicitor which indicates that the property being purchased may be larger or different in scope from the subjects contained in the title[2].

It is, however, the clear duty of the solicitor to acquaint the purchaser of the description of the subjects as contained in the title. This will normally be done by sending the purchaser a copy of the title plan with such comment as is necessary to make it intelligible. The purchaser should be invited to comment on the plan and to indicate clearly if he or she feels that the plan does not accurately reflect the physical position of the property as seen and purchased. In some cases the description of the property may be contained in old deeds which do not have a plan. Where this is the case the purchasing solicitor should still advise the purchaser of the detail of the description, including the boundaries and measurements contained in the titles, even where this description may rely on physical features which have long since changed or disappeared. A solicitor should not accept an ancient description of this type without some further investigation. It is often necessary to insist that a new plan be prepared which sets out the current physical position of the property. This plan should then be attached to the disposition to be granted by the seller and referred to in the dispositive clause, with appropriate wording to link the new plan to the earlier description.

As far as possible, the solicitor should ensure that the new plan and description do not encompass anything to which the seller does not have title. It must be accepted, however, that this will not always be easy and that even the services of a surveyor may be of little use. It is the author's view that in a case of this type a purchasing solicitor will have fulfilled his or her duty to the purchaser if he or she ensures that a new plan is prepared and the seller confirms that he or she has possessed in accordance with the new plan for a reasonable length of time without any interruption or adverse claim. Where a property is about to enter the Land Register for the first time, the purchasing solicitor should submit the deed containing the description with any fresh plan to the Keeper in advance of the transaction settling and ask the Keeper for confirmation that he will issue a Land Certificate based on the new plan without exclusion of indemnity. All plans should be approved by the purchasing client, including any amended plans supplied by the Keeper[3].

1 *Houldsworth v Gordon Cumming* 1910 SC (HL) 49; *The Conveyancing Opinions of JM Halliday* (1992, ed D J Cusine) p 147; *Cusine and Rennie* paras 5.03 to 5.05.
2 See *Brown v Gould & Swayne* [1996] PNLR 130.
3 For examples of negligence claims relating to the extent of the subjects, see *Stewart v J M Hodge & Son* 1995 GWD 12–691; *McManus Developments Ltd v Barbridge Properties* [1996] PNLR 431.

Flatted property

6.31 Where the property being acquired is a flatted dwelling-house there may not be a title plan. In these circumstances the solicitor should report to the client the description of the flat as contained in the title deeds. The situation of the flat in the block or tenement should be noted (for example, northwestmost flat on the first floor) and again the client should be invited to confirm that the description contained in the deeds conforms to the physical situation of the flat as purchased. Any areas of exclusive ground or common ground should also be described, as should the main common parts. If the distribution of the common parts is unusual this requires to be brought to the client's attention. It may also be something which requires careful advice to the client as where, for example, the subjects of purchase are a top flat and the roof is not common property but the sole responsibility of the top flat. It would certainly be negligent to accept a title to a top flat with sole responsibility for roof maintenance without the clearest instructions from purchaser and lender. Special care should be taken when dealing with flatted conversions to ensure that the purchaser understands the areas over which he or she has exclusive ownership and the areas which are held in common. Where there are special features, such as private roads, rights of access, or wayleaves for pipes or drains, these ought also to be brought to the attention of the client and checked with the missives to ensure that the seller is fulfilling all his or her obligations.

Burdens and conditions

6.32 The title deeds of properties in Scotland generally have one or more writ referred to for burdens. Some of the burdens are contained in ancient writs and have little or no application. It is the duty of a solicitor to examine the burden writs and to report on any enforceable burden or condition which may adversely affect the property or the proposed use of the property. Objection should be taken in terms of the missives or in terms of the seller's common law obligation to provide a marketable title where appropriate.

It is also the duty of the solicitor to report the more modern conditions which have been set down for the particular property or the estate of which the particular property forms part. It is a matter for the solicitor's judgment as to whether all or merely some of the conditions require a detailed report or explanation. Where there is a deed of conditions applicable to the property, it is good practice to send a copy of that deed of conditions to the client with a commentary detailing the important conditions. A solicitor engaged in the purchase of domestic heritable property will be entitled to accept conditions which are normal for residential properties, and indeed it is unlikely that a purchaser could object to such conditions once missives have been concluded, unless the missives specifically provide that the title is not to contain certain specific conditions. Common problems which arise in relation to burdens and conditions relate to the consent of superiors to alterations, additions, user, sub-divisions and the like. Obviously, a solicitor would be negligent if he or she accepted a title to a flatted conversion where the feu disposition of the original self-contained property contained a prohibition of sub-division. Similarly, a solicitor engaged in the purchase of a public house would be negligent if he or she accepted a title containing a prohibition of the sale of alcohol.

More difficult questions can arise in relation to more modern prohibitions such as the prohibitions of pets or caravans, power boats or commercial vehicles and the carrying on of trade, business or profession. Modern titles tend to have some sort of restriction on domestic animals and some titles to flatted dwellinghouses contain absolute prohibitions. Much may depend here on whether the solicitor has had notice of the burdens and conditions contained in the title prior to conclusion of missives. If so, the client is entitled to as much knowledge as the solicitor has. If the client is made aware of a prohibition of, for example, pets, prior to conclusion of missives, then the client can withdraw without penalty. A solicitor may therefore be negligent if obvious burdens of this nature are not brought to the attention of the client prior to conclusion of missives. In the view of the author, however, the same will not be the case if missives are concluded in normal terms without the titles being made available at that stage. If on examination the title is found to contain normal residential conditions which include a prohibition of pets, then it will simply be a question of whether that burden is unduly onerous in the circumstances, and that is essentially a question between the purchaser and the seller and not a question of negligence so far as the solicitor is concerned. It is not normal practice for solicitors to insist on production of title deeds prior to conclusion of missives and if the deeds do contain normal residential conditions which, for some obscure reason, the purchaser is unwilling to accept, that will not be the solicitor's fault.

Solicitors should be aware that not all title conditions are enforceable. There are many purported burdens in deeds which are not real burdens at all, either because they do not affect the lands or because they do not comply with the rules laid down for the creation of real burdens and conditions which affect singular successors[1]. In many cases, the seller's solicitor will suggest to the purchaser's solicitor that an offending burden is no longer enforceable due to acquiescence or lack of interest on the part of the superior. A purchasing solicitor should not accept this argument without further inquiry and without advising the purchaser and possibly the lender of the fact that the burden does exist. It is obviously in the seller's interest to take the view that the burden is unenforceable. What the purchaser wants, however, is an assurance that the superior will have no enforcement rights and, perhaps more importantly, that no party buying from the purchaser at a later date will raise a similar objection. The safest course of action is obviously to obtain a waiver or to apply to the lands tribunal. Before a purchasing solicitor accepts the proposition that the superior has lost interest to enforce, he or she should research the law in this regard to ensure that he or she has a clear understanding of what acquiescence actually means. It should also be borne in mind that in many modern estates, neighbouring proprietors may well have rights to enforce feuing conditions by virtue of a *ius quaesitum tertio* which are quite separate from the right of the superior to enforce. A solicitor will also be liable if he or she accepts a title which is subject to an onerous servitude without clear instructions from the client[2].

1 For a discussion of the rules concerning the creation of real burdens and conditions, see *Halliday* vol II para 19–18 et seq.
2 *McLennan v Warner & Co* 1996 SLT 1349.

Preparation of deeds and the nature of the title

6.33 It is clearly the duty of the purchasing solicitor to prepare a valid disposition or other conveyance which transfers the title of the property to the purchaser. The deed should contain all normal clauses, including a non-supersession clause if there is no exchange of non-supersession letters at settlement. The purchasing solicitor should ensure that the deed is properly executed[1]. Where appropriate, the title of the purchaser should be completed by recording or registration[2]. The same applies in the case of the completion and recording or registration of loan documents, including where appropriate, the intimation of assignations[3]. The obligation to obtain a valid marketable title applies in the case of a lender just as it does in the case of a purchaser[4]. If the title turns out to be leasehold rather than feudal, then unless the missives stipulate for a leasehold title, a purchaser is not bound to accept this[5]. If a solicitor accepts a leasehold title without the consent of the purchaser or lender, he or she is likely to be negligent[6]. Many leasehold titles still have enforceable casualty payments which can be collected by the landlord on the entry of a purchaser. A solicitor should not accept a leasehold title of this type but should insist that the seller obtain a discharge of the casualty once and for all or a conveyance of the landlord's title to the *dominium utile*. The general duty of care owed by a solicitor to a purchaser in a modern conveyancing transaction has been described in the following manner in an English case[7]:

'A person who goes to a lawyer with respect to a land transaction is entitled to expect that lawyer to investigate the state of any title that is germane to the matter and to explain to the client exactly what it is that is portrayed by the state of the title.'

Standing that type of general statement of the duty of care, it will be difficult for a solicitor to avoid a negligence claim if there is something wrong with the title, unless the client had advice on the matter and decided to proceed. Clearly a solicitor has an obligation not to hand over the price or a substantial part thereof without ensuring that a title will be available from the parties who are entitled to convey[8].

1 *Currie v Colquhoun* (1823) 2 S 407.
2 *Donald's Trustees v Yeats* (1839) 1 D 1249.
3 *Wallace v Donald* (1825) 3 S 433.
4 *McLeod v Macdonald* (1835) 13 S 287.
5 *McConnell v Chassels* (1903) 10 SLT 790.
6 *Ronaldson v Drummond & Reid* (1881) 8 R 767.
7 *Graybriar Industries Ltd v Davis & Co* (1992) 46 BCLR (2d) 164 at 181.
8 *Di Ciacca v Archibald Sharp & Sons* 1994 SLT 421, 1995 SLT 380 (on appeal).

Non-title matters

6.34 It is often said that a great deal of solicitors' time is now taken up in relation to non-title matters. In many ways, solicitors have brought this on themselves by including a host of non-title matters in offers. The most obvious example of this is the requirement to produce planning permissions, building warrants and completion certificates in respect of either the erection of property or the alteration or extension of property. What is important at the title phase of the transaction is that any protection or safeguard available to the purchaser in terms of the missives is verified. The missives will normally provide that the seller must have a valid marketable title and that the property must not be adversely affected by planning or road proposals. In the course of the title phase, the purchasing solicitor will seek evidence that the seller's obligation has been implemented. This evidence will take the form of the production of title deeds and of an appropriate local authority certificate or certificates.

It seems to the author that the same degree of verification is required for other non-title matters. While it is accepted that in some cases all that the purchaser and the purchaser's solicitor can do is accept the seller's assurance, it may be necessary to repeat requests in the course of observations on title. If, for example, the property being purchased is two years old and the missives provide that the seller has the appropriate planning permission, then it behoves the purchasing solicitor to require the seller to produce the permission. The same would apply to any NHBC guarantee or architect's certificate. In these cases, it is not enough for the solicitor simply to rely on the seller's obligation or warranty in terms of the missives. The solicitor must obtain appropriate evidence to protect the purchaser. In other words, there must be some follow-through from the missives phase of the transaction to the title phase of the transaction, especially where ancillary matters not contained in the titles are concerned.

Discharge of securities

6.35 It is the duty of the purchaser's solicitor to ensure that any securities granted by the seller are discharged either before or at the point of settlement. It must be accepted that it is normal practice to take the seller's solicitor's letter of obligation to deliver a recorded discharge in due course, or to deliver such documents as the Keeper may require to issue a clear land certificate. It is preferable to take delivery of discharges at settlement so that the purchaser's solicitor has control over the recording or registration of the same and is at least aware that the creditor has signed and delivered the discharge.

Problems can arise where a heritable creditor suddenly realises that the sale price is not enough to pay off the loan. Even where the seller's solicitor has granted a letter of obligation, there may be a difficulty if the heritable creditor simply refuses to grant the discharge. Where the letter of obligation has been accepted in good faith, then it is the author's view that a solicitor will not necessarily be negligent if he or she has accepted such an obligation and, in any event, a selling solicitor ought to implement the obligation. In cases where the purchaser's solicitor is aware of some problem with the discharge or feels that there may be some risk, then the appropriate course is to split the cheque for the purchase price into the amount required to redeem the secured loan or loans and the balance, and for the purchaser's solicitor to hand over the cheque or cheques for the former payable to the secured creditors. Alternatively, a three-cornered settlement meeting may be arranged. It would clearly be negligent for a purchasing solicitor to accept a letter of obligation on behalf of the seller in respect of delivery of a discharge. All this does is reiterate the seller's obligation in terms of the missives and at common law, and it has been held that to accept such an undertaking is negligent even where it is common practice among solicitors to do so[1].

1 *Edward Wong Finance Co Ltd v Johnson Stokes & Master* [1984] AC 296, [1984] 2 WLR 36. For a discussion of this case, see *Jackson and Powell* paras 4–29, 4–31.

Searches and incumbrances

6.36 It is the duty of the purchasing solicitor to ensure that the searches are clear in all respects. The appropriate searches will be in the property and personal registers and, where appropriate, the register of charges and the companies register. A solicitor would not be negligent in accepting an ordinary letter of obligation in respect of searches and, where companies are involved, a letter of obligation on behalf of the selling client in respect of charges and companies searches, coupled with an appropriate letter of non-crystallisation from the holder of a floating charge and, if it can be obtained, a letter of warranty from the directors of the selling company. It has to be accepted that there will always be some element of risk where limited companies are involved, and there may well be circumstances where a solicitor will not be negligent if he or she has followed the normal procedures, even if some problem arises between delivery of the deed and recording or registration of the same. A solicitor who does not obtain a letter of non-crystallisation will be liable if a floating charge crystallises before the disposition is recorded or registered[1]. In sasine transactions there used to be a problem because of delays in bringing forward entries in the presentment book to the search sheets. This problem has largely been removed with the introduction of the computerised presentment book. It is now possible to search not only the Register of Sasines but also the computerised presentment book. Any solicitor acting for a purchaser in a sasine transaction who does not insist on seeing a search in the computerised presentment book will be negligent and liable in damages should a security or some other adverse writ be found to have been recorded in the 'blind' period.

1 This was the situation in *Sharp v Thomson* 1995 SC 455, 1995 SCLR 683, where the court held that a receiver appointed under a floating charge took precedence over a grantee holding a delivered but unrecorded disposition.

The title phase: sale

6.37 Most of the obligations in the title phase lie, of course, with the purchasing solicitor, but the selling solicitor does have some obligations to the seller in this part of the transaction. During the course of any conveyancing transaction, it is normal for the purchaser to raise various observations on the title and in relation to other matters covered in the missives. It is important for the selling solicitor to answer any observations accurately. The selling solicitor should bear in mind that the answers which are given are essentially the seller's answers. If there is some point on which the selling solicitor is not sure, then information should be sought from the seller. Answers such as 'confirmed so far as we are aware' should be avoided. If a solicitor confirms something in these terms, then a purchaser will be entitled to assume that the solicitor has at least checked with the seller. If the answers given are incorrect, then the seller may incur some sort of contractual liability to the purchaser and, if this occurs, the selling solicitor may be negligent for having failed to check the position with the seller before answering the observation.

There may be cases where a solicitor exercises a *bona fide* judgment in answering a requisition, and in such circumstances there may not be negligence, especially if the solicitor is acting in accordance with generally accepted practice[1]. It appears from

English authority that in circumstances where an erroneous answer has been given to an observation, it will be difficult for the purchaser to make a claim directly against the selling solicitors, especially where the reply which is given, although wrong, can be regarded as a fair and reasonable reaction to the question[2]. This does not, of course, mean that the seller may not be liable. If the seller is liable to the purchaser, there may still be a liability on the part of the solicitor to the seller as a client. The seller's solicitor should ensure that any draft disposition or conveyance is properly revised on behalf of the seller and that any appropriate consents in respect of occupancy rights are obtained.

1 *Simmons v Pennington & Son* [1955] 1 All ER 240, [1955] 1 WLR 183; *Jackson and Powell* paras 4–45, 4–138.
2 *Gran Gelato Ltd v Richcliff (Group) Ltd* [1992] Ch 560, [1992] 1 All ER 865.

The settlement and post-settlement phase: purchase

6.38 In many ways this should be the smallest part of the transaction and the one in which there is the least scope for professional negligence. As far as the purchaser's solicitor is concerned, he or she should ensure that the appropriate documents are delivered in exchange for the price. In a normal transaction, these will be an executed disposition or other conveyance, executed discharges with the appropriate forms for recording or registration, an exchange of holograph letters keeping the missives alive if there is no non-supersession clause in the disposition, any titles or other documents or land certificates and charge certificates falling to be delivered and a letter of obligation in agreed terms. Even in this age of frenetic conveyancing, it is the obligation of the purchaser's solicitor to check that all the documents have been properly executed and that everything which requires to be delivered has been delivered. It may be the case that some document is not available at settlement. A purchaser's solicitor should also be wary of settling in these circumstances, even where some sort of letter of obligation or undertaking is offered. A purchasing solicitor should bear in mind that a selling solicitor is no longer fully covered by the master policy for non-classic letters of obligation. Accordingly, a purchasing solicitor should not accept a letter of obligation from a selling solicitor which undertakes to deliver a clear planning report or a building warrant and completion certificate. A purchasing solicitor may incur liability to his or her own client if the selling solicitor cannot implement the obligation, no matter what rights the purchaser may have against the selling solicitor[1].

It is clearly the obligation of the purchaser's solicitor to ensure that the disposition or other conveyance is stamped and recorded or registered without any delay. This is particularly important where the sellers are a limited company and there is a letter of non-crystallisation open for a limited period[2]. The solicitor acting for the purchaser should have in mind that he or she may also be acting for a lender. Some solicitors have in the past refused to record or register dispositions and standard securities because the purchaser has not paid the stamp duty. While this might be a defence in a negligence action brought by a purchaser, it would not be a defence to a negligence action brought by a lender. A purchasing solicitor should ensure that he or she is in funds to pay stamp duty and recording or registration dues before settlement takes place. Alternatively, if a solicitor effects settlement and cashes a loan cheque from a lender, the solicitor must be prepared to make the necessary outlay to pay the stamp duty and recording or registration dues to allow the disposition and any security to be recorded or registered in the ordinary course. The purchaser's solicitor should ensure that the missives are kept alive, either by a clause of non-supersession in the disposition or by an exchange of letters. Care should be taken to ensure that no obligations are cut off prematurely by virtue of a general non-supersession clause which lasts for the normal period of two years.

1 See *Edward Wong Finance Co Ltd v Johnson Stokes & Master* [1984] AC 296, [1984] 2 WLR 36.

2 See *Sharp v Thomson* 1995 SC 455, 1995 SCLR 683.

The settlement and post-settlement phase: sale

6.39 As far as the seller's solicitor is concerned, the settlement phase of the transaction should be simple. The purchase price should be received and any secured lenders repaid. The seller's solicitor should redeem the secured loans immediately and will be liable if he or she omits to do so and the seller is bound to pay extra interest or charges. The seller's solicitor should repay any bridging loans with the minimum of delay and should account to the seller for any surplus funds which there may be. Selling solicitors should beware of granting obligations either on behalf of the seller or on behalf of the selling solicitor's firm simply to achieve settlement. The seller's solicitors should, in the first place, ensure that the seller has an obligation to provide the documentation or information which is to be covered by the obligation. Where a letter of obligation is to be granted for what might be regarded as a non-classic matter, the seller's solicitor should check with the seller as to whether the obligation is capable of fulfilment. If there is any doubt, the seller's solicitor should not complicate the contractual issue between seller and purchaser by granting a letter of obligation[1].

1 For an example of the difficulties which can ensue where solicitors grant an obligation which proves difficult or impossible to fulfil, see *Marshall Wilson Dean & Turnbull v Feymac Properties Ltd* 1996 GWD 22–1247.

Recording and registration

6.40 It is the duty of the purchaser's solicitor to ensure that all the appropriate documents are sent for recording or registration. Where a limited company is involved there will be an additional requirement to register in the register of charges if a security is being granted. Such registration should be carried out timeously. In the case of a sasine transaction, all that is normally sent is a discharge, a disposition and a standard security. In the case of a Land Register transaction, however, it is the duty of the purchaser's solicitor to ensure that the Keeper has every deed and document which is required to enable the Keeper to issue a land certificate without exclusion of indemnity.

In the course of the registration process, the Keeper may issue requisitions to the purchaser's solicitor requiring him or her to produce deeds or documentation in support of the application. It is the duty of the purchaser's solicitor to react timeously to such requisitions. Eventually, the Keeper does have the power to reject the application if requisitions are not answered. While it may be that it is the seller's legal responsibility in terms of the missives to produce the deeds and documents required, it is the purchaser's solicitor's duty to ensure that the deeds and documents are provided to the Keeper. If the Keeper rejects an application, the priority afforded by the original date of registration will be lost and it is likely that the purchaser's solicitor will be liable if some intervening deed or diligence appears adverse to the purchaser's interests. In any event, the purchaser's solicitor should ensure that all necessary deeds and documents are available at settlement before the price is paid.

As far as the selling solicitor is concerned, if the purchasing solicitor communicates a request from the Keeper in respect of an obligation for which the seller may still be liable, it is the seller's solicitor's obligation on behalf of the seller to try to ensure that the obligation is implemented. That does not mean to say that the seller's solicitor will be liable if for some reason the seller cannot implement the obligation. It is, however, the duty of the selling solicitor to acquaint the seller of any obligation which may still be outstanding and the likely consequences of failure to implement.

Acting for lenders

6.41 The basic obligation of a solicitor acting for a lender is to obtain a valid and marketable title and a valid and effective security which is capable of enforcement in the event of default by the debtor. The same standard of care will apply as applies in the case of a purchaser, because the lender will potentially be in the same position as a purchaser trying to sell if the security has to be called up. The peripheral duties of disclosure which may arise in lending transactions have already been considered[1].

1 See Chapter 5 above.

Wills and executries

6.42 Solicitors are involved in the drawing up of wills, trust dispositions and settlements, inter vivos trusts and in the winding up of the estates of deceased persons. As far as chamber practice is concerned, the vast majority of negligence claims relate to conveyancing. As far as the preparation of wills and related deeds is concerned, a solicitor will be negligent if he or she fails to interpret correctly the testator's or granter's intentions. The difficulty with this sort of negligence claim, however, is twofold. In the first place, the problem may not arise until after the death of the testator or granter, and in these circumstances there may be no clear evidence of the original instructions given. In the second place, as a matter of causation the negligence may not have resulted in any particular loss to the testator or granter, and at the present time a disappointed beneficiary who fails to benefit because of the negligence of a solicitor does not have a claim against that solicitor under Scots law[1]. The position may be different, however, if an inter vivos trust is involved and the client/granter's position is adversely affected because of the solicitor's negligence. A claim of this nature might arise where the solicitor was giving tax advice as well as legal advice and the deed in question as drawn by the solicitor does not achieve the necessary tax-efficient position. This does not mean that a solicitor will be liable if a revenue statute is subsequently interpreted in an unforeseen manner.

As far as the winding up of estates is concerned, it must be borne in mind that solicitors normally act for the executors and not directly for the beneficiaries. In some cases, a member or members of the solicitor's firm may be the executors or trustees. There is undoubtedly a duty of care on solicitors acting in the winding up of the estate to do so within a reasonable time. If a beneficiary suffers loss because of delays or mismanagement, he or she may have a claim against the executor or trustee. If the delay or mismanagement is the fault or negligence of the solicitors, the executor or trustee has a claim against the solicitors. If the solicitor involved is the executor, then, although the solicitor does not act for the beneficiary directly, the beneficiary may still have a claim against the solicitor for breach of the duties of an executor or trustee if that has resulted in loss.

1 *Robertson v Fleming* (1861) 23 D (HL) 8, (1861) 4 Macq 167; and see paras 4.01 and 4.07 et seq above.

Negligence in other aspects of non-litigation practice

6.43 Solicitors are engaged in a variety of other activities for clients which do not involve litigation or dispute. In relation to all these matters the solicitor must bring to the task the standard of care to be expected of an ordinary solicitor exercising reasonable skill and care[1]. Solicitors should, however, be aware of the fact that the standard which will be applied by a court in a negligence claim is likely to be the standard of a competent practitioner who regularly carries out the type of work which is the subject of the claim. A solicitor engaged in the acquisition of shares in a limited company will be expected to exhibit the standard of care normally exhibited by a practitioner who deals in this type of business.

In company transactions it will be particularly important for the solicitor to realise the difference between a commercial decision and a legal decision, because a great deal of the work carried out by solicitors in such matters is effectively commercial negotiation. The normal procedure in a company acquisition is for the solicitor acting for the purchaser of the shares to prepare a share acquisition agreement and to forward a draft of the same to the solicitor acting for the sellers of the shares. Separate solicitors may also act for any institutions which are funding the acquisition. The agreement should initially contain all the normal warranties, safeguards and indemnities, even though these may be revised and whittled down in the process of negotiation. It would not be sufficient in the normal course of events for a solicitor simply to advise a client that all that is required is for a share transfer to be signed in respect of the shares. A good standard of reporting to clients is essential in commercial matters of this type so that the client understands both the nature of any warranties being given by him or her and the nature of any concessions on these warranties being allowed. Careful notes and records of meetings should be maintained.

1 See para 2.07 et seq above.

Domestic and commercial transactions compared

6.44 It is a salutary fact that most claims made against solicitors both in number and amount seem to relate to conveyancing. Historically, a large number of claims appear to have resulted from security transactions. Although most conveyancing transactions relate to domestic property, it is worth reflecting on the differences which arise in claims which relate to commercial transactions as opposed to domestic transactions. In the first place, although all clients may be said to be claim conscious, commercial clients are more likely than an individual buying a domestic property to investigate a loss with a view to ascertaining whether the loss can be said to have been caused by a solicitor. Some lending institutions have set up departments specifically to examine transactions where a loss has been made following the calling up of a security. In the second place, the amount of any claim in respect of a commercial transaction is always likely to be greater than in a domestic transaction. If a solicitor forgets to include a bedroom carpet in an offer, the amount of the claim is likely to be the cost of a replacement carpet. If the solicitor wishes to be particularly difficult, the amount of the claim may be the value of a secondhand carpet. If, on the other hand, a solicitor forgets to lodge an application for transfer of a licence where a client has concluded missives for the purchase of a public house, the results are likely to be more far-reaching and the amount of any claim large. Depending on how the missives are actually interpreted, the seller may still be entitled to demand payment of the price from the purchaser, whereas without the licence the purchaser may not be able to take possession and trade. Similarly, if a solicitor engaged in the preparation of security documentation fails to achieve a valid and effective security, the claim may relate to the whole sums outstanding by the debtor if the debtor is unable to implement the personal obligation to repay.

Even where there is a solution to a problem which may have arisen from the negligence of a solicitor, the cost of that solution in a commercial transaction may be higher than in the case of a domestic transaction. If, for example, a solicitor omits to notice that there is a strip of ground which is vital for access and is in the ownership of neighbouring proprietors, the cost of putting this right either by acquiring the strip or by entering into a boundary agreement[1] is likely to be greater in the case of commercial property. At best, a domestic neighbour will insist only on his or her legal expenses being met and at worst is likely to insist on a small premium. This is not likely to be the case where commercial interests are involved. If an adjoining proprietor is a commercial entity then the area of ground is likely to become a ransom strip, and if no other access can be found the value of the strip may be stated as a proportion of the value of the commercial site being acquired.

1 See the Land Registration (Scotland) Act 1979, s 19.

CHAPTER 7

Negligence in Matters of Litigation and Dispute

Court work distinguished from chamber practice

7.01 The distinction between an exercise of judgment which has unfortunate results and negligence has already been noted in relation to the general duty of care[1]. As far as conveyancing and other chamber practice are concerned, however, the trend of judicial decision is to hold that most mistakes by a practitioner amount to negligence, especially where an identifiable loss has accrued to the client. It is more difficult, however, to apply a general standard of care to the conduct of a litigation or a dispute before a tribunal, where matters of judgment in relation to the manner of pleading the cause, or the number or identity of the witnesses to be called, will almost certainly be involved. In matters of litigation or dispute there is usually a loser. In some cases where there is a settlement both parties will feel they are losers.

One might deduce from this that a great many negligence claims flow from litigation and similar disputatious matters. After all, the losing side must have been advised that there was at least a chance of victory. Negligence claims arising from litigation and related matters, however, tend to arise only where there has been a clear mistake in relation to procedure or timing. It is difficult to maintain a negligence claim which is based solely on the manner in which the case has been conducted. It must generally be accepted that there are differing levels of skill, both in relation to written pleadings and in relation to advocacy, yet there does not seem to be authority for the view that there is a minimum level of skill in this area below which a solicitor should not fall. Jackson and Powell draw the distinction between matters relating to the conduct of the litigation and matters relating to procedure in the following way[2]:

'The conduct of litigation is in part a matter of routine and in part it is an art. By exceptional ingenuity or foresight the solicitor may secure advantages (sometimes decisive) for his client over the other party. The skilful use of interrogatories or a timely application for specific discovery may bring the other party to its knees in civil litigation. Ingenious pre-trial research and preparation may lead to an acquittal (sometimes an unmeritorious acquittal) in criminal proceedings. However, the solicitor is not negligent if he fails to display exceptional ingenuity in matters of tactics or procedure. What is required of him is reasonable competence and reasonable familiarity with the procedures of the courts in which he practises[2].'

Accordingly, if the client's only complaint is that the opposing party's solicitor performed better on the day in court, he or she is unlikely to be successful in a negligence claim. Although litigation or dispute is unlikely to be as structured as a conveyancing transaction, it is nevertheless convenient to split a litigation or dispute into an instruction phase, a preparation and procedure phase, a conduct of the hearing phase and a settlement phase.

1 See para 2.15 above.
2 Jackson and Powell *Professional Negligence* para 4–115.

Instruction phase

7.02 Ideally, a solicitor should obtain all information from the client necessary for a proper prosecution of the litigation or the dispute. It has been suggested that written instructions should always be obtained from a client before any proceedings are commenced[1]. Jackson and Powell suggest, however, that written instructions will not be necessary if the solicitor takes proper notes of any meeting or telephone call at which the instructions are given[2]. A solicitor, however, cannot force a client to divulge all the information which may turn out to be necessary and there will be occasions where, as a result of embarrassment or some other personal factor, a client deliberately holds back a piece of information which may have a bearing on the dispute. A solicitor is unlikely to be held to be negligent in such circumstances, provided the appropriate questions were asked of the client.

It seems to the author that the question of the funding of the litigation or dispute ought to be discussed at an initial stage. Whether the matter is civil or criminal the prospective litigant ought to be advised as to questions of cost, and eligibility for legal aid ought to be explored. There are some clients who make a natural assumption that if they are without funds they will automatically qualify for legal aid without any application being made. It is, of course, in the solicitor's interests to ensure that there will be funding for the litigation, but it seems to the author that a solicitor will be negligent if a client fails to obtain legal aid because of failure to apply in circumstances where there was elegibility and this matter was not canvassed at the outset. During the instruction phase the solicitor should ascertain certain basic facts, such as the identity of the parties in civil litigation[3]. A solicitor ought also to establish basic questions in relation to jurisdiction and the appropriate forum in which to bring any action[4]. In addition, he or she should ascertain what time constraints are likely to affect the litigation or dispute, especially if a time bar may be involved.

There is probably a duty on a solicitor to advise the client as early as possible whether or not he or she thinks that any proposed litigation has any prospect of success. There is authority for the view that it can be negligence for a solicitor to pursue a litigation which any other solicitor would have regarded as a hopeless case, unless the client has been advised of this and still wishes to persist[5]. There is, however, a fine line to be drawn between a case which is obviously hopeless and a case which turns out to be hopeless once it has gone to proof or trial. It is probably no part of a solicitor's duty to place himself or herself in the position of judge or jury and try to predetermine the outcome of a particular dispute. If a solicitor makes a judgment based on the facts given to him or her at the time of instruction and this judgment is supported by some evidence by way of precognition or statement, then it is unlikely that a solicitor will be liable if at the end of the day a court or tribunal holds that the case cannot succeed[6].

1 *Allen v Bone* (1841) 4 Beav 493.
2 *Jackson and Powell* para 4–118.
3 *Long v Orsi* (1856) 18 CB 610; *Jackson and Powell* para 4–118.
4 *Lee v Dixon* (1863) 3 F & F 744; *Jackson & Powell* para 4–116; Begg *The Law of Scotland relating to Law Agents* p 238.
5 See *Davy-Chiesman v Davy-Chiesman* [1984] Fam 48, [1984] 1 All ER 321.
6 *Jackson and Powell* para 4–121; see *Nestlé v Best* [1996] PNLR 444.

Preparation and procedure phase

7.03 It is perhaps in the preparation and procedure phase of any litigation or tribunal application that mistakes are most likely to occur. In particular, a solicitor will be negligent if he or she fails to meet a time limit of one sort or another. Certain actions must be brought within a certain time in terms of statute[1]. Apart from questions of prescription and limitation there are time limits within which various procedures must be carried through. Obvious examples of these are the entering of appropriate notices of intention to defend, the lodging of applications with employment law tribunals, and the lodging of appeals. It is beyond the scope of this work to list the various time limits which apply at every stage of court or tribunal procedure. Suffice it to say that a solicitor will be negligent if he or she fails to meet one of these time limits in circumstances where the solicitor has instructions to proceed. There are a number of cases which illustrate this point[2]. Jackson and Powell are clear that if the delay is such that an action becomes time barred the solicitor is almost bound to be negligent[3]. It is worth looking at some of the judgments and the remarks of the judges. In *Godefroy v Jay* Alderson J put the matter in fairly simple terms[4]:

'This is a very plain case. An attorney is instructed to defend a cause, and does nothing; and the question is, whether that is not negligence for which he is responsible to his client. If he had any special reason which would justify him in doing nothing, it was for him to shew it in answer to this action. With respect to the amount of damages, it was not for the plaintiff Godefroy to shew, in this action, the circumstances under which he was sued . . . Negligence, therefore, has been proved against him and he has failed to shew that it was immaterial to the plaintiff.'

In *Fletcher & Son v Jubb, Booth and Helliwell* Scrutton LJ said[5]:

'The appellants instructed the respondents to make a claim and, if necessary, to bring an action against the Bradford Corporation for damage done by one of the tramcars of the Corporation. The respondents wrote and for some time continued writing to the Corporation. It is well known that public authorities are willing to avoid litigation if they can settle claims upon reasonable terms, and equally well known that they do not admit claims which they regard as unreasonable . . . What is the duty of a solicitor who is retained to institute an action which will be barred by statute if not commenced in six months? His first duty is to be aware of the statute. His next duty is to inform his clients of the position . . . The time of limitation was running out. The clients did not know this and they were not warned by the solicitors . . . The period of limitation was one of those matters which the respondents as the appellants' legal advisers ought to have borne in mind. It was negligence not to bear it in mind.'

In *Reggentin v Beecholme Bakeries Ltd* Harman LJ said[6] in a case which had been thrown out by the court for want of prosecution:

'I feel very sorry for this plaintiff, but it seems to me that she has a remedy against her own advisers.'

In some cases proceedings are not commenced within an appropriate time limit in circumstances where no instructions have been received from the clients concerned. In *Fletcher & Son v Jubb, Booth and Helliwell* part of the solicitors' defence was that they had asked for instructions on an offer of settlement within the limitation period and had received none from the clients. They had not, however, advised the clients of the limitation period and of the fact that if proceedings were not instituted or the matter settled the claim would be lost forever. The court did not accept that the solicitors had ceased acting because they had not received instructions nor that they had fulfilled their duty in a case where they had not advised the client of the time bar. It seems clear, therefore, that a solicitor can still be negligent in a situation where a client has given no instructions to proceed if the clearest possible advice has not been given to the client that proceedings must be commenced within the appropriate limitation period. Solicitors are not, of course, bound to act, especially in circumstances where it is not clear that the action can be properly funded. That may not, however, be a defence to a claim for negligence that legal aid has not been granted, unless the position has been made entirely clear to the client and the client has been warned of any limitation period. In such a situation it has been suggested that if no funding is available by the expiry of the limitation period, the client should be advised to act in person[7].

It is obviously the duty of a solicitor engaged in a litigation or tribunal application to appear at the appropriate times or to arrange for suitable appearance on his or her behalf[8]. A solicitor will also be negligent if there is a failure to lodge the appropriate documents in court and the client suffers a loss[9]. Thus a solicitor was held liable where a creditor failed to participate in a bankruptcy as a result of a defective claim and affidavit[10]. Although it has been suggested that a solicitor may not be liable for misinterpreting a vague rule of court or practice[11], it is the author's view that solicitors nowadays are likely to be held negligent for failure to comply with any order of the court or rule of court unless there is a clear divergence of view as to how that order or rule ought to be interpreted[12].

Apart from the question of the conduct of the litigation, a solicitor has a duty to ensure that the case is prosecuted with a degree of diligence[13]. Two older cases illustrate a claim for negligence in respect of failure to prosecute a case. In *Dougan v Smith*[14] a writer in Dumfries was found liable for negligence because he had failed, contrary to instructions, to provide aliment for his client's debtor who was then in jail. Because of the failure to aliment the debtor was liberated and the solicitor was found liable for the debt for which the debtor had been imprisoned. The solicitor had apparently gone home without leaving authority with anyone else to attend to his business in his absence. In *Shortt v Lascelles*[15] a country solicitor failed to respond to his Edinburgh agent in relation to a summons and inhibition. Because of this failure the summons fell. The solicitor was held liable for the loss arising to the client. This was an action by the solicitor for payment of his account and the client was held entitled to set the compensation against the account. In the course of giving judgment the Lord Justice Clerk said[16]:

'Now Shortt [the solicitor] was informed that it was necessary that the summons should be prosecuted, and he was asked if it was to go forward. No answer was made; and although the business was committed to other hands, there is no evidence or averment that the new agents were informed as to the state of matters.'

It has been suggested that before raising any action the averments of the client ought to be checked against other available evidence, including the evidence of any other witnesses[17]. The author doubts whether this is a correct statement of the position now. Although there is, no doubt, a duty on a solicitor not to allow a client to commence an obviously incompetent action, it is the view of the author that a solicitor is entitled to accept at face value the statement made by his or her client in relation to the facts at least in the initial stages. If it is the solicitor's view that for some reason the action should not be raised, the client should be advised as to liability for expenses. If the client still wishes to proceed then the solicitor does have the option at this stage of declining to act further.

1 See the Prescription and Limitation (Scotland) Act 1973, as amended by the Prescription and Limitation (Scotland) Act 1984. For a general discussion of prescription and limitation, see D M Walker *The Law of Prescription and Limitation of Actions in Scotland* (4th edn, 1990).
2 See *Godefroy v Jay* (1831) 7 Bing 413 (failure to lodge defences); *Fletcher & Son v Jubb, Booth & Helliwell* [1920] 1 KB 275 (failure to commence proceedings within statutory time limit); *Reggentin v Beecholme Bakeries Ltd* [1968] 2 QB 276 (delay in prosecution of an action once raised).
3 *Jackson and Powell* para 4–126 and the cases there cited.
4 (1831) 7 Bing 413 at 422.
5 [1920] 1 KB 275 at 281.
6 [1968] 2 QB 276 at 279.
7 *Jackson and Powell* para 4–127.
8 See *Swannell v Ellis* (1823) 1 Bing 347.
9 *Morrison v Ure* (1826) 4 S 656.
10 *Brown v McKie* (1852) 14 D 358.
11 *Laidler v Elliott* (1825) 3 B & C 738.
12 See *Frankland v Cole* (1832) 2 Cr & J 590; *Hunter v Caldwell* (1847) 10 Ad & El 69.
13 *Reggentin v Beecholme Bakeries Ltd* [1968] 2 QB 276.
14 3 July 1817 FC 369. (For a fuller report of the case, see (1817) Hume 356.)

15 (1828) 6 S 810.
16 Ibid at 813.
17 See the comments in Begg *Law Agents* p 340.

Conduct of litigation or dispute phase

7.04 The conduct of the litigation will involve the appropriate drafting of pleadings and the appearance by the solicitor in court where appropriate. As far as the pleadings are concerned, it is obvious that they should be accurate and present the client's case in a proper and appropriate manner. When drafting or adjusting pleadings the solicitor should always bear in mind that his or her client's case may be in difficulty if the averments on record are either insufficient to cover the evidence which is likely to be pled in support of the case or, conversely, contain factual allegations which are never going to be supported by the evidence. There can sometimes be a difficulty here in relation to the client's version of events and the pleadings themselves. Many clients give a long and convoluted story containing all they consider vital to their case. It will always be a matter of judgment for the solicitor to decide what is relevant and what is not relevant and in some cases what might even be damaging. So although a solicitor will be liable if some vital part of the case is omitted from the pleadings, a solicitor is not likely to be liable if he or she exercises judgment in relation to some factual matter, especially where there is doubt as to the nature of the evidence available to prove the particular averment[1].

Apart from the actual pleadings witnesses ought to be precognosced in advance of any diet of proof or trial. In *Ritchie v Macrosty*[2] the client averred that she had supplied the solicitors with the names of the witnesses by means of whose testimony a particular action was to be supported, but the solicitor neglected to cite or even precognosce the most important witnesses. The pursuer also alleged that the examination of the witnesses was conducted in an unskilful and unprofessional manner and that various important points of testimony were not covered. The pursuer also alleged that the solicitor had left the proof at an important point, with the result that the commissioner conducting the proof had to adjourn the diet. The Inner House referred the matter to the local sheriff to report on the conduct of the solicitor.

Where a client alleges negligence which relates purely to the drafting of the pleadings or to matters of evidence, it will be necessary for the client to show that the inclusion of the extra information or the calling of the particular witnesses would have made some difference to the case[3]. It is obvious that a solicitor will be negligent if he or she fails to attend court when appropriate. The solicitor may also be liable in circumstances where he or she simply abandons a case without appropriate warning and notice to the client, even in circumstances where the solicitor believes that the case has turned out to have no merit[4]. It is the duty of a solicitor to ensure that vital witnesses are not only precognosced but also cited. As to the choice of witnesses, this is very much a matter of judgment. If it can be shown that a solicitor has given proper consideration to the witnesses to be called, the solicitor is not likely to be held to be negligent merely because the client thinks that a particular witness would have been good for his or her case[5].

As part of the conduct of the litigation a solicitor should take reasonable steps to identify and locate the appropriate witnesses[6]. Once a witness has been located a solicitor should take steps to precognosce that witness so that the strength and direction of the evidence of the witness can be ascertained prior to that witness being cited to any proof or trial[7]. Even in relation to the taking of precognitions, however, the solicitor is still entitled to exercise a judgment as to whether or not the evidence is likely to help the case. Where the solicitor reasonably forms a judgment that there is no point in interviewing a witness because the evidence is unlikely to be favourable, the solicitor will not be negligent[8].

1 *Jackson and Powell* para 4–119; *Re Spencer* (1870) 39 LJ Ch 841; *Ibbotson v Shippey* (1879) 23 SJ 388.
2 (1854) 16 D 554.
3 See *Urquhart v Grigor* (1857) 19 D 853.
4 Ibid.
5 *Godefroy v Dalton* (1830) 6 Bing 460.
6 *Holden & Co v Crown Prosecution Service* [1990] 2 QB 261, [1990] 1 All ER 368.
7 *Hatch v Lewis* (1861) 2 F & F 467.
8 *Roe v Robert McGregor & Sons Ltd, Bills v Roe* [1968] 2 All ER 636, [1968] 1 WLR 925.

7.05 Assuming that all proper preparations have been made for a hearing, be it a civil proof, a trial or a hearing in front of a tribunal, it is extremely unlikely that a solicitor will be found negligent in respect of the manner in which he or she conducts the hearing. It is generally accepted that of all the areas in which solicitors practise, the one where a solicitor is entitled to exercise his or her own judgment to the greatest extent is in the conduct of a hearing in a litigation or other dispute. It has been suggested in England that where a solicitor conducts the case, he or she is entitled to the same immunity enjoyed by an advocate or barrister[1]. It should be remembered, however, that if there is immunity it relates purely to the conduct of the hearing and not to any matters which relate to the preparation. There is a difference between a hearing going wrong simply because of a particular line of argument taken by the solicitor and a hearing going wrong due to lack of preparation.

This matter was considered in the leading English case of *Saif Ali v Sydney Mitchell & Co*[2]. The case is authority for the view that in England, at least, a solicitor acting as an advocate enjoys the same immunity as a barrister. However, the House of Lords refused to extend that immunity much beyond the actual hearing. The case involved a negligence claim against a firm of solicitors for failure to advise the plaintiff to take proceedings against either or both of two drivers involved in a road traffic accident. A barrister had been involved in the claim and the solicitors issued a third party notice against the barrister. The district registrar struck out the third party proceedings as irrelevant. The judge at first instance allowed the solicitors' appeal. The Court of Appeal then reversed that decision, holding that the advice which had been tendered by the barrister fell within the ambit of immunity from an action of negligence available to a barrister in respect of his conduct and management of a cause in court.

The solicitors appealed to the House of Lords and the House of Lords allowed the appeal, although Lord Russell of Killowen and Lord Keith of Kinkel both dissented. Although the case involved a barrister, the principle would apply equally to a solicitor who conducts a hearing and is responsible for the conduct of a case. The House of Lords attempted to define the 'conduct and management' of the case, in an endeavour to draw a distinction between actions which would attract immunity and actions which would not. Lord Wilberforce referred to a decision in the New Zealand Court of Appeal. In the New Zealand case the immunity of a barrister was extended to some pre-trial work, and the judge defined the extent of the immunity in the following way[3]:

> 'I cannot narrow the protection to what is done in court: it must be wider than that and include some pre-trial work. Each piece of pre-trial work should, however, be tested against the one rule: that the protection exists only where the particular work is so intimately connected with the conduct of the cause in court that it can fairly be said to be a preliminary decision affecting the way that cause is to be conducted when it comes to a hearing. The protection should not be given any wider application than is absolutely necessary in the interest of the administration of justice,

and that is why I would not be prepared to include anything which does not come within the test I have stated.'

It is the author's view that Scottish courts are liable to interpret any immunity afforded to solicitors in a restrictive fashion, especially where a mistake at a hearing can be said to have its roots in the preparation for that hearing. Certainly, a solicitor will still be entitled to exercise judgment as to what evidence is to be called[4]. If, however, the hearing goes badly because the solicitor has simply failed to look for witnesses or indeed call appropriate witnesses, then there will be negligence[5]. Problems at a hearing which arise from lack of organisation, such as a failure to instruct counsel or indeed to appear at the appropriate time, will also amount to negligence and will not be protected by any immunity which attaches to the conduct of the proceedings[6].

1 *Jackson and Powell* paras 4–62 and 4–124; see also *Nestlé v Best* [1996] PNLR 444.
2 [1980] AC 198, [1978] 3 All ER 1033; see also *Bateman v White* [1996] PNLR 1.
3 *Rees v Sinclair* [1974] 1 NZLR 180 at 187.
4 *Godefroy v Dalton* (1830) 6 Bing 460.
5 *Dunn v Hallen* (1861) 2 F & F 642; *Reece v Righy* (1821) 4 B & Ald 202.
6 *De Roufigny v Peale* (1811) 3 Taunt 484.

Alteration of advice or pleas

7.06 During the course of a hearing it may become plain to a solicitor that matters are not going well for the client, simply because the evidence has come out in a particular way. In these circumstances a solicitor is entitled to alter the advice originally given as a matter of judgment, without being liable in negligence. The question of advice to change a plea in a criminal trial was considered at some length in the case of *Somasundaram v M Julius Melchior*[1]. In that case a client was charged with maliciously wounding his wife and he instructed solicitors to conduct his defence on the basis that he had no recollection of picking up the knife. The solicitors were advised that their client intended to plead not guilty. Subsequent to this the client advised the solicitors that he remembered getting the knife and hitting his wife on the head with it. Counsel advised that on that basis there was no defence. The client decided to plead guilty and was sentenced to two years' imprisonment. He then sought leave to appeal against conviction. This was refused, but sentence was reduced to eighteen months' imprisonment. The client sued his solicitors, alleging that they had been negligent in the conduct of his defence to the criminal charge and, in particular, had pressurised him to plead guilty. The client alleged that had it not been for this negligence he would have pleaded not guilty and would have been acquitted or would at least have received a lesser sentence because the court would have heard all the facts.

The Court of Appeal dismissed the case, holding that it was in fact an abuse of the process of the court to bring an action which, if successful, would impugn the correctness of a final decision of another court. The Court of Appeal held that the client's claim involved an attack on the soundness of his conviction and the decision of the Court of Criminal Appeal to refuse leave to appeal. In the course of giving judgment, the court also stated that advice as to whether to plead guilty or not guilty was so intimately connected with the conduct of a cause in court as to be a preliminary decision affecting the way the cause was conducted when it came to the hearing. In these circumstances the court stated that barristers giving such advice would be immune but solicitors would not, unless they were at the same time acting as advocates in the case. Accordingly, it would seem that where a solicitor undertakes a criminal trial without counsel and either before or during the trial advises the accused to plead guilty, there are likely to be no grounds for a negligence claim by the accused at a later date.

1 [1988] 1 WLR 1394.

Involvement of counsel

7.07 Where counsel is employed, the conduct of the hearing will be a matter for counsel and there will normally be no possibility of a solicitor being liable in negligence in relation to the manner in which the hearing is conducted. If, however, the hearing goes badly because of a lack of proper instruction from the solicitor to counsel, there may be liability. In *De Roufigny v Peale*[1] the defendant's attorney had a consultation with counsel on the night preceding the hearing but did not deliver any brief to counsel, as a result of which a verdict passed against the defendant. After the verdict had been recorded, the defendant's attorney came into court with a brief to instruct counsel. The court was asked to set aside the verdict and fix a new trial. The court held that it would only be encouraging the negligence of attorneys to grant such an indulgence at the client's expense. The court granted an order for a new trial on payment by the defendant's attorney of the costs.

A solicitor will not escape liability for negligence where counsel is brought in at the last minute, or in other circumstances where counsel is not provided with adequate instructions or information to conduct the case in a proper manner[2]. If counsel has been properly instructed then no liability should fall on the solicitor involved in the case[3]. It has been held that a solicitor can disregard the instructions of a client in relation to procedure where counsel's advice suggests an alternative[4].

In *Batchelor v Pattison and Mackersy*[5] an action was raised against a solicitor and an advocate in respect of alleged misconduct in an action by the client who was a beneficiary under a trust. The action was against one of the trustees who had bought part of the trust property. The client argued that there had been negligence in that his instructions had been disregarded. The solicitor and counsel had consented to a remit to an architect to value the property. The client wished to insist on an actual sale. The counsel and solicitor refused to demand a remit to another valuer after the architect had reported and the counsel and solicitor had consented to a minute fixing the amount of rents instead of asking for a proof. The court held that although a solicitor was generally bound to follow the instructions of a client, when the conduct of a cause was in the hands of counsel the solicitor was bound to act according to the directions of counsel and would not be liable to the client for actions carried out in good faith in obedience to the directions of counsel. The Lord President said[6]:

> 'The general rule may fairly be stated to be that the agent must follow the instructions of his client . . . but above all in importance, as affecting the present question, is the undoubted special rule that when the conduct of a cause is in the hands of counsel, the agent is bound to act according to his directions and will not be answerable to his client for what he does *bona fide* in obedience to such directions.'

1 (1811) 3 Taunt 484.
2 See *Hawkins v Harwood* (1849) 4 Exch 503.
3 *Fray v Foster* (1859) 1 F & F 681; *Somerville v Thomson* (1818) 6 Pat 3.
4 *Megget v Thomson* (1827) 5 S 275.
5 (1876) 3 R 914.
6 Ibid at 918.

The settlement phase

7.08 It might be supposed that since the conduct of a hearing is a matter for a solicitor's judgment, the decision to settle might also be a matter of professional judgment for the solicitor. Older English cases tend to suggest that a solicitor is entitled to exercise his or her own judgment at the settlement phase of any litigation or dispute, and that any settlement agreed will bind the client[1]. Begg, when dealing with the extent of the authority of a law agent to compromise an action, takes the view that there is no definite Scottish authority[2]. Drawing on English, Irish and American authority, Begg tentatively comes to the conclusion that there are grounds for maintaining that law agents or solicitors have an implied power to accept a reasonable settlement, provided that the client has given no definite instructions not to settle or not to settle below a certain sum. In the conduct of any litigation or dispute, the question of settlement is likely to be discussed at various stages of the proceedings. The closer the parties are to a proof or other hearing, the greater the pressure is to achieve a compromise and settle. Indeed, many cases are settled on the day of the actual hearing at the door of the court. There is obviously a great deal of psychological pressure on clients at this stage. Solicitors require to exercise care in how they communicate offers of settlement to clients and how they take appropriate instructions.

There is no doubt in the author's mind that the older cases and authorities, which seem to suggest that a solicitor has some sort of implied authority to settle a court action, are of doubtful validity now. Jackson and Powell take the view that the old cases do not sit happily with the general duty to inform the client as to the progress of an action[3]. These authors cite some obiter remarks in the case of *Waugh v H B Clifford & Sons Ltd*[4]. In that case the Court of Appeal held that a solicitor retained in a court action had ostensible authority as between himself and the opposing litigant to compromise or settle a claim, provided that the compromise had regard only to the subject matter of the claim and not to any collateral matters. On that authority, no matter what the position might be as between solicitor and client, the client might find himself or herself bound to accept any settlement agreed by his or her solicitor. However, as between solicitor and client, the judges certainly appeared to take the view that it would be grossly negligent for a solicitor to settle an action without proper instructions to do so. Brightman LJ contrasts the question of ostensible authority so far as the other litigant is concerned with the question of breach of the solicitor's duty to the client[5]:

'But it does not follow that the defendant's solicitor would have *implied* authority to agree damages on that scale without the agreement of his client. In the light of the solicitor's knowledge of his client's cash position, it might be quite unreasonable and indeed grossly negligent for the solicitor to commit his client to such a burden without first inquiring if it were acceptable. But that does not affect the *ostensible* authority of the solicitor to compromise, so as to place the plaintiff at risk if he fails to satisfy himself that the defendant's solicitor has sought the agreement of his client.'

In assessing the conduct of a solicitor in relation to a settlement of a litigation or dispute, regard must be had to the general standard of care[6]. It must always be remembered that a solicitor must bring to whatever task is at hand the reasonable skill and care to be expected of an ordinary practitioner exercising that degree of skill and care. The question of the general practice of solicitors in relation to any particular matter will also be relevant[7]. As far as general practice is concerned, the Code of Conduct promulgated by the Law Society of Scotland states[8]:

'Solicitors must act on the basis of their clients' proper instructions or on the instructions of another solicitor who acts for the client.'

The code also lays down in the general interpretation of that clause that solicitors act as agents and must have the authority of their clients for their actions. The code also states that solicitors require to discuss with and advise their clients on the objectives of the work carried out on behalf of the clients and the means by which the objectives are to be pursued. Another rule[9] requires solicitors to communicate effectively with their clients and with others. This rule includes an obligation to provide clients with relevant information regarding the matter in hand and any actions taken on their behalf. It also imports an obligation to advise clients of any significant development in relation to their case or transaction and to explain matters to the extent reasonably necessary to permit informed decisions by clients regarding the instructions which they require to give. Given the tendency towards unformity of practice and the formulation of codes and guidelines by the Law Society of Scotland, it seems unlikely now that any court will accept that a solicitor has a general authority to settle an action or a dispute without specific instructions, at least as far as any negligence claim by the client against the solicitor is concerned.

1 *Jackson and Powell* para 4–130 and the cases there cited.
2 Begg *Law Agents* p 95.

3 *Jackson and Powell* para 4–130.
4 [1982] Ch 374, [1982] 1 All ER 1095.
5 [1982] Ch 374 at 387, [1982] 1 All ER 1095 at 1105.
6 See Chapter 3 above.
7 See *Hunter v Hanley* 1955 SC 200, 1955 SLT 213.
8 Code of Conduct (Scotland) Rules 1992, r 5(a).
9 Ibid r 5(e).

Discretionary instructions to settle

7.09 In some cases a litigant or a party to a dispute may give a solicitor a general instruction to settle within particular limits or, in some cases, to settle at all costs. A solicitor should be wary of accepting such an instruction. Litigants and parties to disputes become notoriously nervous as the day of a hearing approaches, but if the action or dispute is settled at a low figure, such litigants or parties very often find that their valour has returned some weeks after the settlement. Solicitors who have settled actions in accordance with instructions of this type may find that their clients somehow cannot believe that a better settlement could not have been obtained if the solicitor had been trying hard or indeed exercising all his or her professional skill. If a solicitor decides to accept a discretionary instruction to settle, then such instruction should be in writing so that any limits on the settlement figure are clearly evidenced. An instruction of this type obviously allows the solicitor to exercise judgment and, provided the instructions can be proved, it is unlikely that a solicitor exercising such a judgment within the ambit of these instructions could be negligent. On the other hand, if a solicitor has an express instruction not to settle beyond a certain figure or indeed not to settle at all, there will be liability if the solicitor contravenes that instruction[1].

1 *Fray v Voules* (1859) 1 E & E 839.

CHAPTER 8

Defences and Mitigating Factors

Introduction

8.01 The most likely defence to an action of negligence whether based on contract or delict is that the solicitor came up to the required standard of care[1]. Apart from this, there may be other defences of a more specialised nature such as the defence that although there has been negligence, there has been no loss[2]. The question of the immunity of a solicitor conducting a court case or hearing has already been considered[3]. In this chapter the author seeks to look at some specific defences which may arise in particular cases, apart from the general defences which may arise in all cases.

1 For a discussion of the level of the standard of care required, see Chapter 3 above.
2 Such defences will be considered in Chapter 9.
3 See para 7.07 above; Jackson and Powell *Professional Negligence* para 4–62.

The defence of following usual and normal practice

8.02 In any discussion of the general standard of care[1] the notion of a usual and normal practice tends to loom large[2]. Even when claims had to be based on gross negligence or *culpa lata,* there still appeared to be a defence that the solicitor concerned was following a normal and usual practice[3]. Older cases suggest that where a solicitor follows the usual practice, he or she will not be liable in a negligence claim, even where the practice is found to be flawed. In *Grahame v Alison*[4] a law agent was instructed by a creditor to bring an action of adjudication in respect of heritable property owned by an heir of entail in possession. Instead of obtaining a decree adjudging the land, he took a decree over the liferent right of the heir. It was held that the agent, having followed the usual practice, was not liable for the debt but only to refund his own fee. It is fair to say that the court accepted that the law of entails was complicated and that the agent had been placed in a difficult situation. Lord Gillies stated[5]:

'The agent here was placed in difficult circumstances; there were various opinions entertained by lawyers as to the steps which it was best and safest for him to adopt; and how can we blame or subject him for following the common course of practice?'

In *Hamilton v Emslie*[6] a law agent was employed to recover a debt from an agricultural tenant and instructed a poinding and thereafter applied for a warrant to sell the stock on the farm to meet the rent. The tenant brought a suspension of the poinding and the poinding was held to be illegal, the debt being only £13.00 and the value of the stock being £72.00. Because too much stock had been poinded, the creditor was found liable in expenses. The creditor brought an action against the law agent. The Inner House held by majority that there was no clear and authoritative rule of law or practice as to infer either gross ignorance or want of skill on the part of a law agent and therefore he was not liable for the consequences of his error. Lord Deas said[7]:

'It is plain that the officer took for granted that the course adopted was the safe and usual course in the circumstances, for he adopted it without any special instructions on the subject . . . The Lord Ordinary did not allow an investigation as to whether what the officer did was in conformity with the usual practice in Ayrshire, and I do not say that such practice, if not followed in other counties, could have afforded a defence for an error this kind if it would otherwise have inferred liability. I am not, however, prepared to say that such an investigation would have been irrelevant if it had been directed to the general practice over the country.'

In fairness, both the cases cited above were decided at a time when a party had to prove gross negligence and not just a failure to come up to the usual standard of care. The author doubts whether these cases are authority for saying that in each and every case where it can be shown that a solicitor has acted in accordance with a normal or usual practice of solicitors, there is bound to be an absolute defence. It is more likely now that a practice will be relevant only in assessing the degree of skill and care required from the solicitors in connection with the particular task[8]. It has been held in England that the fact that a solicitor has adopted a universal practice may not be a defence to an action of negligence if that practice itself carried with it a risk of loss which was foreseeable[9]. In modern English cases some judges do not look favourably on a defence to a negligence claim which consists of a parade of expert and experienced solicitors all giving evidence as to the normal and usual practice[10]. It is also possible to have differing views as to normal practice and in cases where this occurs, a court can choose which evidence to accept[11]. It is the author's view that proof that a solicitor complied with a generally accepted practice will not afford an absolute defence to an action of negligence but will merely be a factor in assessing whether or not there has been a breach of the standard of care.

1 See Chapter 3 above.
2 See *Hunter v Hanley* 1955 SC 200, 1955 SLT 213.
3 Bell *Principles* s 154.
4 (1830) 9 S 130.
5 Ibid at 132.
6 (1868) 7 M 173.
7 Ibid at 176.
8 See paras 2.08 and 2.16 above.
9 *Edward Wong Finance Co Ltd v Johnson Stokes & Master* [1984] AC 296, [1984] 2 WLR 36.
10 *Midland Bank Trust Co Ltd v Hett, Stubbs & Kemp* [1979] Ch 384 at 402, [1978] 3 All ER 571 at 582; see also *Brown v Gould & Swayne* [1996] PNLR 130.
11 *Peach v Iain G Chalmers & Co* 1992 SCLR 423; *Gordon v Wilson* 1992 SLT 849; and see para 2.17 above.

Acting with the benefit of counsel's opinion

8.03 Earlier authorities tend to support the view that if a solicitor places all appropriate facts and documents before counsel and then acts in accordance with an opinion given by counsel, there can be no liability on the part of the solicitor if that advice turns out to be erroneous[1]. It is clear, however, from recent cases that the solicitor does not have an absolute defence to an action for negligence simply because the solicitor acted on the advice of counsel. It has always been the case that a solicitor will be liable if the memorial sent to counsel is in some way inadequate[2]. The view of the courts now seems to be that the matter must be looked at on the basis that a solicitor is a highly qualified professional who must bring to his or her task the appropriate degree of skill and care notwithstanding the fact that counsel may also be involved. A solicitor cannot simply rely on everything that counsel says or advises without applying his or her own mind to the matter[3]. As with other specific defences, it will at the end of the day be a question of deciding whether or not the solicitor concerned exercised that level of skill and care to be expected of an ordinary solicitor.

1 See *Ireson v Pearman* (1825) 3 B & C 799; Begg *Law Agents* p 207; *Jackson and Powell* para 4–65.
2 *Ireson v Pearman* (1825) 3 B & C 799.
3 *Davy-Chiesman v Davy-Chiesman* [1984] Fam 48, [1984] 1 All ER 321.

Acting on clients' instructions

8.04 In *Bell v Ogilvie*[1] Lord Justice-Clerk Inglis stated that when a law agent accepted employment from a client he undertook to perform with due diligence and skill the business committed to his charge. On this basis it might be thought that one of the paramount duties of a solicitor is to act in accordance with instructions and, conversely, that where a solicitor acts in accordance with instructions he or she cannot be held liable in delict or in contract if the result is a loss to the client. In a more modern context Jackson and Powell put it in this way[2]:

> 'It is in general the client's privilege, if he so wishes, to mismanage his affairs. He is entitled to pursue litigation with little prospect of success, to lend on insufficient security, or to enter an unwise bargain if he chooses. The solicitor has a duty to advise on the legal hazards of the transaction but no more.'

In the context of a professional negligence claim the last sentence in the statement made by Jackson and Powell is perhaps the most significant. Many solicitors tend to think that if they get instructions in the form of a nod to proceed then they are bound to be protected no matter what happens to the client. For there to be protection, the solicitor must have given proper advice and not simply asked for instructions where there are legal points involved. The most obvious example of the difficulties which surround this type of defence is the situation where the solicitor sends a copy of a legal document, such as an offer or qualified acceptance, to a client and asks for instructions as to whether or not to accept. In such a case the client may very well give simple instructions to conclude a bargain. If, however, the solicitor has not given appropriate legal advice on the nature of all the clauses in the offer or qualified acceptance, that solicitor will be negligent if the client is then bound to some unusual or risky undertaking or warranty.

In the author's experience this situation often arises in relation to non-title matters in missives. Most offers for domestic property contain a clause to the effect that the seller will produce planning permission, building warrant and completion certificate together with superior's consent in respect of any alterations or additions to the building. It is not sufficient simply to send a copy of an offer containing a clause of this type to a seller and ask for instructions without explaining the nature of the obligation being undertaken. It is the solicitor's duty to go through the offer clause by clause and in connection with alterations and additions to inquire of the seller whether he or she or any predecessors in title have carried out any alterations, and then to inquire as to what permissions and other documentation may be available. If, as is often the case, the seller has only incomplete documentation, the proper advice is not to grant a *de plano* acceptance but to qualify the acceptance in respect of this matter. If this course is not followed and the seller is then found to be in breach of contract for failure to produce the appropriate documentation, the solicitor will be liable even if a copy of the offer was sent to the client and the client instructed acceptance without any qualification.

Once the advice is given it is up to the client to accept or reject the advice. If the advice is rejected, the solicitor can decline to act further if the matter is extremely serious or, alternatively, simply act on the client's instructions on the basis that the client understands the position and has undertaken the risk. In these circumstances it would be wise for the solicitor to record the advice and the failure to take the advice in writing or at least to keep a carefully worded and dated file note. A solicitor was held liable in an old English case where he brought proceedings for debt recovery in a superior court resulting in expenses having to be paid by his client when the case was lost. The case could have been brought in an inferior court at less cost, and although the client was aware that proceedings were being brought in the superior court he had no advice in relation to the choice of forum[3]. The same principles are likely to apply with greater force in a modern age where contracts are more complicated and clients require more advice. It is plain that instructions and advice must go hand in hand and that a solicitor who merely takes instructions without giving appropriate advice will still be negligent, despite having received and followed these instructions.

1 1863 2 M 336.
2 *Jackson and Powell* para 4–71.
3 *Lee v Dixon* (1863) 3 F & F 744.

Prescription

8.05 A right to claim damages from a solicitor, being an obligation arising from liability to make reparation, prescribes after five years[1]. Although the standard of care is essentially a negligence standard, many actions against solicitors are brought for breach of contract or under delict and contract. The same five-year prescription applies to claims brought under contract[2]. The prescriptive period begins running from the appropriate date, which is defined as the date when the obligation became enforceable[3]. For the purposes of reparation, whether arising from breach of contract or form delict, the obligation is deemed to have become enforceable on the date when the loss, injury or damage occurred[4]. Where the client was not aware and could not with reasonable diligence have been aware that loss, injury or damage had been caused, the date of the injury, loss or damage is treated as being the date when the client first became or could with reasonable diligence have become so aware[5]. The prescriptive period begins to run when there is a concurrence of *injuria* and *damnum*. This means that there must be negligence and loss[6]. This does not mean, however, that the *damnum* or loss must be capable of definitive calculation for the period to run[7].

There are various examples of difficult decisions relating to the starting point for prescription[8]. The case of *Beard v Beveridge, Herd & Sandilands*[9] is a particularly interesting one. In that case landlords instructed a firm of solicitors to prepare a lease which was to include a provision for rent review. The lease was executed in 1967 and the first review date was 1987. In 1987 the rent review clause was found to be inoperable because no mechanism was provided for determining the rent failing agreement between the parties. Not surprisingly, in 1987 the tenants simply refused to agree an increased rent. The landlords raised an action against the solicitors claiming reparation for loss arising from negligence in drafting the clause. The solicitors pleaded that any obligation to make reparation had prescribed under s 7 of the Prescription and Limitation (Scotland) Act 1973. Section 7 is the section which deals with the long negative prescription of twenty years, rather than the short prescription of five years which is normally applicable to negligence claims. However, the point relating to the starting date is the same. The solicitors argued that the breach of any duty of care arose on the execution of the lease, because the landlords were at that point bound in a lease which was less valuable than it should have been. Accordingly, the solicitors argued that the landlords could at any time thereafter have raised an action for the difference in value between the defective lease and one with an effective rent review clause, and, although quantifying the loss would have been difficult, the ability to sue demonstrated that there had been a concurrence of loss and breach of duty or *damnum* and *injuria* at the date of the execution of the lease. The landlords argued that there was no concurrence until 1987, when it became clear that the tenants would not actually agree a reviewed rent. Lord Cameron of Lochbroom held that the lease was defective to the loss, injury and damage of the landlords from the date of its execution and that the obligation to make reparation emerged at that time and had prescribed. It was agreed by the parties that the negligence occurred when the lease was drafted in 1967. The problem related to the time of the actual loss. Although the action was brought under s 7 of the Act, s 11(1) applies to s 7, as well as to s 6.

It should perhaps be noted for the purposes of the five-year prescription that although subsections (1) and (2) of s 11 of the Act apply to s 7 in relation to the long negative prescription, subsection (3) does not. Accordingly, if one takes as an example a client who purchases a house with a defective title due to the negligence of his solicitor, the right to claim damages will prescribe after twenty years under s 7 of the Act, as it did in the *Beard v Beveridge, Herd & Sandilands* case, notwithstanding the fact that the client might never know of the defective title until he or she came to sell the property. However, in relation to the five-year prescription the commencement date for prescription cannot be before the client was aware or could with reasonable diligence have been aware that loss, injury or damage had been caused. Accordingly, it would seem that in the example quoted the client can raise an action against the solicitor at any time up to twenty years from the date of the negligence, unless it can be shown that the client was aware of the particular defect or could with reasonable diligence have been aware of the defect[10].

The five-year prescription can be interrupted either by the making of a relevant claim by the client or by an acknowledgment of liability on the part of the solicitor[11]. A relevant claim must be a claim made in proceedings, so there is often a last-minute rush to serve an initial writ or summons on the part of the client just before the expiry of the five-year period, especially where there have been negotiations for settlement up to that point in time. Proceedings will still interrupt prescription even if they are abandoned at a later date[12]. A relevant acknowledgment of liability requires to be either performance towards the debtor which indicates that there is an obligation or a written admission on the part of the solicitor clearly acknowledging the liability[13]. In the case of a solicitor, performance to the client which indicates the existence of an obligation might be attempts by the solicitor to sort matters out within the prescriptive period as where, for example, a solicitor attempts to acquire an extra piece of ground which ought to have been acquired at the time of the original purchase. It is unlikely that a solicitor will give an unequivocal written admission in terms of the legislation. To do so without the agreement of the solicitor's insurers would be foolhardy. Where, however, there is no dispute as to liability but only an argument concerning the quantum of the claim, it may be appropriate for a solicitor jointly with his or her insurers to make such an admission with a view to preventing unnecessary court proceedings or at least to undertake not to plead prescription.

1 Prescription and Limitation (Scotland) Act 1973, s 6, Sch 1, para 1(d).
2 Ibid s 6, Sch 1, para 1(g).
3 Ibid s 6(3).
4 Ibid s 11(1).
5 Ibid s 11(3).
6 *Dunlop v McGowans* 1979 SC 22, 1979 SLT 34.
7 *Duncan v Aitken, Malone & McKay* 1989 SCLR 1.
8 See *Lawrence v J D McIntosh & Hamilton* 1981 SLT (Sh Ct) 73; *Duncan v Aitken, Malone & McKay* 1989 SCLR 1; *Beard v Beveridge, Herd & Sandilands* 1995 SCLR 335, 1990 SLT 609. For a discussion of the short negative prescription in general and how it applies to obligations to make reparation, see Walker *The Law of Prescription and Limitation of Actions in Scotland* Ch 3 and particularly pp 62–66.
9 1995 SCLR 335, 1990 SLT 609.
10 The decision in *Beard v Beveridge, Herd & Sandilands* has been criticised and must surely be questionable: see *Walker* p 64.
11 Prescription and Limitation (Scotland) Act 1973, ss 6(1), 9 and l0.
12 *Hood (George A) v Dumbarton County Council* 1983 SLT 238. For a discussion of the definition of 'relevant claim' see *Walker* p 67 et seq.
13 Prescription and Limitation (Scotland) Act 1973, s 10(1).

Contributory negligence

8.06 As a legal concept, contributory negligence arises in actions based on delictual liability. Where an action against a solicitor is based on contract, there must be an argument that contributory negligence cannot apply, although the client would still have to show that he or she had mitigated the loss. It has been held that it is competent to bring actions which are based on a breach of a standard of care on the basis of contract and delict, and English authority appears[1] to support the view that if the breach of contract is breach of a duty of care which is to all intents and purposes the same as the equivalent delictual duty, contributory negligence will be available as a complete or partial defence[2], no matter what the conceptual or academic arguments may be. Jackson and Powell take the view that it is unlikely that a lay client will be held to have been contributorily negligent in relation to a legal matter[3]. The learned authors cite the case of *McLellan v Fletcher*[4]. In that case 75% of liability was attributed to the client for failing to pay insurance premiums on a life policy and wrongly informing the solicitor that the premiums had been paid. The solicitor did not check this with the insurance company. It is the author's view, however, that the negligence here related more to the mechanics of the transaction than to the legalities. The court held that the solicitor was partly to blame because he failed to check with the insurance company that the premiums had been paid and that the policy was therefore in force. Had the omission been of a legal nature, such as a failure to prepare an assignation, the solicitor might have been in some difficulty.

There is a problem here for Scottish solicitors, given the practice of lending institutions in relation to life policies. Instructions from such institutions generally state that the life policy is not to be assigned but merely deposited with the society or, in some cases, left with the borrowers. The borrowers, however, have taken out the life policy on the basis that it will be used to clear off the loan either on death or maturity. By and large this is what happens, but if the borrower becomes bankrupt then the permanent trustee can simply take the policy as an asset without reference to the lender. Similarly, if the borrower dies and an estranged member of the family such as a separated spouse or *forisfamiliated* child claims legal rights, the proceeds of the policy will require to be taken into account in the calculation of these rights.

The problem can be exacerbated where there is a separation but no divorce, and then a second partner. The author is aware of one case where the husband had a mortgage with a lending institution with an endowment policy which was merely deposited. The husband separated from his wife, but in terms of the separation agreement retained the sole interest in the matrimonial home in exchange for payment of a capital sum to the wife. The husband then left a will bequeathing the house to his new partner. The expectation of the husband and the new partner was that if the husband died the endowment policy would be used to pay off the mortgage and the new partner would be entitled to the house with no heritable debt. When the husband died, however, the executors took the view that the policy simply fell into the residue of the husband's estate which had been left to his children by his earlier marriage. Accordingly, although the new partner received the house, she did so subject to a mortgage which she could not repay. In that case a complaint was made to the lending institution concerned. They merely replied that the solicitor could have insisted on an assignation rather than a mere deposit. No one suggested that the solicitor had been negligent. He had, in fact, followed the ordinary practice of solicitors and might be said not to have foreseen either the separation or the subsequent partner.

What has to be said, however, in this type of situation is that the client would not have been aware of the differences which might arise where a life policy was deposited rather than assigned, and if a claim were ever brought against the solicitor for failing to point out the risks it is unlikely that the client would be held to be contributorily negligent for not insisting on an assignation. Whether or not a successful claim might be brought against the financial institution is a matter of some doubt, even though financial institutions have been warned on a number of occasions by the Law Society of Scotland of the dangers of the practice of merely taking life policies on deposit. It seems to the author that a claim of some sort is likely to be made against a firm of solicitors in the circumstances outlined. It may then depend on whether or not the solicitors can show that they advised not just the lenders of the risks in attempting to take security by deposit but also the borrowers of the possible ramifications of this so far as their own intentions are concerned. It has been held in England that contributory negligence cannot be pled as a defence to an action based on a breach of a specific contractual instruction[5].

1 *Henderson v Merrett Syndicates Ltd* [1995] 2 AC 145, [1994] 3 All ER 506.
2 See the discussion in *Jackson and Powell* para 1–84.
3 *Jackson and Powell* para 4–73.
4 (1987) 3 PN 202.
5 *Bristol & West Building Society v A Kramer & Co* (1995) Times, 6 February.

Contributory negligence in disclosure cases

8.07 Although it may be difficult to show that a client has been contributorily negligent in an ordinary claim where a solicitor has made a mistake of a legal nature, the same might not be the case in relation to claims which are based on the giving of commercial advice or on the failure to disclose matters, especially matters which may affect the value of a security[1]. Cases of this type have arisen where solicitors have not reported recent subsales at lower prices to lenders who are obviously lending on a high valuation[2]. Even if it is now to be accepted that there may be duties of care in this area, there must surely be questions of contributory negligence where a responsible lending institution takes the decision to lend based on a valuation and other investigations carried out by that institution. The problem for the solicitor, however, may be in showing that the lender failed to do something and was therefore negligent. The basis of the disclosure cases is that the lending institution would not have lent *at all* had the solicitor made the disclosure. For contributory negligence to apply, therefore, it would, in the author's view, have to be shown that the cause of the loss was not just attributable to the non-disclosure but also to some other failing on the part of the lender, such as a failure to obtain a proper valuation of the security subjects or a failure to take notice of a valuation lower than the price. It has been held in England that contributory negligence cannot be raised as a defence to a claim where there is an element of deceit or fraud[3]. It has been held that if a lender conducts mortgage business through brokers and allows loan applicants to self-certify their creditworthiness without any independent financial checks, this may be contributory negligence[4].

1 For a discussion of duties of this nature, see Chapter 5.
2 See *Mortgage Express v Bowerman & Partners* (1995) Times, 1 August; *Target Holdings Ltd v Redferns* [1995] 3 All ER 785, [1995] 3 WLR 352.
3 *Alliance & Leicester Building Society v Edgestop Ltd* [1994] 2 All ER 38, [1993] 1 WLR 1462.
4 *Birmingham Midshires Mortgage Services Ltd v David Parry* [1996] PNLR 494.

Shared liability

8.08 In various kinds of transactions solicitors may not be the only professionals involved. In an ordinary domestic house purchase a surveyor will be involved in giving a report on the condition of the property and an estimate of its value. This report may be for the lender alone or it may be for the purchaser and for the lender[1]. In such a transaction there may be circumstances which cause a loss to the client. There will be cases where the surveyor and the solicitor may both have been negligent. If, for example, the subjects of purchase are a house with a large, recently built extension and the surveyor does not point this out in his or her report indicating the need to obtain planning permission, building warrant and completion certificate, then the surveyor would undoubtedly be negligent. If at the same time the solicitor failed to include a clause in the offer requiring the production of such permissions in respect of the extension, the solicitor would also be negligent. In such a case it is for the court to apportion the liability at the end of the day.

The most obvious case involving solicitors and surveyors is the case of property which is grossly overvalued in circumstances where the solicitor has information which indicates an unusual and substantial increase in price in a recent transaction[2]. In a situation of this type it might be thought that the primary liability lay with the surveyor. After all, it is the surveyor's task to value the property either for the client or for security purposes if there is a lender. The solicitor's main task is to obtain a valid and marketable title and a valid and effective security. The problem of apportionment here relates to the question of causation. If the surveyor's valuation is wrong and the solicitor is not otherwise involved, the surveyor will be liable to the extent of the shortfall between his or her valuation and the true valuation. If, however, the solicitor had some information in relation to a recent subsale or some information which makes the overall transaction look questionable it may not simply be a question of valuation. The argument will then be that if the solicitor had passed on the information the lending institution might have formed the view that the transaction was artificial and designed only to raise mortgage moneys. In these circumstances they might not have lent at all.

In this situation courts sometimes apportion a higher liability on the solicitors. The case of *Anglia Hastings & Thanet Building Society v House & Son*[3] is a good example of the problems of apportionment. There was no doubt in the case that the surveyors had given an inaccurate valuation and that this had been the basis on which the building society had decided to lend. It was in fact the surveyors who were originally sued by the building society, but they brought the solicitors in as second defenders because they felt that the solicitors were aware of certain facts which had nothing to do with the valuation but which, had they been disclosed to the building society, might have prevented the building society from lending at all[4]. Ultimately, the court apportioned 70% of the liability to the solicitors and 30% to the surveyors. There is no doubt that the court did not like the flavour of the transactions and felt that the solicitors had acted in an improper way[5].

1 For a discussion on the different types of survey report available, see Cusine and Rennie *Missives* paras 1.02–1.08.

2 This was the case in *Mortgage Express v Bowerman & Partners* (1995) Times, 1 August.

3 (1981) 260 EG 1128.

4 For the facts in the case, see para 5.04 above.

5 For a detailed discussion of the measure of loss in these circumstances, see para 9.10 below.

8.09 Solicitors can also be involved with professionals other than surveyors and, in corporate or commercial transactions, they are often involved with accountants. Solicitors should take care to advise the client whether they or the accountants are giving the appropriate accountancy and tax advice. This is particularly important where pro forma agreements are used, such as in a share acquisition transaction. It is the author's experience that such pro forma agreements often contain a host of tax warranties and indemnities. Solicitors should appreciate that if these warranties and indemnities are contained in a deed which they prepare, primary liability may fall on them and not the accountant, unless the accountant is specifically asked to confirm that the warranties and indemnities are sufficient and the client is made aware that the responsibility for these matters is to rest with the accountant. Similar problems may arise in relation to the preparation of trusts and settlements which are designed to achieve a certain tax efficient purpose. Often stockbrokers or other financial advisers may be involved, as well as accountants. If the solicitor feels that he or she is merely the person who draws up the deed to give effect to the advice of the other advisers in relation to tax and investment, then this is a matter which the solicitor ought to make clear to the client at the outset[1].

1 See *Jackson and Powell* para 4–78.

8.10 Perhaps the most difficult cases of shared liability arise where there have been successive solicitors involved in the same case or transaction, possibly where the client has changed solicitors because of dissatisfaction with the first firm[1]. At first glance it might be thought that since all firms of solicitors in Scotland are covered by the same master policy apportionment is really irrelevant. However, three things must be borne in mind:

1 Different sizes of firms will have different levels of self-insured amounts.
2 The higher the portion of blame, the higher the subsequent premium will be in later years.
3 Solicitors' firms do take claims very much to heart and the apportionment of liability matters to them, especially to the solicitor most closely concerned with the alleged negligence.

Where two or more firms are involved in a negligence claim, different insurers are involved for each solicitor and these insurance companies themselves instruct separate firms to look after their interests and the interests of the respective solicitors involved. Strict confidentiality is observed. Questions of apportionment between successive solicitors are always likely to be fraught with difficulty, except perhaps in cases where delay or failure to meet time limits is involved. Here, it is likely to be similar to a game of pass-the-parcel, and whichever solicitor is holding the file when the prescriptive period stops is likely to be liable or at least to bear the major share of liability. That will not always be the case, of course, and much will depend on what was done or not done by the first solicitors before the hand-over.

In a case where prescription is involved, the period of time actually left to run, as against the amount of work still to be done by the succeeding solicitor, will be relevant. If, for example, the second solicitor takes delivery of a thin file relating to a personal injuries claim where no evidence has been collected and there are four days to go before the expiry of the prescriptive period, the bulk of liability may still fall on the first solicitor, even though it would have been technically possible for the second solicitor to raise an action in time. In these cases it will always be a question of fact and circumstance. In conveyancing matters, once a client discovers that a mistake has been made he or she normally moves on to another firm and, indeed, the first firm should advise the client to do so. The second solicitor may well be involved in trying to sort the matter out, possibly at the client's expense, with a view to them recovering that expense from the first solicitor. Care must be taken in relation to the prescriptive period. If the second solicitor becomes so engrossed in the mechanics of sorting out the problem that he or she forgets to raise an action against the first solicitor within the five-year period, then the second solicitor may be liable in negligence or breach of contract to the client. The second solicitor should also take care that he or she does not perpetuate the mistake by attempting to run erroneous arguments supplied by the first solicitor. The second solicitor should take a clear-cut view of matters and decide what is in the best interests of the client.

1 For a discussion of this, see *Jackson and Powell* para 4–75.

CHAPTER 9

Causation and Damages

Introduction

9.01 Any claim brought by a client against his or her solicitor will be based either on breach of contract or on delict[1]. Either way, for damages to be due it has to be shown that the breach of contract or breach of duty was the cause of the loss or damage and that that loss or damage was reasonably foreseeable. If a causal link can be established, the question of the appropriate heads of loss then arises but only then. The causal link can be interrupted by some *novus actus* and any damages may be reduced if the client has in some way failed to reasonably minimise the loss. The modern trend is to claim not only for actual losses sustained but also for such things as solatium for anxiety and distress[2]. As with damages claims in general, the rule is that if liability is established the client should be put in the same position as he or she would have been had there been no breach of contract or breach of duty by the solicitor[3].

1 *Henderson v Merrett Syndicates Ltd* [1995] 2 AC 145, [1994] 3 All ER 506 makes it clear that concurrent claims under such contracts and delict can be made.
2 See *McAllister-Hall v Anderson Shaw & Gilbert* 1995 GWD 25–1334.
3 Erskine *An Institute of the Law of Scotland* (8th edn, 1871) III, 1, 14; *Hamilton v Dundas* (1710) Mor 3153; *County Personnel (Employment Agency) Ltd v Alan R Pulver & Co* [1987] 1 All ER 289, [1987] 1 WLR 916; Jackson and Powell *Professional Negligence* para 4–152.

Causation

9.02 While it is true to say that, as with any claim for breach of contract or breach of duty, it must be shown that the breach was the proximate cause of the damage, it is sometimes difficult to persuade courts that a solicitor's negligence has not been the cause of the damage where the relationship between solicitor and client is plain, the negligence is obvious and the loss clearly results from the transaction or task undertaken by the solicitor. Nevertheless, questions of causation are important and should still be raised by those defending a claim, because there will be cases in which, even though all these factors can be proved, damages will not be due.

It may be, for example, that a solicitor is negligent in the examination of a title where the description is not as exact as it might be. If the purchaser possesses the property without challenge for ten years, then on the basis of decided cases the defect may be cured if the description is sufficient in respect of its terms to constitute a title to the interest in land or in land of a description habile to include the particular land[1]. Despite the fact that the title has been cured by prescription, it may still be difficult to persuade a purchaser to accept the description in question. In a situation like this, while it may be easy to prove that the solicitor was negligent at the outset, it may be more difficult to show that any loss is attributable to the original failure as opposed to the unreasonable attitude of the new purchaser or his or her solicitor. Not every solicitor fully understands the effect of positive prescription.

Where the alleged negligence relates to a failure to give advice, the causal link will be established only if the client can show that he or she would have taken the advice if it had been given. A client who alleges negligence, whether as a breach of contract or in delict on the part of a solicitor who does not insist on a building warrant or planning permission in respect of an extension or alteration, will require to show that he or she would not have proceeded with the purchase at the same price and on the same terms if appropriate advice had been given[2]. Again, where a client fails in enforcing a debt or obligation against a third party because some document has been negligently prepared by a solicitor, there may be no damages due or nominal damages only in circumstances where the third party is shown to have been incapable of performing the obligation or repaying the debt due to insolvency or some other cause[3]. Even where it is possible to establish a causal link, certain losses may be too remote[4].

Arguments in relation to causation are sometimes difficult to maintain, principally because of the close professional relationship which exists between solicitor and client and the fact that the solicitor is meant to be an expert in his or her field, whereas the client is a layman relying on the solicitor's skill and judgment. As professional people, solicitors may be held to foresee their clients' normal intentions and the fact that, for example, a purchaser of a property will want to sell it at some future date at whatever profit would be reasonable having regard to the market conditions. Where the negligence relates to a title matter, and a subsequent sale cannot go ahead, the causal link is obvious, but it has been extended in English cases to situations where a subsequent sale has simply been delayed but the client has lost interest or paid extra interest because of the delay[5].

Where a solicitor acts for a commercial entity in the acquisition of commercial premises, a solicitor will be held to foresee that the client would intend to use the premises for normal business purposes and will be liable if, as a result of some title defect, the property cannot be used for these purposes. Similarly, a solicitor who acts for a building developer in the acquisition of land must be bound to have in his or her reasonable foresight the fact that the builder will at some future date wish to develop the land and sell it off in individual plots with or without houses erected thereon. If the property cannot be developed because of some title defect, the solicitor will be held to have foreseen that there may be a loss in the capital value of the property and also additional revenue losses due to a failure to develop. As a general rule, a solicitor will be held to foresee that additional legal and other expenses may well be incurred in setting the title right and that revenue or interest will be lost in the interval[6]. Perhaps the classic case of commercial loss is where property is purchased for development and, because of a mistake by the solicitor acting for the purchaser, no right of access is acquired. In cases of this type a whole development can be sterilised because there are no rights over a small strip of ground. There is no doubt in the author's mind that the solicitor in these circumstances would be held to have reasonably foreseen not only the loss resulting from the cost of acquisition of the ransom strip or a right of access over that strip, but also incidental costs such as extra legal expense, surveyors' fees and loss of profit as a result of failure to develop within the developers' original timescale.

It is important to remember that many cases against solicitors are based on breach of contract. As a matter of contract law, reasonable foresight of the party in breach of contract is crystallised not at the time of the breach of contract but at the time the contract was entered into. In the leading case of *Hadley v Baxendale*[7], Alderson B stated that the damages which could be claimed were those damages which fairly and reasonably could be said to arise naturally from the breach, or such as might reasonably be supposed to have been in the contemplation of both parties at the time they made the contract as the probable result of breach. In that case, the court held that carriers could not be held to have foreseen that a mill would inevitably have ceased to function for as long as a broken crankshaft was in possession of the carriers.

It has been recognised that a strict interpretation of this principle in cases involving breach of contract by solicitors can cause problems[8]. A Scottish court will probably take the view that the solicitor's state of knowledge or reasonable foresight at the date of the breach of duty is likely to be more relevant than his or her knowledge at the date of the contract. The reason for this is that a solicitor does not acquire knowledge of a client or his or her affairs at one point in time. A solicitor will amass certain knowledge concerning the client as a continuous process from the date of the original instruction which forms the contract up to the date of the breach of duty. Scottish courts do not appear to have had any difficulty in admitting to probation claims to solatium in circumstances where there might have been an argument that a solicitor could not possibly foresee at the time of entering the contract that a client would suffer anxiety as a result of a breach[9].

1 Prescription and Limitation (Scotland) Act 1973, s 1(1)(b)(i); *Mead v Melville* (1915) 1 SLT 107; *Duke of Argyll v Campbell* 1912 SC 458 at 490; *Auld v Hay* (1880) 7 R 663; *Suttie v Baird* 1992 SLT 133.

2 See *Sykes v Midland Bank Executor & Trustee Co Ltd* [1971] 1 QB 113, [1970] 2 All ER 471.

3 See *Pentland v Wight* (1833) 11 S 804.

4 *Braid v W L Highway & Sons* (1964) 191 EG 433 (client unable to recover stockbroker's fees for selling securities to raise funds); *Nash v Phillips* (1974) 232 EG 1219 (clients refused claim for inconvenience involved in buying another house because negligence of solicitor prevented them from buying the house of their original choice); *Pilkington v Wood* [1953] Ch 770, [1953] 2 All ER 810 (client refused damages for costs of travel to and from a new job where he was unable to sell his house because of a title defect). For a discussion on reasonable foresight and remoteness in general, see Walker *The Law of Contracts and Related Obligations in Scotland* (3rd edn, 1995) paras 33.26–33.32; *Jackson and Powell* paras 4–153, 4–154.

5 *G & K Ladenbau (UK) Ltd v Crawley and de Reya* [1978] 1 All ER 682, [1978] 1 WLR 266.

6 See *Brown v Cheyne & McKean* (1833) 11 S 497.

7 (1854) 9 Exch 341.

8 See *Jackson and Powell* para 4–61.

9 *Paterson v Sturrock & Armstrong* 1993 GWD 27–1706; *McAllister-Hall v Anderson Shaw & Gilbert* 1995 GWD 25–1334; and see *Malyon v Lawrence, Messer & Co* [1968] 2 Lloyd's Rep 539.

Novus actus interveniens

9.03 It is a general principle of the law of contract that where, after the original breach, a further harmful factor intervenes, a question arises as to whether the loss is attributable to the original breach or to the intervening factor. In general terms, the answer to this question is achieved by balancing the importance of the breach with the intervening factor in the chain of causation, with some importance being attached to whether one of the parties was responsible for the intervening act. Thus in *Karlshamns Oljefabriker A/B v Monarch Steamship Co Ltd*[1] it was held that the suppliers of an unseaworthy ship were still liable in damages despite the fact that war broke out during transit. The reasoning was that the unseaworthiness of the ship was the material fact in the delay, and the cause of trans-shipping the cargo was held to be directly attributable to that original breach of contract and not to the intervening declaration of war.

It is the view of the author that where a court is considering a question of causation in a claim against a solicitor and negligence is admitted or proved, any *novus actus* will require to be of a substantial nature before the court will hold that the causal link has been broken. Even where the negligent act could have been retrieved and the client did not do so because of bad advice from counsel, it has been held that the solicitors who had been originally negligent were still liable[2]. Similarly, where a third party is entitled to exercise a remedy against the client because of a failure on the part of a solicitor to protect the client or to give appropriate advice, the fact that that third party chooses to exercise his rights and take advantage of the situation will not be a factor which breaks the causal chain.

1 1949 SC (HL) 1, 1949 SLT 51.
2 *Cook v S* [1967] 1 All ER 299, [1967] 1 WLR 457.

Mitigation of loss

9.04 Where a party is in breach of contract it is the duty of the other party to minimise the loss[1]. Where the claim is based purely on delict, any failure by the client to mitigate loss may amount to contributory negligence. Apart from the general principle of mitigation, it is clear that if the client takes a positive action or omits to do something which makes the loss worse, there may be no claim, or at least the damages will be reduced. If a client fails to insure his property and it burns down, the solicitor will not be liable for the loss merely because some unfortunate dispute held back the sale of the property[2]. Similarly, if a client such as a developer requires to pay money to acquire an extra strip of ground which ought to have been acquired by the solicitor, there may be a reduced damages claim or no claim at all if the developer fails to complete the purchase of the extra ground[3]. As far as the duty to mitigate the loss is concerned, it must also be borne in mind that this is only a duty to take all reasonable steps to mitigate the loss. It does not mean that the client must go out of his or her way to mitigate loss and does not impose on the client an obligation to take a step which a reasonable and prudent man would not ordinarily take in the course of his business[4]. The standard of mitigation required, therefore, is only the standard of the reasonable man. Gloag puts it in these terms[5]:

'A party whose contract has been broken is not bound to make extraordinary exertions to minimise the loss. The purchaser cannot be expected to supply himself with goods if they can only be obtained with difficulty and in remote markets. A ship owner when the charterer fails to supply a cargo does enough if he makes resonable efforts to obtain cargo elsewhere . . . and generally the onus of proving that the best available means to minimise loss were not taken rests on the party who has broken his contract and is seeking to escape the consequences. It is not enough to shew that in the light of subsequent events a different course of action would have been preferable.'

Gloag quotes Lord Collins in *Clippens Oil Co v Edinburgh and District Water Trustees* who said in relation to mitigation[6]:

'I think the wrongdoer is not entitled to criticise the course honestly taken by the injured person on the advice of his experts, even though it should appear by the light of after events that another course might have saved loss.'

It seems unlikely to the author that in the context of a claim against a solicitor failure to mitigate loss will be an issue except in the most obvious of cases. Plainly, however, if the negligent act complained of can be rectified by a modest expenditure, it is the duty of the client to make that expenditure and then seek to recover from the solicitor. A client is not entitled to wash his or her hands of the matter completely and then seek to recover if some reasonable action could have retrieved the situation[7].

The great difficulty with the notion that the client has failed to minimise loss is, of course, that it is raised only in circumstances where negligence has either been admitted or established. Here again one comes up against the problem that the solicitor is supposed to be a professional, whereas the client is a layperson relying on that professional's advice at all times. Vague and general statements on the part of the solicitor that the matter could have been sorted out by the client with a little more effort so that the loss could have been reduced are unlikely to find favour with a court[8]. In most cases of alleged negligence, the client will have changed solicitor, perhaps with a view to pursuing the negligence claim. Accordingly, when possible opportunities to mitigate arise, it is likely that the client will be taking advice from another firm of solicitors. The second firm of solicitors may advise the client in a particular direction. A court is unlikely to accept an argument that a client has failed to mitigate loss if that client is in fact pursuing a course of action after obtaining professional advice from a new solicitor. What is relevant for the purposes of mitigation is not necessarily whether the advice from the second firm of solicitors is completely accurate, but whether the client is acting reasonably in taking that advice and pursuing the course of action recommended by the second firm. Similarly, the duty to mitigate does not mean that the client has to embark on litigation in an attempt either to defend or assert a position which has arisen because of his solicitor's negligence[9].

1 Gloag *The Law of Contract* (2nd edn, 1929) p 688; McBryde *The Law of Contract in Scotland* (1987) para 20–28; Walker *The Law of Contracts and Related Obligations in Scotland* para 33.28; *Jackson and Powell* para 4–217.
2 *Simmons v Pennington & Son* [1955] 1 All ER 240, [1995] 1 WLR 183.
3 See, for example, *Frank v Seifert, Sedley & Co* (1964) 108 SJ 523. For a general discussion of actions of the client which contribute to or increase the loss, see *Jackson and Powell* para 4–155.
4 *British Westinghouse Electric and Manufacturing Co Ltd v Underground Electric Railways Company of London Ltd* [1912] AC 673.
5 *Gloag* p 689.
6 1907 SC (HL) 9 at 14, [1907] AC 291 at 304.
7 See *Joliffe v Charles Coleman & Co* (1964) 219 EG 1608, where solicitors failed to apply for a renewal of a lease and it was held that the clients were unreasonable when they refused a new lease which was offered by the landlords on slightly worse terms.
8 See *Jackson and Powell* para 4–218 and the cases there cited.
9 *Pilkington v Wood* 1953 Ch 770, [1953] 2 All ER 810.

Measure and heads of damages

9.05 So far as the measure of damages is concerned, the general principle is, of course, that the client should be placed in the position in which he or she would have been had there been no negligence or breach of contractual standard. The nature and extent of the damages depend on the type of task entrusted to the solicitor. It is difficult to state general rules in relation to the measure of damages. It is fair to say, however, that the courts have shown considerable flexibility in relation to this matter, generally in favour of the client. The courts are not inclined to accept technical arguments concerning the nature of the loss or the timing of the loss which are designed to reduce an actual loss sustained by the client. This flexibility is illustrated in a number of cases[1]. The case reports, of course, relate only to the question of relevancy: they do not indicate what sums were actually awarded. The cases do, however, indicate a reluctance on the part of courts to restrict the heads of damages which may be claimed. It is convenient to look at the measure and heads of damages in relation to conveyancing matters and litigation matters separately.

1 *Stewart v H A Brechin & Co* 1959 SC 306, 1959 SLT (Notes) 45; *Haberstich v McCormick & Nicholson* 1975 SLT 181; *Paterson v Sturrock & Armstrong* 1993 GWD 27–1706; *McAllister-Hall v Anderson Shaw & Gilbert* 1995 GWD 25–1334; *Di Ciacca v Archibald Sharp & Sons* 1995 SLT 380.

Damages in relation to conveyancing and other matters

9.06 It is often the case that negligence in relation to conveyancing does not come to light until such time as the client wishes to sell the property. The usual case is that a purchasing solicitor then refuses to accept the title because of some defect and a sale is either lost or delayed until steps have been taken and expense incurred to put matters right. The main claim in these circumstances tends to be for a loss in value of the property, with a calculation being made of the value of the property with no title defect as against the price which can be obtained if the defect cannot be cured. On this basis of assessment the main head of claim is the difference between the two figures[1].

In some cases it will still be appropriate to argue that damages should be assessed on this restricted basis. That is, however, only one way of assessing damages and there are other peripheral matters, such as loss of interest and solatium, which also require to be considered. The question of assessment of damages was considered in the leading case of *Haberstich v McCormick & Nicholson*[1]. In that case a firm of solicitors acted on behalf of clients in the purchase of a house in 1968. The disposition which was delivered did not constitute a good and marketable title to the subjects and it was admitted that this was due to the negligence of the solicitors. The defect could have been cured at the time but was not. The property was sold in 1971 and the new purchasers, on hearing that the title was defective, withdrew. The house, which had been improved, was eventually sold at the price of £3,500.00. The clients claimed damages from the solicitors in the sheriff court, assessing their loss at £3,000.00. The sheriff granted decree for £1,500.00 on the basis that if there had been no defect in title, the house would have realised a price of £5,000.00. The solicitors appealed to the Inner House, arguing that the point of time at which damages should be assessed was the point of time at which the breach of contract occurred and not the point of time where the loss was incurred. The solicitors argued that the damages should be the difference between the price which had been paid by the clients in 1968 and what they would have paid had the defect been revealed, and not the difference at the time of the re-sale. The Inner House held:

1 That the clients had suffered loss in selling the house with a defective title.
2 That the loss was a consequence which naturally arose from the solicitors' breach of contract.
3 That there was no general rule according to which the computation of damages should be made in all cases involving negligence of solicitors in connection with the purchase and sale of heritable property.
4 That the true measure of damages flowing from the solicitors' breach of contract involving a continuing operation might fluctuate according to changes in circumstances.
5 That there was no failure on the part of the clients to minimise their loss.
6 That the re-sale of the improved house should have been in the contemplation of the solicitors when they agreed to act in the purchase.
7 That the sheriff had not erred in law in assessing damages by having regard to the price which the clients received on the sale.

In *Paterson v Sturrock & Armstrong*[3] a husband and wife sued their solicitors for damages arising out of the purchase of heritable property in January 1987. The property had been acquired for operation as a guest house catering for up to eleven guests and this was known to the solicitors. After the purchase, the clients discovered that they required planning permission, change of use permission, a fire certificate and a building warrant and had also to provide car parking, a disabled toilet and carry out certain adaptations to comply with fire regulations. The clients claimed damages for breach of contract and delictual negligence on the part of the solicitors in respect of failure to inquire into the necessity of obtaining the various permissions and consents. The solicitors argued on the procedure roll that the clients had adopted an erroneous measure of loss. The clients claimed loss of profit, architects' fees, the cost of fire extinguishers and fees paid to the local authority. The clients also averred that since they were unable to finance the alterations, they had to sell the guest house. They also claimed the difference between the actual sale price and the price at which they would have sold the premises as a guest house had it had all the necessary consents. The solicitors argued that there were a number of methods which the clients could choose by which damages might be assessed but that these methods were mutually exclusive and that the clients were not entitled to claim both for loss of value on re-sale, for the costs incurred towards solving some of the problems and loss of income which might have been generated had the clients been able to run the property as a guest house. The clients also claimed solatium in respect of anxiety and stress and the solicitors argued that this was inappropriate where the transaction was a contract for carrying out commercial activity with a view to profit and not a personal matter.

The court allowed a proof before answer and was not prepared to hold as a matter of relevancy that the three methods which the solicitors argued could be used (difference in value basis, cost of putting right the defects basis and no transaction basis) were mutually exclusive. The court also refused to hold that the claims for loss of profit and for the expense incurred towards solving the problems were necessarily excluded, although the question of double counting was still a matter for proof. As regards solatium, while the court accepted that the question of solatium in a claim over a commercial matter was a difficult one, it was not disposed to hold that no claim for solatium could exist, especially where the clients had intended to live in the guest house as well as run it as a commercial enterprise. The court was therefore not prepared to hold that the venture was of so purely a commercial character as to exclude any claim for solatium resulting from anxiety on the failure of the enterprise.

In *McAllister-Hall v Anderson Shaw & Gilbert*[4] solicitors failed to check that a building warrant had been obtained in respect of alterations to a boarding house. The clients claimed that as a consequence they had to carry out further alterations which resulted in the loss of three letting bedrooms. The heads of loss were diminished capital value, loss of profits and solatium for anxiety and distress. The solicitors argued that the clients' averments of loss were irrelevant and that a claim for diminished capital value was exhaustive and must exclude all other heads of loss. The solicitors argued that in carrying out a calculation of a diminished capital value there was bound to be an overlap with any separate claim for loss of profits and therefore double counting in the assessment of damages. The clients averred that they would not have purchased the property had they known the true state of affairs, but that they subsequently changed their minds and decided to operate at reduced profit. The solicitors argued that the clients had not minimised their loss or, alternatively, that they had caused a *novus actus interveniens* which broke the causal chain. The solicitors also argued that since the contract to purchase the property was not for pleasure or relaxation, solatium should not be awarded. In this case the solicitors relied heavily on the English case of *Hayes v Dodd*[5]. Again the court allowed a proof before answer, taking the view that the English authorities did not support any general rule and holding that a claim for diminished capital value was not necessarily exhaustive of all heads of claim. The matter of failure to minimise loss was held to be a matter for proof, and since the clients had averred that they intended to use the property as their home as well as a guest house, the claim for solatium was admitted to probation.

In *Di Ciacca v Archibald Sharp & Sons*[6] purchasers of a dwelling-house sued their solicitors alleging breach of contract and negligence, in that the solicitors had allowed them to take entry to a property on payment of a substantial deposit in circumstances where it was eventually discovered that the seller had no title. The solicitors argued that damages should be restricted to the amount which had been paid and not recovered from the sellers and that the other averments of loss which did not relate to the price or parts of the price were irrelevant. The Lord Ordinary allowed a proof before answer on the whole averments of loss. The solicitors appealed to the Inner House. In addition to claiming the moneys which had actually been lost, the clients claimed the additional cost of borrowing when they had to move to a larger house for family reasons, compared with the cost of borrowing which they would have incurred had they been able to sell their previous house at market value with a clear title. The Inner House refused the appeal, holding that the heads of loss were ultimately a matter of fact and that it would be inappropriate to exclude any of the averments from probation. Having seen that the Scottish courts are prepared to take a very flexible view of what are the appropriate heads of damages in conveyancing transactions it is now appropriate to look at some of the individual heads.

1 *Stewart v H A Brechin & Co* 1959 SC 306, 1959 SLT (Notes) 45.
2 1975 SLT 181.
3 1993 GWD 27–1706.
4 1995 GWD 25–1334.

5 [1990] 2 All ER 815.
6 1995 SLT 380.

Loss of value in property

9.07 This is normally the main head of claim where a property has not been re-sold or has been re-sold at a lower figure because of some defect in the title or lack of appropriate permission. In these circumstances the normal measure of damages is the difference in value of the property with or without the title or other defect[1]. This, however, cannot be regarded as an absolute rule and it has been held in England to be only one method of calculating the loss in such situations[2]. It is likely that any claim will be looked at on the basis of the facts of the case and, although there is still scope for arguing this restricted measure of loss in appropriate cases, a Scottish court is unlikely to rule out any head of claim without allowing proof. There may be matters which, in addition to affecting the value, affect the use of the subjects and this, as has been seen in the Scottish cases, may result not only in a claim for a diminution in capital value but also in a claim for loss of use or loss of profit, especially where the solicitors knew or can be held to have reasonably foreseen the use to which the client intended to put the property. An obvious example of additional claims of this nature is where a client purchases a public house as a going concern and the solicitor does not notice a prohibition in the titles of the sale of alcohol. Assuming a waiver cannot be obtained, there is a claim for a loss of capital value, and there may also be a claim in respect of loss of profit while matters are sorted out at the Lands Tribunal. Similarly, if a client buys a vacant plot of ground with the express purpose of erecting a house or indeed a housing development and is precluded from so doing because of some title defect, the main claim will be for the loss in capital value of the land but, if building has commenced before the defect is noticed, the claim is also likely to relate to the actual value of any structure, it being in the reasonable contemplation of the solicitor that something was to be built on the land.

1 *Stewart v H A Brechin & Co* 1959 SC 306, 1959 SLT (Notes) 45.
2 *County Personnel (Employment Agency) Ltd v Alan R Pulver & Co* [1987] 1 All ER 289, [1987] 1 WLR 916.

Actual loss where property disposed of

9.08 In some cases the title or other defect cannot be cured and the client simply decides to cut his or her losses and dispose of the property at whatever price can be obtained. In the event of the transaction involving a lease or some other agreement which has been entered into on the wrong terms as a result of a solicitor's negligence, the client may settle with the landlord or other party and pay a sum of money which allows the client to be released. In these circumstances it would be difficult to apply a strict diminution in value rule and, provided the client has acted reasonably, the court may award damages based on the loss which has actually been sustained. This is what happened in the English case of *County Personnel (Employment Agency) Ltd v Alan R Pulver & Co*[1] where the clients were bound to a lease which had no capital value as far as the tenant was concerned, so that the actual diminution in capital value could not be assessed. The clients obtained the landlords' agreement to a renunciation and the loss was held to be the cost incurred to the landlords in this respect. In the other leading English case of *Hayes v Dodd*[2] the defect related to the absence of an access right to property. The clients were entitled to recover all the damages and expenses which they had incurred while they attempted to dispose of the property.

1 [1987] 1 All ER 289, [1987] 1 WLR 916.
2 [1990] 2 All ER 815.

Loss of commercial income

9.09 The Scottish cases indicate a willingness on the part of the Scottish courts to admit to probation claims in respect of loss of profit or a lessening of profit where the negligence arises in the course of a commercial transaction. Two of the Scottish cases involved guest houses where the heads of claim included loss of profit due to the inability of the client to carry on the business at all or on a restricted basis because of a reduction in the number of letting rooms. In these circumstances it seems likely that such heads of claim will be held to be reasonably foreseeable. It should be obvious to the solicitor concerned in most cases that the property is being acquired with a view to commercial profit. The same appears to be the position in England[1].

1 *Jackson and Powell* para 4–181; *Simple Simon Catering Ltd v JE Binstock Miller & Co* (1973) 228 EG 527.

Loan transactions

9.10 Where solicitors act for lenders and prepare an invalid or ineffective security, there will be a claim for the amount of the loan plus interest and expenses under deduction of any sum recovered from the debtor by way of his or her personal obligation, provided it can be shown that the value of the security subjects would have covered these amounts. As with other heads of damages, the client is entitled only to be placed in the same position as he or she would have been had the solicitor correctly performed the task. Thus if the negligence arises from a failure to notice a prior security, the liability of the solicitor will be restricted to the amount required to discharge that security so as to place the client in the position of having a first-ranking security[1]. Problems arise where the nature of the alleged negligence is not a failure to obtain a security or a properly ranked security but a failure to disclose something to the lender which, if disclosed, might have affected the lender's original decision to lend. Examples of this type of liability have been considered earlier[2].

The difficulty here is that if it is accepted that, in the particular circumstances of the case, matters came to the notice of the solicitor which ought in accordance with the standard of care to have been disclosed to the lender, the measure of loss may not necessarily be restricted to the value of the security. In *Mortgage Express v Bowerman & Partners*[3] surveyors as well as solicitors were involved. It was alleged that the valuation given by the surveyors was inaccurate. In calculating the damages due by the surveyors, it was held that a natural fall in property values would require to be deducted from the claim. So far as the solicitors were concerned, however, it was held that no such deduction was appropriate because the lenders would not have lent at all had they been in possession of the information relating to a back-to-back sale at a lower figure. The lenders argued that they would have incurred no loss whatsoever because they would not have lent and questions of the value of the security or a fall in the property market did not enter the equation. Similar arguments might have arisen in the *Bank of East Asia Ltd v Shepherd & Wedderburn, WS*[4] case, where the bank argued that had it been aware that the clients in a building contract which was assigned to it in security would be entitled to deduct sums due in respect of bad workmanship by the builder, it would never have made the loans on that security. This case is, however, no longer going to proof.

Recent English cases suggest, however, that this basis of assessment in lending transactions, often referred to as the 'no transaction' basis may not always apply. In *South Australia Asset Corporation v York Montague Ltd*[5] the House of Lords held that a 'no transaction' basis of assessment was inapplicable where valuers had been negligent in the provision of a valuation. The Court of Appeal had held that in a case where the lender would not have lent but for the valuation, the correct measure of damages was the difference between the sum actually lent together with reasonable interest and the sum eventually recovered by the lender. The valuer therefore took the whole risk of the transaction, including any natural fall in the property market. The House of Lords reversed this decision of the Court of Appeal, holding that the valuer was not responsible for all the consequences of overvaluing a property but only for the actual loss arising from the foreseeable consequences of that action. Accordingly, the valuer was not held to be responsible for that part of the loss attributable to the natural fall in the value of the property. The damages awarded therefore depended on whether the actual loss was within the difference between the actual valuation and a proper valuation, in which case the whole loss was recoverable, or greater than this difference, in which case the damages would have to be restricted to the actual difference between the negligent valuation and a proper valuation. The case relates to negligence on the part of valuers and not solicitors and leaves open the question of total liability in the case of fraud or fraudulent misrepresentation.

It might be argued that this case impliedly overrules *Mortgage Express v Bowerman & Partners* because of the general nature of the statements made in the only judgment delivered by Lord Hoffmann. The author doubts, however, whether the case is definite authority for saying that solicitors will never be found liable in damages on a 'no transaction' basis. The difficulty is that where valuers are concerned, the negligence is closely connected to the question of valuation of the property. Accordingly, the most that can usually be said as far as a valuer is concerned is that if a proper valuation had been given, the lenders would have been relying only on that amount for security. Where a solicitor fails to disclose something to a lender, it may be that the lender would have lent a restricted amount, in which case there may now be House of Lords authority for saying that the solicitor should not be liable for the whole amount of the loan less the amount actually recovered, but only for the difference between what a reasonable lender would have lent had the disclosure been made and the amount recovered.

In the case of *Bristol & West Building Society v Mothew (Stapley & Co)*[6] the Court of Appeal held that where a lender sued a solicitor who had acted for borrower and lender for negligence in giving incorrect information, the lender did not have to prove that it would not have lent if it had known the true facts. The lender did, however, require to establish what it had lost as a result of the existence of a second charge. The judge at first instance had awarded the building society damages based on the amount lent of £59,000.00 less the amount they received on repossession. The solicitors argued that the building society was entitled only to damages calculated on their actual loss. The building society's case was based on breach of trust or fiduciary duty. The building society argued that the normal common law principles of causation and remoteness of damage did not apply in such a case and that it was not necessary for it to prove that it would not have proceeded with the transaction if it had been informed of the true facts. The Court of Appeal agreed that the building society did not need to prove that it would not have lent, but held that it had to prove an actual loss and even accepted that it might well be that the building society would fail to establish any loss.

Taking these two recent English cases together, it may be thought that the position in England is moving away from the 'no transaction' measure of damages, even where solicitors are concerned. English cases are sometimes complicated with notions of breach of trust or fiduciary duty which do not apply in Scotland. In the author's view, there will probably still be cases where the 'no transaction' basis of assessment is appropriate, but these may be restricted to circumstances where there has been non-disclosure of something so material (such as a mortgage fraud) as to lead to the inescapable conclusion that the lenders would never have lent had they been aware of the circumstances. In other cases, it is likely that the lender will in each case require to prove the loss actually attributable to the negligent act or omission. There are always likely to be difficult arguments in relation to the measure of loss in non-disclosure cases even where liability is admitted or proved.

1 *Campbell v Clason* (1840) 2 D 1113.
2 See Chapter 5 above and *Anglia Hastings & Thanet Building Society v House & Son* (1981) 260 EG 1128; *Mortgage Express v Bowerman & Partners* (1995) Times, 1 August; *Target Holdings Ltd v Redferns* [1995] 3 All ER 785, [1995] 3 WLR 352; *Bank of East Asia Ltd v Shepherd & Wedderburn, WS* 1995 SCLR 598, 1995 SLT 1074.
3 (1995) Times, 1 August.

4 1995 SCLR 598, 1995 SLT 1074.
5 [1996] 3 All ER 365.
6 (1996) Times, 2 August.

Incidental expenses caused by delay

9.11 In some cases a defect in title or in the handling of a purchase will result in delay in a future transaction involving a resale. In these cases the client will be entitled to recover incidental expenses, such as mortgage interest and the interest which could have been obtained on the sale proceeds. Where there is a purchase and a sale involved, there may be a question of bridging interest to consider and, in the author's view, it is reasonably foreseeable that if a sale is delayed, the client may have purchased in advance and therefore will have to take out bridging finance. In any computation of loss under this head, however, there should be no double counting of interest and the client would not, for example, be entitled to charge interest on the full sale price and at the same time charge interest on an outstanding loan[1].

In many cases the defect which has been caused by the solicitor's negligence can be remedied or rectified, albeit at some expense. It is clear that it is in line with the client's duty to minimise his or her loss to take such steps as can reasonably be taken to rectify the situation to allow the property to have its proper value or to allow a re-sale to proceed at the sale price agreed. If, for example, a developer has acquired a site with no right of access and the solicitor is held to be negligent, the reasonable cost of obtaining such an access will be an appropriate head of claim. Similarly, if a solicitor fails to obtain a building warrant or a superior's consent for an alteration at the time of purchase but these are subsequently obtained at some expense from the local authority or the superior, the amount of this expense will clearly form an appropriate head of claim. A claim under this head is often only part of a larger claim involving loss of interest and other expenses due to delay, but in general terms, where a solicitor acts for a purchaser and the title is not good, the solicitor will be liable for the cost of making the title good and for any incidental expenses which may have arisen as a result of any delay[2]. Such expenses are also recoverable in England[3].

Liability under this head may also arise where a solicitor, in acquiring a property for a client, accepts an unusual form of title. There are, for example, pockets of leasehold title in Scotland and for many years some members of the legal profession have tended to treat leases for 999 years as equivalent to feudal titles. It is fair to say that such titles have been and are marketable in the commercial sense of that word. It must always be remembered, however, that if the missives stipulate for a feudal title or are silent, the purchaser need not accept a leasehold title even if the lease is for 999 years[4]. Problems have recently arisen in relation to casualties exigible under these long leases[5]. In certain cases a seller may find it difficult to force a purchaser to accept a leasehold title, especially where there is a casualty. In these circumstances, unless the client clearly agreed to accept the leasehold title at the time of the purchase and unless the nature of the casualty was clearly explained, there may be a claim against the solicitor for the cost of acquiring the landlord's title so as to render the title feudal and remove the casualty forever. This may be an alternative head of claim to a straightforward diminution in value claim based on the different nature of the title.

1 See *G & K Ladenbau (UK) Ltd v Crawley and de Reya* [1978] 1 All ER 682, [1978] 1 WLR 266.
2 See *Donald's Trustees v Yeats* (1839) 1 D 1249; *Brown v Cheyne & McKean* (1831) 9 S 573.
3 See *Jackson and Powell* para 4–199; *Creech v Mayorcas* (1966) 198 EG 1091; *G & K Ladenbau (UK) Ltd v Crawley and de Reya* [1978] 1 All ER 682, [1978] 1 WLR 266.
4 *McConnell v Chassels* (1903) 10 SLT 790.
5 See Sinclair 'Casualties: Suitable Cases for Treatment' 1996 SLPQ 125.

Recovery of solicitors' fees

9.12 It is apparently the position in England that where negligence has been established the solicitor is not entitled to the fees which were charged for the transaction over and above the actual damages resulting from the negligence[1]. This can be categorised as a wasted expenditure or as repayment under an obligation of restitution, the purpose for which the solicitor was instructed having failed as a result of the negligence. In practice matters of this nature are more likely to be dealt with by the Law Society of Scotland ordering a full refund or a mitigation of fees under the inadequate professional services regulations[2].

1 *Jackson and Powell* para 4–208.
2 See Chapter 11 below.

Solatium for inconvenience, anxiety and mental distress

9.13 The question of whether solatium should be awarded in respect of breach of contract has always been a matter of some difficulty. On the one hand, it has long been recognised that where a breach of contract is established the innocent party must at least be entitled to nominal damages to cover the trouble and inconvenience which, of necessity, flows from a breach[1]. On the other hand, in breach of contract cases the basic rule has tended to be that no damages are recoverable in respect of the manner of the breach or for hurt feelings, at least in the case of breach of a commercial contract[2]. Damages can be recovered, however, where disappointment or distress are the main essence of the loss suffered[3]. McBryde states[4] that although it may be suggested that damages can rarely be recovered for the mere affront caused by a breach of contract, beyond the breach there may be injury to feelings or pain or discomfort which flow naturally from the breach.

This matter was considered in a negligence claim against a solicitor in *Watson v Swift & Co's Judicial Factor*[5]. In that case a husband and wife had purchased a flat, lived there for two years and then decided to move to a bigger house. They entered into missives for the purchase of a house and for the sale of their flat. It was discovered that the disposition of the flat had been granted by adjudgers under an adjudication which was capable of being redeemed. The former owner raised proceedings for declarator that the sum due in terms of the decree of adjudication had been repaid, for discharge of the adjudication and for the removal of the husband and wife. As a result, the husband and wife had to resile from both sets of missives and, after four years of negotiation involving the solicitors who had acted for them in the purchase of the flat, they eventually obtained a valid title from the previous owner. Not surprisingly, the husband and wife then made a claim against their former solicitors for professional negligence. They sought to recover the higher price required to purchase the sort of house they had intended to buy in the first place and also damages for upset. The defenders argued that the claim was irrelevant in so far as it related to the increased cost of acquiring a new house and in so far as it related to the claim for anxiety, depression and frustration in being unable to move until the title dispute had been resolved. The court held that it was reasonably foreseeable that loss would result to the pursuers from the delay occasioned by resolving the problem with the titles and that the delay could cause mental suffering. In the course of giving judgment Lord Morison said[6]:

> 'The matter is again to be determined only by reference to the test of reasonable foreseeability and the particular circumstances of the case. I have already held that the delay imposed on the pursuers in moving house was foreseeable and I consider that the anxieties and difficulties to

which they were exposed in this connection were such as could well be foreseen as likely to lead to mental distress. If substantial distress can be proved to have been incurred as a direct consequence of the failure in duty I see no reason in principle or authority to exclude it as an enforceable element of claim.'

Lord Morison appeared to accept that a claim for solatium might not lie where the contract was primarily commercial, but he held that the husband and wife's contract with their solicitors related very much to their personal and family interests. It is fair to say, however, that the case was based on delict as well as on breach of contract. A proof before answer was also allowed in the case of *Black v Gibson*[7]. This was a claim against a firm of builders for alleged failure to follow up working drawings and for defective workmanship. The claim included an amount for trouble, inconvenience, anxiety and stress which had caused a heart attack. The court held that the averments relating to damages for anxiety or worry were relevant, since the claim alleged fault as well as breach of contract.

In the case of *Palmer v Beck*[8] the court refused to allow a claim for breach of warrandice, but in the course of judgment the court held that had the claim for fraudulent misrepresentation succeeded then damages could have been awarded not only for financial loss but also for solatium. The court held that no solatium would have been due in respect of a breach of warrandice and in this regard did not follow the dictum of Lord Morison in *Watson v Swift & Co's Judicial Factor*. However, that related to the question of warrandice alone. The facts of the *Palmer v Beck* case were complicated, but basically purchasers of a property found that they did not have title to the whole of the garden. Because of this there were various complications in the transaction and the purchasers eventually moved out. In the course of giving judgment Lord Kirkwood said[9]:

'In this connection there is no doubt that, as a result of title difficulties which emerged, she understandably suffered anxiety and distress and required medical treatment. She has not, however, demonstrated that there was any need for her to move out of "Summerside" when she did and her husband gave evidence that the property had been vacated on the advice tendered by their solicitor. I am not satisfied that, viewed objectively, it was reasonable for her to have moved out in January 1976. Further, it is not easy to assess how much of her anxiety and distress could be said to be attributable to the defenders' alleged fraudulent or negligent misrepresentation and how much was attributable to the other things which went along with the transaction. In the circumstances I would have been disposed, so far as solatium was concerned, to make an award of £5,000.'

Although *Palmer v Beck* was not a negligence case involving solicitors, it was a claim arising from title difficulties and accordingly the remarks of Lord Kirkwood and the fact that he would have been prepared to make an award of solatium of a fairly reasonable amount are relevant to cases involving negligence by solicitors, at least in cases where the claim is based on delict as well as on breach of contract. Although the Scottish courts may not have recognised that every breach of contract is bound to cause distress to the innocent party, they have certainly recognised that where the transaction involves something personal, such as the purchase of a residence or even the purchase of a business with residential accommodation, a claim for solatium for inconvenience, anxiety and distress will be relevant[10].

The question remains as to whether solatium can be recovered where the negligence arises in a purely commercial transaction, where the claim is based on breach of contract and not on delict or both. English authority would tend to suggest that solatium may not be recoverable in these circumstances[11]. In the leading English case of *Hayes v Dodd*[12] clients purchased commercial premises and it was discovered that there was no proper right of access. The client sued the solicitors and included a claim for mental distress. This was rejected as being too remote. Part of the basis for rejection was the fact that the acquisition of the commercial premises could not be said to be for the comfort or pleasure or the relief of discomfort of the client but was simply a commercial acquisition with a view to profit. Jackson and Powell are of the view that if the transaction is the acquisition of a domestic property there will be a claim for solatium[13].

It seems to the author that the distinction between a commercial purchase, which has no bearing on the comfort or pleasure or relief of discomfort of the client, and a transaction which does have such a bearing, may not be easy to draw in every case. If, for example, a client is made redundant and decides to sink the whole of his or her redundancy payment in the acquisition of a public house, can it really be said that solatium would not be due if, as a result of a solicitor's negligence, the client were unable to open the public house because of a prohibition of the sale of alcohol in the title? It seems to the author that in circumstances like these there would be bound to be foreseeable personal distress. It would, of course, be different in the case of an individual who had a large portfolio of business premises, all of which were let.

In such circumstances there would be likely to be no claim for solatium if, say, in a portfolio of twenty properties one of the properties had a defective title as a result of a solicitor's negligence or breach of contract.

1 *Webster & Co v Cramond Iron Co* (1875) 2 R 752.
2 *Addis v Gramophone Co Ltd* [1909] AC 488.
3 *Diesen v Samson* 1971 SLT (Sh Ct) 49; *Jarvis v Swans Tours* [1973] 1 QB 233, [1973] 1 All ER 71.
4 *McBryde* para 20–99.
5 1986 SLT 217.
6 Ibid at 219.
7 1992 SLT 1076. See also *Martin v Bell-Ingram* 1986 SLT 575 and *Fraser v D M Hall & Son* 1996 GWD 31–1874, both cases involving surveyors.
8 1993 SLT 485.
9 Ibid at 491.
10 *Paterson v Sturrock & Armstong* 1993 GWD 27–1706; *McAllister-Hall v Anderson Shaw & Gilbert* 1995 GWD 25–1334.
11 See *Jackson and Powell* paras 4–211 to 4–216.
12 [1990] 2 All ER 815.
13 *Jackson and Powell* para 4–215. In *Mill v Iain Smith & Partners* (unreported) there was an award of solatium arising from the bankruptcy of the client.

Damages for negligence in litigation or disputes

9.14 Damages may be awarded against solicitors either where they fail to bring an action within an appropriate limitation period or where they fail to prepare the action adequately so that it fails. Similarly, there may be negligence if a solicitor fails to lodge the necessary appeal within the required time limit or fails to enter an appearance or defences on behalf of a defender. It is necessary to look at the question of damages in each separate situation.

Time-barred proceedings: evaluation of a chance

9.15 The commonest type of negligence claim arises where solicitors have failed to bring an action within a prescriptive or limitation period. In these cases the question of the quantum of damages involves an evaluation of the likelihood of success had the action been raised timeously. Although it would not be true to say that there is a proof within a proof in such matters, the court has to assess the likelihood of success in the original action and the likely recovery in money terms. The test to be applied in such cases has been considered in one important English case and several Scottish cases[1]. The English authorities are well discussed in Jackson and Powell[2].

In the English case of *Kitchen v Royal Air Force Association* the Master of the Rolls set out two types of case where he thought the question of assessment of damage involved no difficulty[3]. Generally, if it was plain that an action could have been brought and must have succeeded, the client would recover the full amount of the damages lost by failure to bring the action; if, on the other hand, it was plain that the client never had any cause of action and that there was no case which the solicitor could reasonably have formulated, the only damages which could be recovered would be nominal damages for the irritation caused by the failure to raise the action. Unfortunately, many cases lie in between these two extremes, in which the client would have faced some sort of difficulty in maintaining the original action but might have had some prospect of success even on the basis of a settlement. In such a case the Master of the Rolls held that the loss of the right to bring the action was in itself valuable. So far as Scots law is concerned, the matter was summed up by Lord Avonside in *Yeoman's Executrix v Ferries*[4]:

> 'Where a solicitor has been negligent, in a case like the present, he has, in my opinion, been guilty of depriving his client of a right, the right legitimately to press a claim for damages. I consider it would be grossly unjust to that client to say that that right had no value because, years after it should have been pressed, if necessary, to action and trial, it was held that the action of the pursuer failed at a time when, and in a court in which, it would not have been judged, but for the negligence of the solicitor concerned.'

Lord Avonside was of the view that it could not be said that the pursuer would have failed in his original action. He thought that the odds were that a jury would have given him a verdict and, further, that his employer would have made an offer of settlement. Lord Avonside went on to say[5]:

> 'I consider that a judge in a case of this kind, having heard the evidence available to him, is entitled to draw on his own experience in a field in which probabilities are open to decision and practice within knowledge. The purported application of narrow limits of legalistic rectitude to preserve a solicitor from the consequences of his admitted negligence is at once distasteful in suggestion and unjust in result. I see no difficulty in a judge coming to a proper decision on all the facts and circumstances of a case, in so far as those lie within the field of the test of probability.'

In the case parties had agreed that the most which the pursuer would have been awarded in his reparation claim was £3,000. Allowing for contributory negligence Lord Avonside held that the potential value of the claim had the case gone to trial could moderately be put at £1,000. Further, he considered that a figure in the region of that sum would have been offered by way of settlement by the clients' employers.

In *Siraj-Eldin v Campbell, Middleton, Burness & Dickson*[6] a petroleum engineer was dismissed by his employers for knowingly taking alcohol on to an off-shore oil rig. He instructed solicitors to lodge an application for unfair dismissal. The solicitors failed to lodge this timeously. The engineer brought a damages claim against the solicitors, pleading that if the complaint had been timeously presented to the tribunal it would have been upheld. The Lord Ordinary found in the solicitors' favour and the client appealed to the Inner House, submitting that the question was whether upon the evidence it appeared that there was a reasonable prospect that an industrial tribunal might have upheld the complaint. The Inner House refused the appeal, holding that there was no prospect of the employers settling with the employee and that the question for the Lord Ordinary was whether it would have been open for a reasonable industrial tribunal to hold that no reasonable employer engaged in an off-shore oil industry would have dismissed the pursuer in these circumstances and so make an award. On the evidence that in the circumstances of this particular case dismissal was an option open to the employers, the view that a tribunal would have refused the application was reasonable.

In *Kyle v P & J Stormonth Darling*[7] a client had been a defender in a court action where decree had been pronounced against him. The decision had been appealed unsuccessfully to the sheriff principal and thereafter an appeal was marked to the Court of Session. That appeal was subsequently held to be abandoned through the admitted failure of the solicitors to lodge papers. The solicitors admitted breach of contract and negligence but argued that the pursuer's averments of loss were irrelevant, in that he did not offer to prove on the balance of probability that he would have obtained a favourable outcome in the appeal to the Court of Session either by decree or compromise. The client averred that the appeal had a reasonable prospect of success and that even if it had no reasonable prospect of success there was a reasonable prospect that the action would have been settled. The court held that the loss alleged was a loss of the legal right to continue with the original appeal, and that where the pursuer had been deprived of that legal right that in itself constituted a completed wrong which was capable of valuation quite apart from the question of evaluation of the chances of success in the appeal. The court allowed a proof before answer. Lord Prosser drew a distinction between the loss which might have resulted because the appeal did not proceed and the loss of the actual chance to appeal. He said[8]:

'If a claim would probably have succeeded, the value to be put upon its loss was indeed the amount which would probably have been obtained if the claim had been pressed, but even if the best that could be said was that the claim had a real prospect of succeeding by decree or by settlement, the court would be entitled to put a value upon the loss of the claim . . . I am, however, satisfied that a distinction can be drawn between cases . . . where some opportunity or chance has been lost which is not itself a matter of legal right, and cases . . . where the lost opportunity or chance is itself a matter of legal right. In the former category it will not be appropriate to value the lost opportunity or chance and in order to prove a completed wrong, it will be necessary to show, on a balance of probabilities, some loss flowing from the loss of opportunity. In the latter category, however, where there has been a deprivation of a legal right, that will in itself constitute a completed wrong and one will be entitled, as a matter of valuation, to take into consideration all reasonable prospects of success if they exceed nuisance value, even if they fall short of probability.'

An analysis of the Scottish cases would indicate, therefore, that some damages may be due simply for the loss of a legal right either to bring a case or to prosecute an appeal, and that damages under this head are separate from damages which attempt to value the lost opportunity. Where a court decides that in addition to the loss of the right to bring the action there was a reasonable prospect of success, any valuation of the chance will be made by the court on the basis of the evidence available. Thus, where there was a failure to raise an action for personal injuries within the triennium, damages were calculated on the basis of what would have been awarded for the loss of the sight of one eye and various fractures[9].

1 *Kitchen v Royal Air Force Association* [1958] 2 All ER 241, [1958] 1 WLR 653; *Yeoman's Executrix v Ferries* 1967 SC 255, 1967 SLT 332; *Siraj-Eldin v Campbell, Middleton, Burness & Dickson* 1988 SC 204, 1989 SLT 122; *Kyle v P & J Stormonth Darling* 1992 SLT 264.
2 *Jackson and Powell* paras 4–182 to 4–191.
3 [1958] 2 All ER 241 at 250, [1958] 1 WLR 563 at 574–575.
4 1967 SC 255 at 264, 1967 SLT 332 at 336.
5 Ibid.

6 1988 SC 204, 1989 SLT 122.
7 1992 SLT 264.
8 Ibid at 268.
9 *McLean v Ross Harper & Murphy* 1992 SLT 1007. The judge in the case made a calculation of damages as a matter of academic interest only. He had previously held that there was no liability on the part of the solicitors.

Matters to be taken into account in the evaluation

9.16 In England there have been a great many cases following *Kitchen v Royal Air Force Association*[1]. It is fair to say that the Scottish courts have not gone into the basis of evaluation to any great extent, preferring to leave this to the discretion of the judge in each particular case. It is therefore difficult to state with certainty which factors may be relevant in evaluating the chance of success. Certainly, the claim which has been lost must be more than mere nuisance value: it has to have some prospect of success[2]. In *Siraj-Eldin v Campbell, Middleton, Burness & Dickson*[3] the test was whether or not a reasonable tribunal would be likely to have made a client an award. Where that test is not satisfied, the damages will be only for loss of the actual right to bring the claim, to prosecute the appeal or to defend the action. Where the test is satisfied, the court will require to decide the likely award and whether or not that requires to be discounted in respect of other factors. English case law suggests that there may be discounts for the risks of litigation and, possibly, even for the costs involved in the original action[4]. It is the author's view that Scottish courts are unlikely to apply anything other than general rules relating to the prospects of success to each individual case.

1 [1958] 3 All ER 241, [1958] 1 WLR 563.
2 See *Buckley v National Union of General and Municipal Workers* [1967] 3 All ER 767.
3 1988 SC 204, 1989 SLT 122.
4 *Jackson and Powell* paras 4–186, 4–187.

Damages in respect of failures after commencement of proceedings

9.17 Where a case is dismissed as a result of the negligence of the solicitor concerned, there will again require to be an evaluation of the chance of success in the action, although in practice such a claim might be dealt with in some cases by the raising of an appeal at the expense of the solicitor. If an evaluation has to be made, the fact that the action has actually been raised may lead to a presumption that the solicitors themselves thought there was at least a prospect of success. Accordingly, it will be very difficult in these circumstances for solicitors to argue that there was little or no prospect of success[1]. If the client is successful in a court action and instructs a solicitor to enforce a decree by diligence, there may be liability if the solicitor fails or delays to do this and the other litigant in the meantime becomes insolvent. Again in a case like this there would require to be an evaluation of the solvency of the other litigant at the time the decree was issued. Older Scottish cases suggest that the solicitor may be liable for the full amount of the decree in such circumstances[2]. It is submitted, however, that if the matter came before a court now, the court would require to make some sort of evaluation of the solvency of the other party.

1 See *Jackson and Powell* para 4–192; *Allen v Sir Alfred McAlpine & Sons Ltd* [1968] 2 QB 229, [1968] 1 All ER 543.
2 See *McMillan v Gray* 2 March 1820 FC 110.

Additional costs and expenses

9.18 Where, through a solicitor's negligence in a litigation matter, a client incurs extra expenses, they will normally form part of the claim. In accordance with the principle that the client requires to mitigate the loss or damage, the expenses incurred would require to have been reasonably incurred. It might be reasonable to lodge an appeal where a decree has passed because of the negligence of a solicitor, but it might not be reasonable to raise proceedings in a claim for personal injury after the triennium has expired, although the court does have a discretion in these matters[1]. Where the fault lies squarely with the solicitor, the courts appear to be unwilling to exercise the power to extend the period, on the basis that the pursuer in the reparation action will normally have a clear claim against the solicitor concerned[2].

1 Prescription and Limitation (Scotland) Act 1973, s 19A.
2 See *Donald v Rutherford* 1984 SLT 70; *Forsyth v AF Stoddard & Co* 1985 SLT 51; *Forbes v House of Clydesdale Ltd* 1987 SCLR 136.

Damages in respect of solatium for inconvenience and distress

9.19 Where a party is involved in a litigation or dispute it could be argued that they are bound to be more personally involved than where they are simply engaged in a conveyancing transaction. Accordingly, there seems little doubt that solatium will be a valid head of claim where there has been negligence in the raising, prosecution or defending of the court action or tribunal application, especially in cases which allege delictual as well as contractual liability[1]. As with other heads of damages, the test will be foreseeability, but in the author's view it would be accepted by everyone that when a person consults a solicitor either to raise or defend proceedings in relation to some important matter, the object of the exercise is to obtain advice and reassurance and not upset and distress.

1 See *Heywood v Wellers* [1976] QB 446, [1976] 1 All ER 300.

CHAPTER 10

The Conduct of a Claim

Introduction

10.01 Any client or indeed any solicitor who has been involved in making or defending a claim may be forgiven for wondering if there is any law involved. In this respect claims against solicitors are probably no different from other civil claims. There are two opposing sides, there are two sets of advisers who may include counsel and there are, at least at the start, two opposing points of view. If the matter goes to court, there will be some form of summons or initial writ and there will be defences. The pleadings will be adjusted over a period of months and in some cases, a period of years before the matter either comes to debate or to proof or is resolved by settlement. There is no doubt that a claim against the solicitor involves stress and anxiety for the client and the solicitor, sometimes over a lengthy period of time. In many cases the claim is settled after a period of negotiation in which the opposing sides' legal advisers weigh up the possibility of success or failure. It is appropriate to look at the conduct of a claim against the solicitor both from the standpoint of the client making the claim and from the standpoint of the solicitor defending the claim.

Making a claim: preliminaries

10.02 Any claim which is made against a solicitor will normally be intimated by another solicitor. The disappointed client may have gone to that other solicitor to resolve a problem and on its resolution at some expense, sought to recover from the previous solicitor. Alternatively, the previous solicitor may have finalised the transaction or the litigation but the client may not be satisfied and may feel that he or she has suffered some form of loss as a result of negligence or breach of contract. Whatever the position is, it is up to the succeeding solicitor to carry out an initial investigation in the same way as he or she would do in relation to any other form of claim. This will involve the taking of an initial statement from the client and from anyone else involved, such as a spouse, relation or indeed another adviser who may have useful evidence.

It is important, in the author's view, for the solicitor handling the claim to be frank, as regards both the merits of the claim and the likely recovery. In some cases solicitors are too diffident in dealing with the client because they do not wish to give the impression that they are playing down a claim simply because it involves another solicitor. This attitude does not help the conduct of the claim at a later date, especially if it has to be abandoned or settled for an amount of money far below the client's expectations. Solicitors handling claims should be wary of making immediate judgments without learning all the facts and indeed seeing all the files and documents which may be relevant. Accordingly, if the solicitor conducting the claim feels that there may be some merit in the claim, the next step is usually to recover all files and papers relative to the transaction or the litigation from the previous solicitor. This can usually be done fairly easily, although there are sometimes difficulties involving unpaid bills. If, however, there appears to be a *prima facie* case of negligence, the normal professional rule is that the files should be surrendered for examination.

At this point it would be prudent for the solicitors conducting the claim to discuss the question of legal expenses with the client. Perusing a lengthy file is time-consuming and can be costly. It is important that the client understands that the making of a claim against the solicitor is not a public service. Clients can sometimes become confused between the role of the Law Society as a public body in dealing with complaints and the instruction of an independent solicitor in a negligence claim. The Law Society's complaints procedures are funded by the profession; a negligence claim must, like other claims, be funded either by the Legal Aid Board or by the client. The solicitor conducting the claim should ensure that the client understands the risks and costs which may be involved in civil litigation. The client should also be made to understand the difference between judicial and extra-judicial fees. The client should also be made to understand that in the event of any claim being settled, it may be settled on the basis that no expenses are to be paid to or by either party. These preliminaries are more important in a claim against solicitors than in any other civil litigation. The solicitor handling the claim should realise that the client is already disillusioned with the legal profession. It does not take much for the client to become disillusioned with the solicitor handling the claim. There are instances of clients maintaining claims not just against the first solicitor in relation to the original matter, but also against the second solicitor in respect of the handling of the claim.

The intimation

10.03 Once the solicitor conducting the claim has taken the initial statements and perused the files and documents, the claim may be intimated in the normal way. There is sometimes a tendency to rush at an intimation. Naturally, if the prescriptive period of five years is about to run out, not only will a claim require to be intimated, but an action will require to be raised. However, if there is still plenty of time, it is often useful to delay the intimation until all the facts are known and have been properly evaluated. If a claim is simply intimated without research, it will undoubtedly be met with an aggressive response. This sets the tone and it is sometimes difficult to introduce reason at a later date. If, on the other hand, the claim has been properly researched, the intimation of the claim can be made on a proper and reasoned footing.

The detail of the claim can sometimes be set out. There is a school of thought which holds that in matters of civil litigation it is good to keep certain information back. It is the author's view that in relation to claims against solicitors, this is often counter-productive. If the claim can be set out in detail at the start, it can often be resolved at a much earlier date and this can only be to the good of the client and of the solicitor concerned. This is also the view of the insurers under the master policy and the solicitors who act for the insurers in relation to claims. At seminars on risk management organised by the Law Society of Scotland, the panel solicitors always state that it is preferable to give as much information as possible as early as possible in relation to the basis of the claim. Ideally, the claim should intimate the circumstances which are alleged to have given rise to the claim. This does not simply mean stating baldly that things have gone wrong in a transaction or a litigation and that therefore the previous solicitor must be liable. The intimation should indicate not only the facts and circumstances but also the involvement of the solicitor. In other words, the claim should state where and to what extent the solicitor is allegedly in breach of the contractual or delictual standard of care. If the intimation contains these particulars, the causal link between the alleged breach of duty and the loss should be plain. If it is not, then the intimation should make the link clear. In some cases it is not possible to quantify the loss at this stage, but in many cases it is. If the loss is quantifiable, it should be intimated at the same time so that the solicitor concerned and his or her insurers can take a realistic view at an early date. Ideally, an intimation of claim in relation to alleged negligence in a conveyancing transaction might be in the following terms[1]:

'We have been consulted by Mr and Mrs John Smith for whom you acted in 1994 in the purchase of the cottage known as Treetops, Oildrum Lane, Anytown. We recently attempted to conclude missives on behalf of Mr and Mrs Smith for the sale of the said subjects. The titles were made available by us to the purchasers' agents during the process of conclusion of missives. The purchasers refused to accept the title in that there did not appear to be a valid right of access over the private road. In addition, it was discovered that the dormer conversion which was carried out in 1991 by our clients' predecessors did not have planning permission, building warrant or completion certificate. In an attempt to rectify the position and minimise loss, we were able to obtain a deed of servitude from the adjoining farmer over the private road for a consideration of £2,000.00, plus the farmer's legal expenses. Our clients also engaged the services of an architect who was able to obtain retrospectively the appropriate permissions, but only after certain additional work was carried out to the staircase leading to the dormer extension. The purchasers were not prepared to wait until these matters were sorted out. Our clients had purchased another property and had to obtain a bridging loan to settle that purchase. Eventually, Treetops was re-sold but at a lower price than had been originally offered by the first purchasers.

We have to intimate to you that our clients hold you to have been in breach of your contractual obligations to them as solicitors and in breach of the general standard of care, in that no solicitor of ordinary competence acting with reasonable skill and care would have failed to notice that there was no servitude right of access over the private road nor failed to make inquiry in relation to the existence or otherwise of planning permission, building warrant and completion certificate in respect of the dormer extension. As a result of these failures, our clients have suffered considerable loss. They have also been subjected to strain and anxiety. We append hereto a note of our clients' losses for which they hold you liable although we must intimate that our clients reserve the right to maintain other claims for loss which may emerge. The list of heads of claim is therefore not to be taken as exhaustive. We also enclose copies of the original offer which did not proceed and copies of the concluded missives showing the lower price, a certificate from our clients' bank showing the amount of bridging interest suffered and copies of invoices in respect of legal expenses from the farmer's solicitors and from ourselves in respect of the extra work involved. We also enclose herewith copy invoice from the architect and copy receipted account from the builders in respect of the dormer extension. We enclose a medical report in respect of Mrs Smith showing that she has required to be treated for depression.

We should be grateful if you could acknowledge receipt of this letter and at the same time pass a copy of it to your insurers from whom we look forward to hearing in due course.

Yours faithfully,

Note referred to:

1	Shortfall on price	£5,000.00
2	Cost of obtaining deed of servitude from farmer	2,000.00
3	Farmer's legal expenses in connection with deed of servitude, including VAT	440.63
4	Our legal expenses in connection with abortive sale, obtaining deed of servitude, liaising with architect in connection with dormer and all other extra matters necessary to rectify the situation, including VAT	940.00
5	Bridging interest incurred from date of entry in relation to the abortive sale to date of entry in the second sale	2,795.89
6	Extra interest paid on our clients' existing building society loan from date of entry in original abortive sale to date of entry in the second sale	1,295.37
7	Architect's fees in connection with obtaining of permission for the dormer extension, including fees paid to local authority	3,795.00
8	Builder's account for carrying out work to stair leading to dormer extension	5,729.87
9	Solatium for stress and anxiety – Mr Smith	3,500.00
10	Solatium for stress and anxiety – Mrs Smith	5,000.00
		£30,496.76'

1 This style of letter is an indication of the various items which *may* be included in a claim. Not every item claimed will necessarily be accepted and there are always likely to be arguments over solatium, especially where the claim is based on breach of contract. The defenders might also try to restrict the basis of the claim to the difference in value of the property with and without the defects at the date of purchase, as discussed in para 9.06 above.

The use of experts

10.04 In many cases a claim may be met with the assertion that there has been no breach of the standard of care because the problems would have arisen no matter what any solicitor did in the circumstances. In such a case it is often useful and in many cases imperative to obtain a report from another solicitor of experience and standing in relation to the particular transaction, litigation or dispute. The purpose of obtaining such a report or opinion is to show that there is evidence available that the solicitor has in fact failed to come up to the standard of care and has been negligent. It is often a good idea to obtain a report of this nature at an early date. If such a report is available, a copy can be sent to the solicitor concerned or to anyone acting on behalf of the insurers. Not all experts agree on matters of practice and it is perfectly possible for two solicitors of standing and experience to take different views on what a reasonable solicitor would have done in any particular set of circumstances. Solicitors who are conducting a claim should therefore not advise the client that a favourable opinion from an expert necessarily means that the claim will be successful to its full extent. It should also be remembered that reports of opinions of this nature relate purely to practice. Questions of causation and quantum are quite separate.

Raising court proceedings

10.05 Even if a very full intimation is made at the outset, there will be cases where liability is denied for various reasons. In some cases there are inevitable delays while the solicitor concerned consults with his or her insurers and their legal advisers. If the reason for the delay is a lack of information in relation to the claim or to the amount of the claim, the solicitor conducting the claim should attempt to furnish the information as soon as possible. It is often said that insurers delay claims for their own reasons, hoping that the claimant will become weary and settle for a low figure. I doubt if this is true in every case and certainly not in every case involving claims against solicitors.

Many claims are held up simply because of lack of information. If, however, the solicitor conducting the claim feels that all appropriate information has been made available and no response is being made, court action should be raised. This will have the effect of crystallising the minds of everyone involved. It also brings the question of judicial expenses into the argument. The solicitor conducting the claim would be wise to warn or re-warn the client in relation to expenses if court action is to be raised. There is no doubt that matters become more complicated once an action has been raised. Inevitably, after the initial effect there is likely to be further delay while defences are lodged and pleadings are adjusted. The client should be warned by the solicitor conducting the claim that the raising of a court action does not mean that a cheque in respect of the claim will be sent by return of post. It is often very difficult for a client to grasp the nature of court procedure. If the matter goes to proof, the solicitor conducting the claim should ensure that all relevant witnesses will be available and that their statements will be relevant. If an expert witness who has made an original report is to be called, some consideration should be given as to whether such an expert ought to be present at any consultations with counsel.

Settlement

10.06 It is a salutary fact of life that most cases which begin in court end in settlement. There is always pressure on both parties to settle as the date of a proof approaches. There is the expense of the proof to be considered and, as counsel will always point out, no civil litigation is without risk. In many cases, serious moves to settle are not made until close to the date of the proof: indeed, some settlements are made at the door of the court or half way through the proceedings. It is the author's view that it is preferable to try to take a reasonable view of the question of liability or the quantum of loss as early as possible. If an offer has been made by the insurers, it should be seriously considered and appropriate advice given. That is not to say that every offer made by the insurers should be accepted. There is almost bound to be an element of negotiation in claims of this type. It is helpful, however, if the solicitor conducting the claim can at least take a reasonable view of the quantum. Clients often assume that the purpose of the damages claim is to punish the solicitor as well as to obtain redress. Solicitors conducting claims should make it clear to clients that this is not the case. For this reason it is preferable to have started with a reasonable claim. If a large amount of money is picked out of the air at the start, the client will fix his or her mind on that amount and it may be very difficult to persuade that client at a later date that a smaller sum is in fact appropriate. Again, where any settlement is being discussed, the question of expenses must be borne in mind and if a figure is being offered with no expenses, the solicitor conducting the claim should advise the client that there will be a bill for his or her services and for those of counsel.

Defending a claim

10.07 No one likes to receive bad news, particularly in the form of an allegation that some task has not been performed in a proper or competent manner. Although it might be said that we live in the age of the claim, the author doubts whether any solicitor or indeed any professional person receives intimation of a claim for professional negligence with calmness and equanimity. Almost inevitably the initial response will be emotional, especially if the intimation of the claim lands on the desk of the party whose professional competence is called into question. It may be, of course, that there has been a flow of initial correspondence leading up to the intimation so that the actual letter comes as no surprise. Nevertheless, it is important to adhere to certain ground rules when dealing with a claim. No one would pretend that responding to a negligence claim is easy. However, if the ground rules are observed, the distress can be lessened.

Obtain all files and papers

10.08 It is often tempting to respond immediately to the first intimation of a claim. Most solicitors feel that they give a reasonable service to their clients. There are many cases where things go wrong without it being the fault of the solicitor. However, everyone's recollection is faulty and a solicitor should never respond to an intimation of a claim arising from circumstances which are three or four years old without drawing together all the files and papers and subjecting them to detailed re-examination. Many intimations of claim start with words which indicate that the solicitor acted in a particular transaction or matter at a particular time. No response should be made based on a hazy recollection of some difficult transaction which went off the rails, or of some difficult title which, according to the solicitor's recollection, was eventually accepted both by the client and by the building society. The first step should always be to collect all the necessary papers relating to the transaction and to ensure that they are in order and available, before any response is made. Even when the files have been obtained and perused, it may not be a good idea to respond in any detail to the claim before advice has been taken from the insurers or from solicitors appointed by the insurers. No solicitor can be impartial in the assessment of his or her own conduct. Accordingly, the first response to the intimation of claim should simply be an acknowledgment and a statement that the matter is being looked into or will be referred to the insurers and that in the meantime liability is not admitted.

Advise other partners in the firm

10.09 For the individual solicitor concerned a negligence claim, like a complaint to the Law Society, can be a profoundly embarrassing matter. There is no doubt that in some cases the initial reaction is to conceal the intimation from other partners and attempt to persuade the solicitors acting for the former client that there is no merit in the claim. The logic, if it is logic, is that if the claim can be made to go away, then the solicitor concerned will be spared embarrassment and his partners need never know. This is a strategy which in the view of the author never works and when, as always happens, the other partners in the firm find out, the embarrassment is heightened. Many firms have designated complaints partners who deal with Law Society complaints or indeed complaints in general. It is often appropriate for the complaints partner to take over the file relating to the claim. In no circumstances is it appropriate for the solicitor most closely connected with the claim to deal with the correspondence on behalf of the firm or to deal with the defence of any action which results. While no one in the firm is likely to be able to take a totally impartial view of the claim, a partner who has not had an involvement in the subject matter will certainly be more impartial than the partner most closely connected to it.

Advise the insurers

10.10 It is an obligation of solicitors covered by the master policy to advise the insurers as soon as any claim is intimated. Many solicitors fear that intimation of a claim will have an immediate effect on the premium which they pay to the insurers. Where, therefore, the claim is likely to be settled within the solicitor's self-insured amount, there is a tendency not to intimate. Similarly, where solicitors are confident that they will be able to see off the claim they sometimes feel that it would be preferable to leave the insurers out of account. It should always be remembered, however, that where a claim is intimated to the insurers, the insurers will fix a reserve amount on that claim and it is only if that reserve amount exceeds the self-insured amount that there will be any effect on the premium. It is never really wise to conceal claims from the insurers. Claims have a habit of increasing with age and if intimation is not made, the solicitor concerned will not have the benefit of advice from the insurers and from solicitors appointed by the insurers. Late intimation may also affect the cover itself. In many cases the insurers will be able to take matters out of the office entirely by responding to the correspondence. This has two beneficial effects. In the first place, it ensures that any answers will be given after due professional consideration and not as a result of some emotional response. In the second place, it removes some of the correspondence from the office which can relieve stress on the particular partner or solicitor concerned.

Accepting service of a writ

10.11 In some cases matters will not be settled and a writ may be served. Often a writ is served because the prescriptive period is about to end. Service of a writ is an unpleasant matter. If, however, the insurers have been advised at the outset, service of the writ may be accepted without embarrassment by a firm of solicitors appointed by the insurers and thereafter all court proceedings may be dealt with by that firm of solicitors. There is no doubt that solicitors who act in their own defence have bad lawyers and stupid clients.

Taking advice

10.12 Firms of solicitors which act for the insurers under the master policy are experienced in the law relating to professional negligence. They are prepared to offer advice and very often come to the solicitor's office to discuss matters. They are skilled in giving advice both on liability and on quantum and can offer this advice not only with tact and diplomacy but also with the benefit of a great deal of experience. Where the action has been raised in the Court of Session, counsel will also be involved. In the initial stages, the solicitors for the master policy will require to examine all files, papers and documents, including any notes of meetings or telephone calls which may have taken place. In many cases, it will also be necessary to take a statement from the solicitor or solicitors most closely concerned. No piece of evidence or fact or circumstance should be left out. It is up to those advising to determine the significance or otherwise of anything which has been said or written.

The advice given will normally come in two parts. First, the question of liability will require to be examined in detail and a view formed. Secondly, if liability is to be accepted, the question of the quantum of the claim will arise. No one case is the same as another and it is therefore difficult to formulate general rules. It is fair to say, however, that many solicitors simply cannot accept that they have been negligent in any way. A failure to face up to this possibility can delay a reasonable settlement and disposal of the claim. Once a solicitor accepts that there may be liability, the question of quantum can become an easier matter to discuss. It remains a fact, however, that solicitors are often the most difficult clients of all.

Questions of liability

10.13 Liability depends on proving negligence, either as a delictual matter or as a breach of contract. The standard of care is not a fixed standard but depends in general terms on the standard which would be adopted by an ordinary practitioner exercising reasonable skill and care[1]. The problem which often faces solicitors is that they regard their own practice or perhaps the practice in their own town or area as sacrosanct and do not readily accept that it may fall below the general standard of care adopted by practitioners in other parts of the country. Thus, for example, a solicitor practising in Lanarkshire where difficult mineral reservation clauses and leasehold titles are common may not be easy to persuade that he or she has been negligent in accepting a particular type of title which has been accepted by generations of practitioners in Lanarkshire. Similarly, solicitors are adept at working out complicated legal reasons as to why a particular title should be accepted, even though there is evidence that three or four other firms of solicitors have already refused to accept the title when acting for a new purchaser. It must always be remembered that what is to be obtained for a purchaser is not a title over which six different firms of lawyers can argue but a title which is valid and marketable and which will be accepted without the need to go to the Inner House of the Court of Session for a declarator in a special case. Sometimes, of course, the advice may be that there is no liability, or at least that the question of negligence is far from clear as a matter of law. In these circumstances, the solicitor should take the advice offered and proceed to defend. In some cases the question of liability will depend very much on the evidence as to what advice was or was not actually given and what instructions followed from this advice.

1 See Chapter 2 generally.

Opinions and reports from experts

10.14 In many cases the solicitor will be advised that an opinion should be sought from a solicitor experienced in the particular field of law. The purpose of this is to obtain a totally unbiased view of the conduct of the solicitor measured against the standard of care. If the point is a narrow one, the matter may be covered by a memorial to the expert. If it is a broader one, the expert may well require to consult all the files and papers in the case. The report of the expert will be either that the conduct of the solicitor has come up to the required standard of care or that it has not. Where a claim is to be defended, a report by an expert confirming that the conduct has come up to the required standard of care will be valuable. Where the solicitor refuses to accept that he or she may be liable even after advice from solicitors appointed under the master policy, an independent report confirming that the conduct has not come up to the standard of care may at least serve to persuade the solicitor that the matter must be settled. Reports and opinions of this nature do, of course, depend on the facts and evidence presented to the expert. In most cases which go to court, each side has a different interpretation of the facts. It is therefore not uncommon to find experts on both sides of a litigation who have come to differing views on whether the solicitor has come up to the required standard in what are or what should be the same set of circumstances. It should also be remembered that a court need not accept an expert's view that there has been no breach of the standard of care[1].

1 See *Brown v Gould & Swayne* [1996] PNLR 130.

Causation and quantum

10.15 If it is accepted that liability exists, then the question of causation may still play a role in determining whether there is any claim to be met. Even if there is negligence, that negligence may not have caused the actual loss suffered[1]. If that is the case, the claim may still be defended. It is fair, however, to point out that courts are not particularly fond of technical defences by solicitors in circumstances where there has been negligence and some sort of loss has resulted at the end of the day. As far as damages are concerned, this will be a matter of assessing the loss properly and checking that the claim is vouched.

1 See Chapter 9.

Settlement

10.16 Many claims against solicitors are settled either before they go to court or during the course of the litigation. As with other claims of this nature, some are not settled until a few days before a hearing. This can be a particularly difficult period of time for the solicitor concerned, especially if the advice which he or she has obtained is that there may be a defence to the claim either on liability, causation or quantum[1]. The solicitor involved should be prepared to listen to and to take advice from the panel solicitors and counsel appointed by the insurers. In dealing with questions of settlement, the following should always be borne in mind:

1 No matter how strong the case may be, no civil litigation is without risk.
2 The advice which has been given was given on the basis of the evidence of one side only and without the benefit of hearing the evidence of the other side.
3 Those advising the solicitors have experience of how a court may react to a particular set of circumstances and whether or not in the light of that it may be prudent to make some offer.
4 A lengthy proof involving a partner or partners or other personnel is costly both in time and in loss of fees, no matter what the result.
5 Any publicity which arises from a proof is almost bound to be adverse, even if the court ultimately finds in favour of the solicitor.
6 Where the amount claimed is above the solicitor's self-insured amount, the insurance company is entitled to a view on whether settlement should or should not be effected.
7 Where the amount claimed exceeds the self-insured amount of the solicitor, the insurers are entitled to a view in relation to the expenses involved in going ahead with a hearing, given the fact that the insurers pay the expenses.

1 See Chapter 9.

CHAPTER 11

Inadequate Professional Service and Negligence

Introduction

11.01 On 29 January 1989 ss 42A to 42C of the Solicitors (Scotland) Act 1980 came into effect[1]. Until then the jurisdiction of the Law Society of Scotland in relation to the actings of solicitors related purely to matters of conduct. Prior to that date, if a complaint was received which alleged incompetence or a lack of proper service, then unless this amounted to unprofessional conduct or professional misconduct, the Law Society of Scotland could not and did not entertain the complaint. Section 42A allows the Council of the Law Society of Scotland to entertain a complaint from any person having an interest to the effect that professional services provided by a solicitor have been inadequate. If the Council of the Law Society, after inquiry and having given the solicitor an opportunity to make representations, is satisfied that the services rendered have been inadequate, it may take the various steps set out in s 42A(2). The steps which the Council can take are to reduce fees and outlays or have them waived altogether, to direct the solicitor to rectify errors or omissions, to direct the solicitor to take action in the interests of the client as specified by the Council and to direct the solicitor to pay the client compensation not exceeding £1,000.00. A solicitor who is unhappy with a determination that he or she has provided an inadequate professional service may, within 21 days of the date on which the determination or direction is intimated, appeal to the Discipline Tribunal[2]. It will be obvious that there must be some correlation between the provision of an inadequate professional service and the concept of professional negligence. The correlation is, however, far from clear and a determination by the Law Society that there has been inadequate professional service does not necessarily mean that there has also been negligence[3].

1 These sections were inserted by the Solicitors (Scotland) Act 1988 and were further amended by the Law Reform (Miscellaneous Provisions) (Scotland) Act 1990 with effect from 3 June 1991.
2 Solicitors (Scotland) Act 1980, s 42A(7).

3 The term 'negligence' is used in this chapter to cover claims based on breach of the contractual standard of care and claims based on breach of a delictual standard of care.

The statutory definition

11.02 Section 65(1) of the Solicitors (Scotland) Act 1980 defines inadequate professional services as professional services which are in any respect not of the quality which could reasonably be expected of a competent solicitor. There are obvious similarities between this statutory definition and the common law standard of care to be expected of an ordinarily competent solicitor exercising due skill and care. There is, however, not the same degree of similarity between the statutory definition and the definition of the standard of care based on the notion of general practice as set out in *Hunter v Hanley*[1]. Although the test in that case refers to deviation from a general practice, it allows that there may be no negligence unless it can be shown that no ordinary solicitor would have taken the course of action taken if exercising reasonable care. It seems to follow, therefore, that negligence and the rendering of an inadequate professional service are two different things. For example, it may be inadequate professional service to fail to answer telephone calls from a client, but there may be no negligence involved and indeed there may be no loss involved, merely annoyance and inconvenience. This may be compensated in one way or another in terms of the statutory powers. Accordingly, a solicitor may go through a transaction without being negligent but still find himself having to lower or waive his fee or indeed pay compensation up to the statutory maximum in terms of the statutory provisions.

It is the view of the author that standing the statutory definition of inadequate professional service it is possible to have inadequate professional service without negligence. Whether it is possible to have negligence without inadequate professional service has been a matter of some debate. On the one hand, it would seem clear that if a solicitor has been negligent then he or she must have provided an inadequate professional service. To take an obvious case, if a solicitor fails to raise an action for damages within the prescriptive period, that solicitor will not only have been negligent but will also have provided an inadequate professional service. The counter argument is that the two matters are entirely separate, and that a solicitor can provide an adequate mechanical service in the sense of returning calls, answering letters, preparing deeds and the rest but may make a mistake of principle which is 'pure negligence'. In these circumstances, it has been argued that if the mechanics of the service are in order then no complaint should lie in terms of the statutory provisions and the only claim should be in negligence. The author finds this latter argument difficult to follow. Even if a solicitor performs correctly mechanically, the service provided must be inadequate if a mistake is made which amounts to negligence. In other words, it can surely never be professionally adequate to perform services in a negligent manner.

1 1955 SC 200, 1955 SLT 213; and see para 2.07 above.

The conduct of a complaint

11.03 Complaints are dealt with initially by the Complaints Secretariat of the Law Society of Scotland. They are then normally referred to a committee if conciliation between solicitor and client cannot be achieved. That committee will consider the complaint and the solicitor's files and will issue a statement of facts and invite the complainer and the solicitor either to agree that the facts as set out in the statement are accurate or to make other representations. Thereafter, on the basis of the agreed facts, the committee will come to a view as to whether there has or has not been inadequate professional service. It is the current practice of the Law Society of Scotland to inquire from complainers whether or not they intend to intimate or to pursue a negligence claim. If the complainer indicates that this is so, the Law Society advises the complainer that it will not deal with the complaint until the negligence claim has been finalised. The reason for this is that the Law Society has powers to demand files and explanations from solicitors. In the course of making an honest response to a complaint, the solicitor may give information which could be useful to the complainer in a negligence claim and which information would not in the normal course of events be made available on a voluntary basis.

Although there is no statutory basis for this policy, s 56A(1) of the Solicitors (Scotland) Act 1980 states that the taking of any steps under s 42A(2) or s 53A(2), which relates to the powers of the Council and the Discipline Tribunal where inadequate professional service has been established, shall not be founded on in any proceedings for the purpose of showing that the solicitor has been negligent. The author, however, takes the view that the point of s 56A(1) is to allow the Law Society to entertain a complaint in relation to inadequate professional service at the same time as a negligence claim is ongoing, rather than to bar such a procedure. If the Law Society's determination and direction cannot be used in evidence in the negligence claim, there should be no prejudice to the solicitor. Similarly, s 56A(2) states that although a direction to pay compensation shall not prejudice the right of the client to claim damages for negligence, any award made by the Law Society or the Discipline Tribunal may be taken into account in the computation of compensation in the negligence proceedings. In fairness to the Law Society's current policy, however, it has to be said that all s 56A(1) states is that the applying of a sanction by the Law Society or by the Discipline Tribunal cannot be founded on in negligence proceedings. Before a determination has been made that inadequate professional services have been provided the solicitor will have provided a great deal of information to the Law Society and this is normally copied to the complainer. It cannot be denied that the complainer may be able to make some use of this in any negligence claim.

General principles of inadequate professional service

11.04 It is fair to say that there are no discernable general principles in relation to what is or is not an inadequate professional service. Suffice it to say that in the handling of complaints in relation to this matter the Law Society of Scotland has considered almost every aspect of practice, from the taking of telephone calls to the preparation of completion statements. Each complaint is treated on its own merits and the most common form of sanction is a reduction in the amount of fees and outlays, sometimes coupled with a direction to complete unfinished work or to hand the files over to another solicitor for this purpose. Compensation awards have, however, been made in a number of cases including awards up to the maximum of £1,000.00. What the Law Society is concerned with is the general handling of the transaction or the litigation or other dispute. Lack of effective communication between solicitor and client is a common feature of complaints.

No need for loss

11.05 For a negligence claim to succeed, it has to be shown not only that the solicitor failed to come up to a required standard or was in breach of contract, but also that that failure or breach caused a loss to the client. In considering a statutory complaint that there has been an inadequate professional service, matters of loss and indeed causation are irrelevant. Even where the Law Society awards compensation, there is no need to prove that the client has lost anything, even a sum up to the amount of the compensation. Awards of compensation are made on the basis that the client is bound to have suffered inconvenience and possibly anxiety and distress because of the inadequate professional service provided. There is no need to aver this or indeed to prove that this has occurred.

The effect of settlements or discharges of claims

11.06 Where a negligence claim has been disposed of and the Law Society then takes up consideration of a complaint that there has been an inadequate professional service, it seems that the terms of any settlement or decree or discharge in the negligence claim will be irrelevant and will not bar the Law Society from considering the complaint. In a long-drawn-out negligence case, the fact that a complaint may have been brought to the Law Society some time ago is often forgotten in the terms of the settlement. It may be that a negligence action is settled by a payment to the client which is stated to be in full and final settlement of all claims. It may even be that the settlement is made on an *ex gratia* basis without admission of liability. Despite the terms of any joint minute or discharge, the Law Society will still be able to consider a complaint in relation to inadequate professional service and make an award of compensation or alternatively require fees which have been paid to be reduced or waived. Whether it is theoretically possible to obtain a valid discharge of a right to complain to the Law Society in terms of an overall negligence settlement must be a matter of some doubt, even where the client is separately represented and advised throughout. The difficulty is that in terms of s 33 of the Law Reform (Miscellaneous Provisions) (Scotland) Act 1990, the Law Society has a statutory duty to investigate any complaint relating to professional misconduct or to the provision of inadequate professional services and must after investigation make a written report to the complainer and to the solicitor of the facts of the matter as found and the action proposed to be taken. It is difficult to see how the signing of a discharge or the settlement of an action by joint minute can override the statutory duty of the Law Society to investigate a complaint relating to inadequate professional services and make a determination in terms of the statutory provisions.

Index